The Algorithmic Code of Ethics

Technological Prospects and Social Applications Set

coordinated by
Bruno Salgues

Volume 2

The Algorithmic Code of Ethics

Ethics at the Bedside of the Digital Revolution

Jérôme Béranger

iSTE

WILEY

First published 2018 in Great Britain and the United States by ISTE Ltd and John Wiley & Sons, Inc.

ISTE Ltd
27-37 St George's Road
London SW19 4EU
UK

www.iste.co.uk

John Wiley & Sons, Inc.
111 River Street
Hoboken, NJ 07030
USA

www.wiley.com

Library of Congress Control Number: 2018949174

British Library Cataloguing-in-Publication Data
A CIP record for this book is available from the British Library
ISBN 978-1-78630-306-6

FSC
www.fsc.org
MIX
Paper from responsible sources
FSC® C013604

Contents

Foreword

Welcome to a new world where mankind joins forces with machines through *digital technology*. To understand this new world, there is only one guide: the book of Jérôme Béranger.

Both lighthearted and serious, clear and complex, a source of hope as well as concern, the author's reflections allow us to navigate between the questions and interests that digital technology and its applications raise.

This reconciliation of contradictions is easily achieved as the author helps the reader to ask the right questions by suggesting that they refer to a Code of Ethics.

Digital technology allegedly originated in nature where, *in fine*, all becomes one. Following the example of a matrix, nature is allegedly only a visual envelope which reflects a virtual reality. How can we then make sense of it, if not by relying on what is most fundamental and common to us? The answer is: *ethics*. As such, the author suggests inserting ethics into the meandering of digital technology, in order to come up with an algorithmic ethics, an applied ethics and a renewed ethics; an ambition which is sometimes difficult to consider for a lawyer with a Cartesian mind. To come to terms with it, returning to the word's definition is necessary. Thus, French dictionaries commonly define ethics as all the principles of morality that are the basis for a person's behavior. Ethics is thus generated by a moral that people question, challenge, contradict, and then accept and apply in order to comply with it. It is therefore a reference specific to each person.

Consequently, can codifying this ethics and creating an algorithmic ethics be considered?

With a strong, scientific demonstration, using mathematical and philosophical concepts, the author convinces the reader as to the need for a regulation of the digital world. This regulation cannot be exclusively legal; it must also be ethical. Thus, Jérôme Béranger suggests a digital governance laying the foundations for a responsible and empowered society whose foundation would be an algorithmic code of ethics.

Along the lines of a social pact within a digital society, Jérôme Béranger thus humbly lays down the foundations for our future societal model.

Lina WILLIATTE
Professor of Law – Université Catholique de Lille
Lawyer at the Lille bar – Cabinet WT Avocat

Acknowledgments

I wish to seize this literary opportunity to express my deep appreciation and my sincere gratitude to:

– The ADEL corporation (Frédéric, Conrad, Guillaume and Jérôme), JMC Investment (Jean-Marie and Tom) and Team 4 of the UMR 1027 (public health and epidemiology research center) of the INSERM (French National Institute of Health and Medical Research) mixed unit/Paul Sabatier University (in particular Emmanuelle) for their support and trust in my research, as well as for providing me with the best possible conditions – in terms of material and human resources – in order to develop my innovating and forward-thinking vision of a digital ethics;

– Cédric Villani and Gilles Babinet, who have supported me from the very beginning of my work and reflections on the subject;

– Lina Williatte, who was so kind as to write the foreword of this book;

– All persons who have, directly or indirectly, taken part in the completion of this work;

– My family (Madeleine, Jean-Noël, Stéphanie, Christophe, etc.) and my friends (Yannick, Marie-Ève, Élodie, Marjorie, Mathieu, Danaé, Emma, Nicolas, Marie, etc.) for their encouragements and patience. I dedicate this book to them…

Without all these people, this book would never have seen the light of day!

Introduction

"Everything changes, nothing remains without change".

Buddha

"In nature, everything always has a reason. If you understand this reason, you do not need any more experience".

Leonardo da Vinci

"It has become appallingly obvious that our technology has exceeded our humanity".

Albert Einstein

"Information is the resolution of uncertainty".

Claude Shannon

I.1. Preamble

In the 1950s, IBM sought to introduce the word "computer" in France. Philosopher Jacques Perret, mandated by the American giant, came up with the idea of using an ancient Latin word from the Middle Ages: *ordinateur*. This term referred to a quality that the Church Fathers assigned to God – *Deus Ordinator* – meaning "God Orderer" [ALI 17].

Over half a century later and after the emergence of algorithmic systems, one could wonder if the use of this name was premonitory. Indeed, biblical texts say that "God is everywhere, in each one of us [...] and guides our choices". Two thousand years later, this quote is still relevant, with an aging God who has taken a digital form: "Algorithm is everywhere, in each one of us [...] and guides our choices!"

For the historian Yuval Noah Harari [HAR 17], the 21st Century will witness the emergence of a new religion focused on data, "dataism", in order to fill a spiritual void, and whose premise claims that the universe consists of a data stream and that the value of each phenomenon or entity is determined by its contribution to data processing.

By inventing the binary code a few years ago, human beings had certainly not considered that they would become themselves a series of 0s and 1s. In fact, nowadays, algorithms are omnipresent within us and our environment in a natural and artificial manner, whilst governing us directly or indirectly. Information is everywhere and the algorithm enables mankind to interact with this information environment. In 2014, GSMA Intelligence announced that there were more connected devices than human beings on the planet. All the ins and outs of theirs uses are not known.

The "datafication", "algorithmization", or even "gamification"[1] of our society inevitably result in a dematerialization of relationships, a disintermediation and a transfer from property value to use value. This data society is no longer built on meaningful knowledge, but on data aggregates, which contribute to the disruptive nature of our societies [STI 15].

Algorithms are now an integral part of the citizen's daily life with the hierarchical organization of the information on billions of people's consumption on Google (PageRank), the selection of information present on Facebook's newsfeed (Edgerank), product recommendations (Amazon), the optimization and geolocation of movements, disease detection and so on. They represent the basic operation tool of most current websites and software, and the operating source of connected objects[2], information

1 Neologism referring to the application of the principles and mechanisms of games in non-entertaining situations. The idea is therefore to attract the attention and interest of the user in order to try to retain them as long as possible. An example is the development of serious games to train professionals, in particular in health-related fields.

2 Connected objects (known as "Information Technology 3.0") operate via algorithms to study traffic data and enable a car to be autonomous, to analyze health and well-being data, or also to

systems (IS), future digital ecosystems and technologies (big data, Artificial Intelligence (AI), platforming, IoT (Internet of Things), Blockchain, biometric system, virtual or even augmented reality, Nanotechnology, Biotechnology, Information Technology (IT) and Cognitive Science (NBIC), quantum computing, three-dimensional bioprinting[3], etc.).

These algorithms are probably one of the most valued immaterial creations of our modern economy. Nearly all market participants base their model on their algorithms' performance. All these algorithmic actions include within each of them a moral process containing their own value system, their own way of reading and understanding reality and its interrelationships, as well as their own subjectivity. Algorithms have no qualms about invading people's privacy and studying their behavior. In these conditions, designing, implementing and using these algorithms cannot remain neutral due to their societal and economic impact. Consequently, this digital transformation introduces a change of contextual landmarks and perspectives focused on information and its financial valuation potential. From now on, the value of data is conditioned by a set of transversal parameters and criteria, such as its accessibility, integrity, reliability, legitimacy, purpose, confidentiality, and so on.

In our current digital world, compliance with the law and regulations is no longer sufficient. The ethical dimension of algorithmic data processing[4] must be reviewed. Governing and regulating New Information and Communication Technologies (NICTs) must go way beyond the rigid, purely technological and normative aspect, in order to embrace the transversal, flexible and mobile dimension of algorithmic ethics. This is why it is essential to consider an in-depth, wide and multidisciplinary analysis, in order to provide recommendations and clarify the social debate as to how modern society should face this technological challenge.

analyze the food consumption of a person or enable a connected refrigerator to stock up automatically.

3 The three-dimensional bioprinting of organic elements, which uses copies of patients' cells and collagen "biobands" to fix successive rows of living cells, should be available soon. It will allegedly facilitate the supply of tailor-made human anatomical elements.

4 Let us note that we understand by "algorithmic processing" any operation or set of operations – including at least one algorithm – performed or not performed using automated processes and applied to digital data.

Therefore, confronted with this change in paradigm of our society, how should mankind evolve? It is obviously complicated to project in a future which is, by definition, uncertain, especially since we are in a transition period marking the beginning of the Fourth Industrial Revolution in human history. The whole point, essence and purpose of this book are actually based on this issue. We are convinced that, on the basis of our ethical approach, we can provide some responses regarding the main course offered to us, along the path of our neo-Darwinian evolution.

This book is a follow-up to two previous books entitled *Medical Information Systems Ethics* [BÉR 15] and *Big Data and Ethics* [BÉR 16] published by ISTE. It is the last part of our trilogy on ethics in the digital ecosystem. Over these years of achievements and reflections, our line of reasoning evolved from "digital ethics" to "algorithmic ethics" and ended up with "quantum ethics". Regardless of the name, form and application of our ethical vision on the subject, the intrinsic essence and content emerging are first and foremost what prevails. Our literary quest aims at pursuing our vigilance and our epistemic, civic and moral approach regarding the societal issues to which we are confronted, as they involve our future, and whose risks, challenges and limits, beyond an apparent semantic modernity, seem *a priori* obscure and meaningless.

We are fortunate to be at the beginning of a new era based on the digitalization of society. It is therefore essential to be able to seize this opportunity to define a human framework of confidence and outline a new moral space focused on ethical principles and the accountability of all concerned participants, by developing, implementing and using NICTs. This is what is called ethics by design!

Hence, the main goal of this book is to provide readers with the first building blocks in the interest of the people, which go with this digital revolution, in order to obtain a more meaningful and better harmony between the intentions, implementations and purposes of technological tools. The balance between the promise of useful innovation and the risk of algorithmic prejudice is at stake. Therefore, by highlighting a background focused on a new ethical and technical approach, our book aims, on the one hand, to provide the backbone for a substantial change in attitudes surrounding the digital environment of society and, on the other hand, to contribute to the intelligibility of this digital revolution and ponder the impact of our digital representations in terms of social, economic and industrial practices, construction of standards and relationship with civic action.

Finally, our reasoning about the establishment and integration of an "algorithmic code of ethics" will include two essential steps, which are both separate and complementary. The first stage will argue that "Code is Ethics", following the example of the legal expert Lawrence Lessig's famous quote that "Code is Law" [LES 99]. The author stresses that code has gradually been set up as an active regulator of behaviors and of the online dematerialized transactions of the collaborative economy which, *de facto*, supersedes the law. The encoder is generally solely responsible for their choices and is the only one who can determine whether this choice is ethical. For instance, this is the case for the quantity of data they will use to perform algorithmic processing, for which they will have to carefully think about the really useful data and encode the algorithm accordingly. Technology is likely to set the standard without any democratic debate. Its value also comes from the fact that code is a workspace for developers and, as such, reflects the culture of their team and company. The influence of computer code on our daily lives and the overriding of the law by the algorithm can be witnessed. Digital technology generates numerous ethical questions of its own, as it alone produces a regulatory system equivalent to that of the law.

Then, a second phase will demonstrate that "Ethics is Code", adapting Primavera De Filippi and Samer Hassan's expression [DEF 16]: "Law is Code", suggesting that blockchain (distributed public register) could be the technical source making it possible for code to become a way of enforcing the law. This regulatory perspective of digital technology must be the subject of an ethics of attention, which could highlight dilemmas between the standards produced by digital technology and our own standards or value systems. However, this ethics is likely to be insufficient. Indeed if, as Lawrence Lessig [LES 99] has said, the code regulates, and if it regulates poorly, if the intentions of the programmers are not in line with a certain ethics, regulating or rebalancing this normative vision will be difficult *a posteriori*. Under these conditions, an autonomous platform or expert system could initiate technological solutions allowing the code to become a means of expression for ethics. As part of a neo-Darwinian approach, this platform, or even AI[5], would be the embodiment of our idea of an "algorithmic code of ethics", both scalable and universal. This is then called ethics by evolution!

Lastly, the particularity of this book is its focus on both NICTs animated by algorithms themselves and the best ethical requirements and recommendations regarding their design, development, use and control, while encouraging the latter.

I.2. Technical revolutions through time

Initially reflecting the circular movement of a star returning to its point of origin, the term "revolution" has changed with time and now refers to a radical break or change in our structural patterns and our framework for reflection. This semantic insight reflects the cyclical nature seen in a revolution through time, which results in different forms. If the industrial sector is associated with it, this revolution is defined by a collection of important changes which successively transformed industrial production devices and work, significantly affecting the employment, economy, consumption and environment. This definition clearly explains that the change in our vision of the world is the result of each Industrial Revolution and is currently taking place again.

Over the centuries, science has made the discovery of new energy resources and raw material possible, facilitating the appearance of more efficient machines and technological innovations, as well as novel production methods. Therefore, the technological evolution of mankind has been driven by new knowledge and innovations created, acquired and used by humans. This necessarily leads to a phenomenon of obsolescence[6] of the actors' knowledge, which is inevitably outdated and superseded by NICTs. Consequently, in a perpetually shifting and evolving world, it is essential that everyone avoids keeping the same bases and rather enriches them, in order to develop their expertise within the society. The different realms, the Western European countries and then the "New World", have mainly sought,

5 AI can be described as the capacity enabling machines to imitate human beings' way of thinking and progressively acquiring knowledge, instead of only executing specific commands.

6 Obsolescence is when a product is outdated and, therefore, loses part of its value only due to technological evolution or a trend, even if its operating state is perfect.

during each major phase of their history and through their multiple mutual influences (economic, political, spiritual, cultural, social, etc.), a great common and shared goal, whose structure, which is spatially and temporally quite homogeneous, provided the development of a society model each time [DOS 15].

For the record, it is worth remembering that Europe was the birth place of what we call the "Western model" up to the end of the 19th Century (in particular with its colonial development policy). Then, the United States appeared on the international scene (via its globalization policy) during the 20th Century. Finally, the latest projections and trends predict that the United States and various Asian countries, especially China, will extend their influence worldwide.

Technical progress led humankind to improve its industry throughout its history and increasingly rely on it, but also reinvent it as soon as new resources provided new technical means. Therefore, industry was the subject of qualitative and significant progress representative of its time, which can be associated with "revolutions". Thus, we see that the cyclical history of mankind – which endlessly starts over – currently accepts four main industrial and technical revolutions, which are fully interdependent:

– The First Industrial Revolution took place at the end of the 18th Century in the United Kingdom and then France: it emerged with the advent of mechanization which resulted in industry becoming the cornerstone of the economy, sidelining agriculture. The invention of the steam engine associated with the massive extraction of coal contributed to a new essential energy (patented by James Watt in 1760) for the development of material, economic and human exchanges via the expansion of railways. The first railway steam engine was built and then patented in 1815 in the United Kingdom by George Stephenson. Other significant inventions, in particular in textiles (mechanized sewing machines, the Jacquard loom created by Joseph Jacquard in 1801) or in metallurgy (metal and cast iron work, use of coke and invention of puddlage) and in the steel industry (in France, the pont d'Austerlitz was the first metal bridge built in 1807), amplified this phenomenon of society industrialization.

We then witnessed a rapid development of economic growth driven by the unprecedented increase in production generated by major discoveries in the knowledge sector. Urban centers were gradually built and grew. The establishment of different companies in the same place made it possible to improve the profitability of productions. Technical innovations were always renewed, constantly increasing the industrial output. This therefore led to major economic and social disruptions. Finally, this First Industrial Revolution emerged in a specific context favorable to progress and during which the capitalist spirit increasingly developed. It is thus that, up to 1830, significant economic, technical and social changes reshaped Great Britain, before extending to Europe and the United States.

– The Second Industrial Revolution emerged at the end of the 19th Century in Germany and the United States: after an economic depression (Vienna crash) over several years (1873–1896), a Second Industrial Revolution was born. It started at the very end of the 19th Century and only ended in 1914 with the beginning of WWI.

This Industrial Revolution began again with the appearance of new energy sources (gas, electricity and oil) which made the creation of new technological innovations and inventions possible, such as the internal combustion engine, artificial textiles, the incandescent light bulb, the telephone (by Bell), the telegraph (by Morse), the automobile, the plane, and so on. These means of communication and transport facilitated the creation of international trade.

This was the beginning of a period where the economy and industry were based on new methods of production and management devised by Taylorism and Fordism, and from which the steel industry developed steel and aluminum. Likewise, the economy adopted a new model with the emergence of trusts, cartels and the increasing number of shareholders. Therefore, this period is marked by great innovations which facilitated the economic growth of countries and productivity gains.

Consequently, this Second Industrial Revolution contributed to the emergence of major technical progress, the creation of large companies, especially in the United States, the beginning of globalization and commercial (mainly international), financial and human (human migrations) development. It was accompanied by a reduction of inequalities in industrialized countries and a gradual increase of the workers' standard of living.

– The Third Industrial Revolution emerged during the mid-20th Century in the United States: as before, it was the appearance of a new energy, nuclear generated electricity (Uranium), that marked the beginning of this new Industrial Revolution. This source of energy resulted in the development of revolutionary materials (silicones, ceramics, resins) and contributed worldwide to the structuring of new electronic means of transmission (micro-processor and transistor: see "Information Technology 1.0"[7]) and information technologies to automate production. This opened the way for component miniaturization, which then made electronics one of the main areas of the economy. This period was characterized by the production of ever smaller materials and tools, which had an impact and opened up new prospects, especially in the aerospace, aeronautic and biotechnology industries. Let us note that some experts consider that the history of electronics started with the invention of the vacuum tube by Fleming in 1904, followed by the invention of the triode by Lee de Forest in 1907.

It was in the United States, more specifically in California in Palo Alto, that this revolution really started at the beginning of the 1940s with the creation by William Hewlett and David Packard of the first company based on digital technology, which resulted in the emergence in 1971 of the Silicon Valley, the first global technopole. At the end of WWII, the engineer Vannevar Bush invented a memorizing machine storing microfilms. At mid-decade, in the United States, the Citizen-Band (or "CB") activity appeared, which was the first involvement of amateurs in the field of telecommunications. In 1957, the USSR put the first artificial satellite into orbit, Sputnik 1. This stage was decisive in the age of telecommunications, especially for the implementation of the Internet a few decades later. The process of component miniaturization – as the image of the integrated circuit (or "electronic chip") invented by Jack Kilby (of Texas Instrument), or the modem (by Bell) making it possible to disseminate binary data – relentlessly continued. This phenomenon increased production cost reduction, while programming languages were more and more elaborate via increasingly powerful algorithms. Computer commercialization had only just started and only concerned the business field.

Finally, in 1969, thanks to the research of Léonard Kleinrock (at the MIT) on the use of packet switching for data transfer, the ARPANET (Advanced Research Projects Agency Network) project was created. The

7 "Information Technology 1.0" represents an IT device which transfers voice, data and images on the same network.

implementation of this device within the US Department of Defense took place in the context of the Cold War with the USSR. The challenge of this system was to develop a structurally decentralized military telecommunications network able to operate despite the destruction of some devices or line breaks. Its development and use at the level of the whole society, which was never considered at the time, marked the arrival of the Internet and, along with it, the beginning of the Fourth Industrial Revolution or "Digital Revolution", at the beginning of the 1990s.

– The Fourth Industrial Revolution took place at the end of the 20th Century in the United States and China: this revolution was directly associated with the emergence of the massive development of information technology, namely the fact that any information can be expressed through a combination of numbers (namely 0s and 1s). We consider that this Fourth Industrial Revolution appeared at the beginning of the 1990s, with the appearance of the most famous form of Internet today, the Web[8].

Let us note that the philosopher Luciano Floridi [FLO 14] also referred to the Fourth Revolution in his book entitled *The Fourth Revolution*, in order to characterize this new ecosystem focused on digital information reconciling nature (*physis*) and technology (*technè*). The author assumed that human beings represent informative organisms (*inforgs*) [FLO 07] among others, which are not very different from material entities, natural or artificial agents, smart systems, or modified connected objects.

It can be noted that in 1991, China was one of the pioneers of this digital revolution with the design of the first TCP/IP[9] network, called the TUNET, at Tsinghua University. Three years later, a first connection to the Internet was designed by linking the electron spectrometer of Beijing to the linear accelerator of Stanford University.

Today, we are right in the middle of the period characterized by a fusion of NICTs, which blurs the lines between physical, digital and biological spaces worldwide. Digitalization facilitates the construction of a new, virtual world from which it is possible to drive the physical sphere, especially

8 The Web is also called the "World Wide Web" (WWW). It represents a public hypertext system operating on the Internet. It can be described as a set of HTML pages mixing text, links and images, that can be sent via a URL and accessed through the HTTP protocol.

9 The TCP/IP suite represents all the protocols used for data transfer on the Internet.

thanks to the analysis of databases and big data. Therefore, data represents the raw material of this digital revolution. In fact, it is often compared to oil, which is itself the main element of the Second Industrial Revolution.

Thus, these industrial revolutions helped to develop new products and new technologies. This can be illustrated by the creation of personal computers (see Information Technology 1.0) (1980s), the exponential growth of Internet uses, such as websites, forums and social media (see Information Technology 2.0[10]) (1990s), and the appearance of connected objects, smartphones, tablets, the Industrial Internet of Things (IIoT), (see Information Technology 3.0[11]) (2000s). For example, it can be said that NICTs, such as connected objects, play the same catalytic role for big data as chemistry and automobiles for oil.

This Fourth Revolution is the first one to directly impact and modify the everyday space–time landmarks of people. There is indeed a real digitalization and "platformization" of society (AI, Programmable Logic Controller (PLC), self-learning expert systems, biotechnologies, three dimensions (3D), and robots, Uber, Airbnb, BlaBlaCar, smart cities, etc.) (See Information Technology 4.0[12]) (2010s). In fact, all big cities in the world are starting to fully integrate the digital aspect. These smart cities are made possible through the installation and widespread usage of sensors (along with its inhabitants), as well as networking these sensors via telecommunications operators. The objective is to provide new services, improve the quality of life and security, and have a more sustainable city (urban planning, transport management, citizen integration, etc.). The installation of sensors on buildings makes it possible, for example to obtain interesting data on pollution levels in the air, energy consumption, and so on. In Singapore, the city has placed building-integrated sensors, which generate useful, reliable and instant data for the prevention and management of natural disasters (climate data, space data, photographs of urban areas, etc.).

---

10 "Information Technology 2.0" makes the exchange and sharing of information possible between persons through digital networks.

11 "Information Technology 3.0" corresponds to "Information Technology 2.0" enhanced with a digital data location capacity.

12 "Information Technology 4.0" is defined as being "Information Technology 3.0" in which we can now integrate the information derived from the space and environment context, namely the "infosphere".

The latest technological progress has helped to develop the generation, collection, storage, processing and dissemination of various forms of digital data at an unprecedented significant speed [HAM 07]. Moreover, it can be noted that coltan is one of the major sources of tantalum production (especially niobium) used for its high resistance to corrosion. This raw material is essential for making electrical components, especially surface wave capacitors and filters, used in the manufacturing of mobile phones and laptops.

Nowadays, we refer to "Industry 4.0"[13] which tends to connect together all the means of production and makes their interaction in real time possible in an open space with no defined border. This is made possible thanks to NICTs, such as cloud computing, blockchain, augmented reality, big data analytics or the Internet of Things. This period sees the emergence of new actors such as the American giants GAFAM (Google, Apple, Facebook, Amazon and Microsoft), GAFAMITIS (Google, Apple, Facebook, Amazon, Microsoft, IBM, Twitter, Intel and Salesforce), or even the Chinese NATU (Netflix, Airbnb, Tesla and Uber) and BATX (Baidu, Alibaba, Tencent and Xiaomi) which represent the emblematic companies of the digital "disruption"[14]. According to a Gartner survey, by 2021, 20% of all human individual activities will be directly linked to at least one of the GAFA and BAT members. As an example, we can consider Apple with the launch in 2007 of the iPhone, which resulted in the creation of a market based on smartphones. On the other hand, China has developed big data in the maritime sector with the creation of a "smart ocean". Therefore, Tsinghua University has set up a marine big data remote sensing center, taking into consideration the airwaves of oceanic storms, monitoring internal inundations and including an early warning system.

13 The concept of "Industry 4.0" was first described during the Trade Fair for Industrial Technology in Hannover, in 2011. It corresponds to a new way of organizing the means of production from technological bases, such as the Internet of Things, big data technologies and cyber-physical systems. The objective is to set up smart factories able to better adapt their production and better use the resources at their disposal.

14 Etymologically, this term comes from the Latin *disruptus*, past particle of the verb *disrumpere* or *dirumpere*, which means "burst, break apart, destroy, sever". In economy, this term is used to describe a sudden break, especially when a company introduces a new completely innovating product or service, which disturbs the strategy of the company and breaks the market codes by causing a disruption, a new economic model, a new market, and therefore new consumption behaviors.

Thus, Wu Lixin, the Director of the Qindao National Laboratory for Marine Science and Technology, proposed the project called “Transparent Ocean”, which is driven by satellite sensing, intelligent buoys, underwater gliders and robots, deep-sea space stations, and other various NICTs. The main challenge is to be able to, on the one hand, obtain overall information on the marine ecosystem at different depths in certain locations in real or normal time and, on the other hand, guarantee safety in inlets, at the level of environmental ecology and marine resources, the prevention of maritime disasters and weather forecast. Finally, the Chinese Government made blockchain technology one of its priorities. As an example, we can consider the implementation of this NICT for the collection of social taxes and the issue of Chinese e-invoices.

Unlike previous ones, this industrial revolution is, on the one hand, driven by a digital raw material which cannot be depleted – on the contrary, it is exponential – and, on the other hand, does not have the disadvantage of being energy-intensive – in terms of non-renewable energies – since it is increasingly associated with models powered by alternative resources. With the convergence of nanotechnologies, biotechnologies, IT and cognitive science, we have transitioned to the age of technoscience and data centrism. The living and non-living worlds, interconnected through an Internet of all things, are inexhaustible sources of data and of generation of information streams. The body, the human brain, movements, behaviors, feelings or emotions are a wealth of information constantly collected and processed through arithmetic and logic operations [GHE 18].

Over the years, databases have continued to increase, statistics are going to become more and more accurate, algorithmic processes more defined, and decision-making more fair. In fact, we can legitimately think that, if these predictive NICTs increasingly earn human trust via their performances and efficiency, is mankind not in the process of gradually delegating its decision-making role and therefore a bit of its free will? A vision of the world based on the exploitation of data generated by the user, but also collected and produced from partly interconnected algorithmic systems and processors without its knowledge. In fact, without realizing it, the citizen encourages and feeds the knowledge of self-learning algorithmic systems, AI development, and even the applications based on transhumanism. Such a model prevents us from thinking and using other patterns, since our autonomy is gradually colonized by NICTs.

As history is constantly repeating, as it has done over the previous centuries, this colonization process – which would partly consist of depriving the colonized persons of their natural resources, while maintaining them in a state of inferiority and dependence – still continues nowadays in the form of a "digital colonization" in which raw material is represented by digital data.

In addition, when we study the succession of these industrial revolutions, we notice that the duration of their sequence is getting shorter, going from several centuries to less than half a century. The cyclical pace of these industrial revolutions is then accelerated as time passes. At the same time, we see that the more industrial revolutions follow one another, the more energy sources and their main innovations are decreasing. We are inevitably moving towards the infinitely small, or even the dematerialization of physical structures. We are witnessing the transition and material exploitation of the macrocosm towards the environmental microcosm and, in another sense, from the visible world to the invisible world.

At the same time, the more we move forward in industrial revolutions, the more technological progress has an impact, or even a hold, on the individual. Thus, for the first time in our human history, the Fourth Industrial Revolution – in which we are now – directly affects the essence, nature and status of the human being. Indeed, with the development of AI, we see that the machine directly competes with neurons and the human brain. This can be illustrated by transhumanism, which keeps amplifying relentlessly (see Table I.1).

	1st Industrial Revolution	2nd Industrial Revolution	3rd Industrial Revolution	4th Industrial Revolution	5th Industrial Revolution?
Date of emergence	End of 18th Century	End of 19th Century	Mid-20th Century	End of 20th Century	Mid-21st Century?
Country of origin	United Kingdom and France	Germany and United States	United States	United States and China	China and United States?
World population*	0.8 to 1.1 billion	1.5 to 1.8 billion	2.5 to 3.3 billion	4.4 to 5.7 billion	8.5 to 11.1 billion?

Sources of energy and raw materials	Coal	Gas, electricity and oil	Nuclear (uranium) and electronics (silicones, ceramics, resins)	Coltan, digital technology (big data and database)	Quantum?
Main inventions	Steam engine	Internal combustion engine, incandescent light bulb, telephone	Nuclear power plant, micro-processor, transistor	Computer, robot, Internet, IoT, NICT, blockchain	Computer, teleportation, avatar and quantum cryptology?
Nature of the information	Analog	Analog	Digital (Information Technology 1.0)	Digital (Information Technology 1.0, 2.0, 3.0, and 4.0)	Digital (Information Technology 4.0), Quantum? (Information Technology 5.0)?
Nature of the law	Civil Code	Labor Code	Charter of Fundamental Rights, bioethical law, DVB-T	Robot and Digital Ecosystem Code? Cyberspace International Treaty?	Environmental and Quantum Transformation Code?
Nature of the ethics	Utilitarian ethics	Positivist ethics	Bioethics	Algorithmic ethics?	Quantum ethics?

Table I.1. *Industrial revolutions through time (*sources: UN (World Population Prospects: The 2015 and 2017 Revision))*

Furthermore, when we look at the world population for each emergence of this event, we note, on the one hand, that the number of people nearly doubles each time compared to the previous one and, on the other hand, that the time between the succession of these technical revolutions is increasingly shorter with an acceleration coefficient between 1.3 and 1.5 (see Figure I.1).

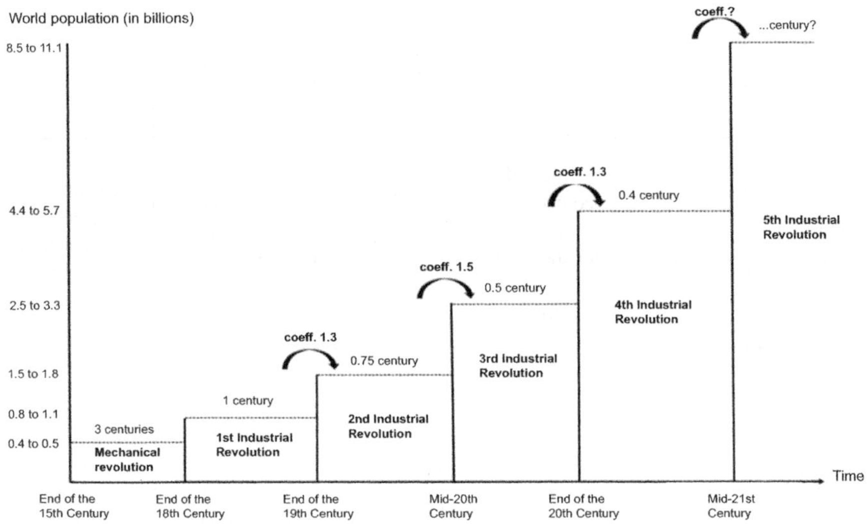

Figure I.1. *Main technical revolutions of mankind through time (sources: UN (World Population Prospects: The 2015 and 2017 Revision))*

We note that this rule partly works with the mechanic revolution, with the invention of the typographical printing press by Johannes Gutenberg around 1450, a period during which the world population was estimated between 0.42 and 0.54 billion people. Even if the appearance of printing is not considered by historians as a real industrial revolution, it also had a disruptive nature for society during the Renaissance. According to the historian Elizabeth Eisenstein [EIS 91], in 50 years, between 1457 and 1500, almost eight million books were printed, namely the equivalent of all that had been produced by European scribes since the founding of Constantinople. Thus, printing made it possible to set texts and contributed to spreading ideas, in particular those of humanists, and then those of the Reformation. The Bible could be read and understood thanks to its full translation in German, French and English.

On the other hand, according to the archeologist Jean-Paul Demoule [DEM 17], the Neolithic revolution with the invention of agriculture and animal husbandry facilitated a sedentary lifestyle and resulted in an unprecedented demographic boom. Thus, on average, female hunter-gatherers had one child every three or four years compared to one every year for female farmers (even if some of these children died as infants). We can therefore consider and assume that our demographic rule regarding the doubling of the world population also applied between the emergence of the Neolithic revolution and the beginning of the Secondary Products Revolution[15].

Further study of this observation could perhaps imply a law on the emergence of a new industrial revolution pursuant to, on the one hand, an established doubling of the world population and, on the other hand, an acceleration coefficient of 1.3–1.5 compared to the emergence of the previous industrial revolution. However, it can be noted that it is highly likely that this "law" will reach its limits after the Fifth Industrial Revolution. In fact, numerous studies estimate that Earth cannot accommodate more than 10 billion coexisting human beings, due to its limited resources. The future of the number of people on the planet could then highly depend on future innovations in terms of natural resources, as well as the eating and environmentally friendly habits of individuals.

Thus, if we make a projection from the estimates of the world population (according to *The 2017 Revision* study and UN average scenarios), with an acceleration coefficient around 1.3–1.5 between the period of the two technical revolutions, the next industrial revolution (the fifth one) should emerge around the first half of the 21st Century (around 2040). In fact, according to the UN demographic estimates, it is very likely that we will reach 10 billion people in the next 20 years. We suspect that the major energy source that will be exploited is *quantum* (see quantum physics) with the creation and implementation of technological innovations such as the quantum computer, quantum teleportation, quantum imaging, quantum avatars[16], and quantum cryptology. We note that this quantum and cognitive information technology represents a new step in the development of machines

---

15 According to the English anthropologist Andrew Sherratt, the Secondary Products Revolution, after the Neolithic revolution, occurred when Neolithic people became aware that animals could provide several other products useful for mankind.

16 Quantum avatars correspond to a system intermixing digital identities, connected relationship, avatars and principles of quantum mechanics. They are an implementation of an interactive device and a networked digital system derived from a metaphorical transposition of the principles of quantum physics. This will make it possible to study the relationship dynamics of living beings through time and space.

and computerization. These quantum NICTs are developed to reach, or even circumvent, the standard limits in space and time metrology, magnetic fields, gravitation, and so on. This list of fields of application and range of possibilities will only be limited by the imagination of mathematicians, physicists, computer scientists and engineers.

On the other hand, this Fifth Industrial Revolution will mark the advent of "Industry 4.0" and cybernetics[17], and therefore of "Society 5.0"[18] since quantum computing will allow us to exploit all the possible uses of "Information Technology 4.0" – focused on big data – by fully integrating the whole space context and digital ecosystem. We can imagine that with the new quantum applications, especially thanks to quantum computers and quantum teleportation, we will see the emergence of an "Information Technology 5.0" for which developers managed to bring the integration capacity of the time context within "Information Technology 4.0". The generated information will be of a quantum nature. This next industrial revolution could become the scene of the planned obsolescence of the human being.

Finally, countries where this new revolution might emerge could well be the United States and China, which are already well in advance in the R&D work focused on quantum applications. We can consider the example of China which, a year after launching Mozi – the first quantum communications satellite – managed, in 2017, the first quantum teleportation over long distances and from space.

In addition, when we closely analyze all these technical revolutions through time, we notice that they all have an informational nature:

– *mechanic revolution*: developed the information support (with printing): analog information;

– *1st Industrial Revolution*: accelerated the information transport (with the steam engine for people and post): analog information;

---

17 Cybernetics describes itself as the government science or also the information management aiming at piloting systems. This discipline partly took off thanks to the work of the mathematician Norbert Wiener.

18 It is defined as the "society of intelligence" where physical space and cyberspace are highly involved and integrated. This society represents the will to optimize the research of the four previous societies (1.0, 2.0, 3.0, and 4.0).

– 2nd *Industrial Revolution*: created information means (with the telephone and telegraph): analog information;

– *3rd Industrial Revolution:* invented information tools (with the microprocessor and transistor): digital information;

– *4th Industrial Revolution:* deploys information objects, networks and the information ecosystem (with the computer, robot, IoT, Internet, blockchain): digital information;

– *5th Industrial Revolution:* leads to information transformation (with the quantum computer, quantum teleportation and quantum avatars): digital and quantum information.

According to the economist Jeremy Rifkin [RIF 11], a change of civilization is activated from the moment a revolution appears in three sectors: communications, energy and transport. These three pillars all have one point linking them, namely information. Finally, it is all about information. When reading about the chain of these technical information revolutions, we realize that each invention or creation has an informational nature, and is itself governed and dedicated to the development and expression of information as such. A certain logic seems to emerge from the succession of these revolutions, where each corresponds to a step whose outcome moves towards a total information miniaturization and transformation of matter.

We go from a macroscopic state (governed by classical physical laws) respectively illustrated by the information support, transport, means, tools, objects, networks and ecosystem, to a microscopic state (driven by the laws of quantum physics) embodied by the information transformation. From that to saying that the final step is only the revelation of what we really are – that is to say information – is only one step away! Because in the end, we see that everything is information and at its service, whether these are living beings, the environment, or Nature and the physical laws structuring it.

The whole universe is governed by information laws, and everything existing in the universe is driven by information. The latter determines the behavior of atoms, electrons, life and the universe itself. Each subatomic particle, each atom, each molecule, each cell, each living species, each planet, each star and each galaxy is full of information. Information is part of each interaction occurring in the universe, and Nature is structured and revealed through the use of information and algorithmic systems.

As the history of humanity is cyclical, it is justified to wonder if our law regarding the doubling of the world population and the acceleration coefficient of 1.3–1.5 between two technical revolutions would not be the consequences of an algorithm[19] on a global, or even universal, scale. It is the same for the quantum theory which, we know today, is nothing other than an information theory for which information is not an abstraction, but a physical thing whose property is concretely expressed in matter and energy. Under these conditions, we can offer the hypothesis that the whole history of mankind can be considered as a single data processing algorithmic system, of which mankind would be an integral part, as an information transmitter and receiver, and even as a processor. Each area of the world macrocosm is connected to the life microcosm, where information must freely flow. This data-centric approach of the world can seem extravagant at first, or even a bit provocative. However, it has the merit of asking real questions about humankind's evolution.

In addition, all these (r)evolutions are accompanied by social and human progress, with a time of transition and adaptation. In the end, they always resulted in productivity gains and the creation of more jobs than they destroyed. Of course, industrial revolution means creative destruction. This mutation disrupts all the global geopolitical rules, established concepts, the global economy and, more directly, the way citizens see the world (see Culture), behave with other people (see Mores and attitudes), and consider themselves (see Representation). Each industrial revolution therefore supports the emergence of a new form of Law. Thus, we see that the First Industrial Revolution was accompanied by the creation in France of the Civil Code (or Napoleonic Code) – promulgated on March 21, 1804 – regrouping all the French civil laws, namely all the rules determining the status of persons (book I), that of property (book II) and that of relationships between private persons (books III and IV). As for the Second Industrial Revolution, the latter saw the emergence of the Labor Code. We can consider the example of the French Labor Code entitled *Code du travail et de la prévoyance sociale*, whose first book was adopted on December 28, 1910. This Code is an organized compilation of most of the laws and regulations

19 This idea of Nature integrating codes, programs and algorithms will be further developed in Chapter 2 of this book.

applicable to labor law, and which mainly concern employees under a private law employment contract, as employees from the public sector are generally subject to special statuses.

After these first two industrial revolutions, the Human Rights Movement preserved and ensured the general social good by reducing barriers to the respect for the natural person. With the Charter of Fundamental Rights of December 7, 2000, and following the Universal Declaration of Human Rights and the European Convention for the Protection of Human Rights, the European Union has focused on the inviolability of human dignity. In addition to being a fundamental right in itself, this human dignity is a pillar which supports other rights and freedoms, including the rights to the protection of personal data and privacy[20]. At the same time, the Third Industrial Revolution was marked, in our opinion, by the creation of two other major instruments:

– on the one hand, the first law on bioethics which was voted in 1984, in the State of Victoria, Australia, the Infertility Treatment Act, aiming at regulating *in vitro* fertilization practices. This legislative and statutory text provides an official legal framework which changes according to scientific discoveries and ethical reflections;

– on the other hand, the Treaty of the Non-Proliferation of Nuclear Weapons (NPT) which corresponds to an international treaty recorded and signed on July 1, 1968 by a great number of countries. It aims at reducing the risk of nuclear weapons spreading through the world, and its implementation is guaranteed by the International Atomic Energy Agency (IAEA). This text is the first one to partly regulate the uses of this energy source, namely nuclear power.

As the Fourth Industrial Revolution is still ongoing, we can only make assumptions. However, some signs make us think that we are heading towards the implementation of a "Robot Code"[21], a *Lex robotica* allowing

20 See Article 1 of the Charter of Fundamental Rights which is a declaration of fundamental rights adopted on December 7, 2000 by the European Union and implemented by the Nice Treaty.

21 In his 1942 short story entitled *Runaround*, the science-fiction author Isaac Asimov set out three robotics laws, which are ethical rules. This became the cornerstone of dozens of other novels and stories from the same author [AZI 50, AZI 85]. They are more like the rules of a game than the bases of a legal system. These three laws eponymous of robotics are that

law texts to better understand and anticipate the change in paradigm of the modern world that is being established. In fact, the school of thought of "robotarians" [BEN 15b], which is getting stronger, wishes that robots have a full legal status, similar to human beings and the "humanitarian" movement [LOI 15, MEN 16].

In fact, the Committee on Legal Affairs (JURI) of the European Parliament adopted, on February 16, 2017, a resolution project demanding from the Commission, European rules on robot law and its digital environment. This instrument is directly influenced by the development of robots and AI, which keeps increasing along with a number of both legal and ethical problems. Finally, we could imagine the creation of an International Cyberspace Treaty with a Cyberspace Geneva Declaration which, for example, could set out in its preamble that "men and women of all nations recognize that mankind must provide cyberspace with what is best, asserting their obligations, regardless of any consideration of race, nationality, belief" [GHE 18].

As for the Fifth Industrial Revolution, we can assume that we might need to create a Code of the (physical and temporal) environment and quantum transformation, in order to monitor and control the use of quantum applications of all kinds (computers, teletransportations, transactions, telecommunications, avatars, etc.), which are going to disrupt, at the global level, the space-time relationship of mankind.

Furthermore, we note that, as each emergence of a new industrial revolution occurs earlier and earlier, this results in making the adaptation of individuals to society more complex and difficult, due to an increasingly shorter transition time.

Finally, since forever, periods of change have created both enthusiasm and concern. The modification of landmarks, uncertainties, and disregard about the close future of society, fuel people's doubts. Under these conditions, these industrial and social disruptions are always accompanied by an ethical framework applicable according to the environment and fields of application.

"a robot may not injure a human being or, through inaction, allow a human being to come to harm", "a robot must obey orders given it by human beings except where such orders would conflict with the First Law", "a robot must protect its own existence as long as such protection does not conflict with the First or Second Law".

Thus, we notice that the First Industrial Revolution was more framed by utilitarianism from the legacy of the Age of Enlightenment and a deep influence of the English Empire via Jeremy Bentham. It was characterized by a pattern of thought which, failing to be able to objectively define what is Good and Evil, offered to ignore it by using "usefulness" as the first principle of so-called rational action. Regarding the Second Industrial Revolution, we saw a philosophical doctrine founded by Auguste Compte being developed, "positivism". This ethics reflected the mistrust of great hypotheses, or even the simple thought to only focus on the most immediate certainties and the most concrete goods. The Third Industrial Revolution saw the emergence, in the 1960s, of bioethics, arising from the ethical questions posed by the use of new medical technologies (biomedicine and technoscience) and the power struggles they highlighted. This field of ethics was at the junction of three old disciplines anchored in society, which are (religious or philosophical) morality, politics and science. Nowadays, the Fourth Industrial Revolution forces actors to rethink and reinvent the existing ethics, in order to move towards an algorithmic ethics mainly applied to digital technology. This ethics becomes crucial in order for all the people concerned to find the right balance between a rational and measured processing of digital data respecting privacy, and an over-processing which would be counter-productive for society. Algorithmic ethics would make it possible to give meaning to the digitalization of the world, by relying on the concept of Responsibility by Design or Ethics by Design, which we will describe later in this book. This is necessary in order to better understand, accompany and regulate this Industrial Revolution. Because, as Max Weber explained, "Revolution is not a carriage one can get off at will". We cannot escape it!

Like its predecessor, we can imagine that the future Fifth Industrial Revolution will have to be driven by a quantum ethics, namely an ethics whose scope of action will be directed towards innovations concerning the quantum sector. Just like the previous one, this ethics is to be built and implemented. It will probably rely on the same bases and parameters as quantum mechanics, namely space, time and the infinitely small.

In the end, we see that these technical revolutions have direct consequences on the organization of work, the economy and social relationships in general, but also contribute (or should contribute) to mankind questioning its future and the meaning of the world it is building.

I.3. Emergence and multiform omnipresence of NICTs in society

The digital world is characterized by its instantaneity, its information density, its omnipresence, in contrast with the concrete world of things. Nowadays, with the multiplication of the means of connection, the cost reduction of technologies, the new capacities of data collection and processing, we realize that we can make elements of our environment communicate, which were up to now silent. We see the multiform development of New Information and Communications Technologies (NICTs) illustrated by the emergence of technologies associated with big data, connected objects, algorithms, Nanotechnology, Biotechnology, Information technology and Cognitive science (NBIC), blockchain, Artificial Intelligence (AI), virtual and augmented reality, and even quantum computing in all the areas of activity of our contemporary society. Digital technology can even be found in the world of art, which is often depicted as the sphere reserved to mankind. Thus, autonomous computers allowed artists to design melodies, harmonies or voices from music tracks or extracts that they forwarded to different software. We can also consider the example of the music album *Hello World* for which the Belgian artist Stromae used AI to compose two music tracks. The universe of painting is no exception with an autonomous deep learning machine able to study the paintings of prestigious artists to understand their styles and to reproduce them from a photo. This algorithmic system can then generate works of art from masters such as Picasso, Van Gogh or Leonardo da Vinci.

This multi-faceted digital phenomenon is gathering different worlds by adding the speed, intelligence and ubiquity specific to digital technology to objects associated with these NICTS. This technoscientific context is favorable to the development of an increasingly significant international cultural and intellectual movement, namely transhumanism, whose objective is to improve the physical and mental features of the human being by relying on biotechnologies and other emerging technologies. This school of thought considers that some states of the human condition such as disease, disability, pain, aging or death are not inevitable *per se* and can be corrected, or even eliminated.

Thus, technological revolutions made a change in scale possible [CAM 04] in the exploitation of digital data, especially in the genetics field. They can be produced in great quantity, in an increasingly accurate way and be indefinitely stored. The aim of digital data processing is to reveal information hidden within large volumes of data. We see that progress in IT made possible, thanks to the creation of specific programs, the interoperability of databases, thereby facilitating the fusion of data from various and multiple sources. We can add to this the development of new modes of access to data, in particular through the multiplication of data sources of all kinds. If we consider the biomedical and medical sector, crowdsourcing[22] becomes one of the new devices providing easier access, in real time, to health data in order to develop research [KHA 15].

Finally, with the digitalization of the world, which results in excessive hyper-connectivity, a permanent automation and multiplication of exchanges, networks and information flows, mankind no longer lives with machines, but is learning to live in a technical-humanist cyberspace.

I.3.1. *Big data*

Mankind generates and exploits data at varying scales, with the knowledge and technologies of the time. History tells us that clay tablets from Mesopotamia probably represented one of the first databases and information bases in sectors as diverse as literature (*The Epic of Gilgamesh*), mathematics (Babylonian geometry and algebra) and commerce (accounting).

According to the European Union, big data can be defined as "large amounts of different types of data produced with high velocity from a high number of various types of sources. Handling today's highly variable and real-time datasets requires new tools and methods, such as powerful processors, software and algorithms"[23].

Generally, computer scientists more often use the term data than "information". This comes from the fact that data are mainly characterized by their type, which can be digital, alphabetical, temporal, binary, alphanumeric, and so on. Nowadays, more than 90% of data are semi-structured or

---

22 In France, participative production is defined by the French Commission of Terminology and Neology as "the embodiment of a project or product involving the contributions of a large number of people, usually Internet users", *OJFR* No 0179 of August 5, 2014, p. 12995, text No 91.

23 Communication of the Commission at the European Parliament, the Council, the European Economic and Social Committee and the Committee of the Regions, Towards a thriving data-driven economy, /* COM/2014/0442 final */, Introduction point 2. http://eur-lex.europa.eu/legal-content/FR/ALL/?uri=CELEX:52014DC0442.

non-structured. By nature, data are only individualized and neutral residues from an effort of de-contextualization [ROU 14].

Every day, significant quantities of data are collected by means of our browsing history, our activity on social media, or even through sensors associated with connected objects. We estimate that the volume of data stored in the world doubles every four years [BLO 13]. In 2013, mankind stored more than 2,000 billion gigabytes of new digital data.

Data only has content and a type. It has no meaning in itself as it is objective and real. It is built from facts, observations and gross elements. Without processing, its meaning is low. These big data say a lot about the individual, such as their age, health condition, financial and insurance capacity, location, even their interests and behaviors. Once collected and analyzed, big data are very valuable in sectors such as advertising, marketing, urban planning, finance or even health. Thus, thanks to the information collected, some companies are often able to offer personalized products more in line with the habits and tastes of their customers. From a merchant point of view, big data transform consumers' activities into information in order to document the market's players. They therefore represent a documentation process.

Let us note that these big data can be considered and understood as secondary data, in that the majority is not collected in order to answer research questions identified in advance [KIT 14]. These big data imply what is covered by the acquisition of analytical and heterogeneous data, whose exploitation requires the use of the latest technological and algorithmic progress (machine and deep learning). Under these conditions, a lot of information can be digitally recorded and can provide information on, or even direct, our behaviors via NICTs and self-learning dynamic algorithms. After a deductive reflection, in a probabilistic bottom up approach directly at odds with classical scientific visions which are mainly hypothetical and deductive, big data can be represented not only by the production of a large quantity of data, but also by the potential benefits (for health, economy, education, ecology, etc.) which the use of these technologies could have. Indeed, we estimate that the value produced by the data provided by European citizens could represent 1,000 billion euro in 2020, namely 8% of the European GDP[24].

24 Available at: http://europa.eu/rapid/press-release_SPEECH-13-788_en.htm.

Now, all data are personal. Even the most insignificant data can reveal the identity of a person if it is crossed with numerous other data, made possible by the Internet. The main danger of big data is not only the risks to privacy and confidentiality of the individual, but also the risk that society is led to judge people not according to their actual behavior, but their tendency to behave as data claim they do.

Since the development of NICTs and algorithmic technologies, we see the increasingly frequent appearance of so-called "non-structured" or "semi-structured" data[25] which are supplementing and enriching structured data from traditional computer applications (ERP, CRM, SCM, etc.). These data will be identified and called non-structured as soon as they undergo a more complex transformation, before revealing their meaning and expressive value. The exploitation of these data, which is often in real time, systematically goes through powerful algorithms and can, in some situations, be the core of the information to be analyzed [BEN 14]. After being processed, data are transformed into information which is more characterized by its meaning, whose understanding and acquisition naturally result in knowledge. This knowledge represents what makes it possible to locate information, contextualize it and globalize it, namely to locate it within a set. From an etymologic point of view, information provides a knowledge that the recipient does not have or cannot predict. It helps to reduce uncertainties and clarify things.

Therefore, the diversity of the multifaceted character of data is one of the main benefits of a big data project. The interest is in the comparison and crossing of numerous sets of very different non- or semi-structured data[26] from various origins such as:

– electronic messages (e-mails and instant messages), forums, social media and websites, elements entered and traces left on the Web, the digitalization of contractual documents, and conversations with call centers;

– data associated with mobility: identifiers (SIM card, IMEI identification number, UID, etc.), browsing history, and geolocation;

25 The source of "non-structured" data can be pictures, videos and sounds, whereas "semi-structured" data come more from email messages, logs, etc.

26 According to Gabriel Siméon, in the newspaper *Libération* in 2012, "mankind produces as much information in two days as it did in two million years. The future belongs to those who know how to make use of this profusion".

– data from connected objects: machines, sensors, home automation, "smart" cars and meters, personal biometric systems, set-top boxes (Internet gateways of operators, box of cable operators, etc.);

– data produced and shared outside the traditional communications circuits of a structure and organization via the social Internet [BÉR 16].

These data are derived from different sources such as energy meters, RFID, financial transactions, volume commercial operations, social media, blogs, industrial sensor networks, Internet indexing, telephony, details of calls made to call centers, GPS routes, medical files, e-commerce, the Internet of Things (IoT), embarked information technology, data from massively online games, biological data, surveys, logs, emails, and so on.

This variability of the intrinsic character of data reflects both the value added and the complexity of carrying out an algorithmic processing of digital data requiring multidisciplinary actors within the company.

Today, the exponential growth of data cannot be separated from its context and environment. This phenomenon is directly and/or indirectly associated with:

– data generation by sensors and machines;

– the change in number of final users[27] of IT solutions;

– the fineness of the information traced;

– the development of the areas covered and uses (mobiles, satellites, 4 or even 5G, etc.);

– the development of the data history available;

– the increase in operational volumes.

Beside the gross or quantitative information it has, it gives information on the quality of the one disseminating it. Now, we query what digital data say about the ethics of the structure providing it. Indeed, big data include a paradoxical intrinsic value: on the one hand, they reinforce the idea of seeing

27 Final users can be characterized as either direct (private individuals and professionals) or indirect (employees or students whose respective career (see HR software) and orientation (see admission after High School Certificate (APB)) progress is allegedly driven by an algorithmic system).

information exit the structure and, on the other hand, they present the risk of a Big Brother effect.

In both cases, we are dealing with the field of visibility, which requires an additional control of the announced NICT validity. Multi-sector applications around big data are numerous: predictive maintenance, assistance with decision-making in real time, optimum coordination between trades, analysis of the purchase behaviors of a person on an e-commerce site and suggestion in real time of products, live monitoring of mechanical parts to predict the best time to replace them, prediction of criminal acts (within one hundred meters) in Los Angeles, selective destruction of archived documents, automatic diagnosis of pathologies in real time [SER 16], anticipation of stock management according to production progress, and so on.

We can consider the example of *in silico*[28] clinical trials, where therapeutic choices are tested and evaluated on a digital twin (a kind of avatar), created from very elaborate mathematical models established on the basis of big data. This digital twin can, in particular, facilitate "virtual" clinical tests, or even avoid unnecessary interventions.

Coupled with genomic sequencing, such an approach would then help to create predictive and customized medicine. It is the case of the Insigneo Institute – based in Sheffield, Great Britain – which works on the Virtual Physiological Human (VPH), namely a virtual physiological twin of the human.

On the other hand, we see projects gradually developing the "smart" city, such as SystemX in Lyon (France), which targets smart territories, in connection with the actions conducted by the Greater Lyon area on the smart metropole.

The objective is to develop decision-making assistance tools able to add value to urban data. This project will use big data technologies to focus on everything related to connected and smart urban mobility: traffic management sensors, goods tracking in the city, urban lighting, car park dynamic management, security, the Internet of Things (or IoT), etc.

---

28 The term *in silico* corresponds to a neologism of Latin origin referring to a research or test carried out by means of complex computations or computer models.

These are innovations which slightly improve production tools on a daily basis and suggest unlimited possibilities for the future of "Industry 4.0", a crossroads of a global interconnected process.

I.3.2. *The Internet of Things*

The Internet of Things (or IoT) corresponds to the objects connected to the Internet which disseminate digital data through radio-frequency (RFID) chips. These objects can communicate between themselves. They can be found in everyday objects (home automation, connected pedometers, smart electric meters, etc.), cars and planes, cities, the sport medical sector, construction, mass consumption business, insurance and financial trade, and so on. In short, these connected objects invade all fields of society. The value of the Internet of Things overlaps three main levels: objects, connectivity (networks) and data processing (intelligence).

According to an EMC-IDC study in 2015, the IoT will have the effect of "doubling the size of the digital universe every two years, which should weigh 44,000 billion gigabytes in 2020, that is 10 times more than in 2013". According to the McKinsey firm, the Internet of Things has a market which should reach 6.2 trillion dollars in 2025. Connectivity should become a standard feature, with more than 50 billion connected objects present in the world in 2020[29] in industries from automobiles, drones or semi-autonomous aircrafts, through telemedicine, to smart meters facilitating the construction of smart cities [BUT 15]. Their use might lead to serious interferences with privacy and have a dissuasive effect on the freedom of expression of people.

It is important to point out that the real benefit of the IoT does not simply lie in the object and its related technology, but in the services it will provide. This phenomenon is creating new uses and reshaping our lifestyles. We cannot say that the Internet of Things is a revolution in itself from a strictly technological point of view. Thus, autonomous vehicles[30] are probably going to disrupt the way individual's journeys are performed and organized, and could make the distinction between public and private transport unclear.

29 Source: *World Economic Forum*.

30 According to the Boston Consulting Group firm, it is estimated that, by 2035, Europe will have 12 million fully autonomous vehicles and 18 million partially autonomous vehicles.

The true revolution lies mainly in the uses and economic models enabled by this Internet technology. Nowadays, the IoT looks like one of the cornerstones of the transformation of the economy into an economy of services and functionality, in which actors no longer sell objects intended for a given use, but for support, skills and the guarantee of use. Big data from sensors are then designed to continuously produce services in a customized way. Now, the user – person or structure – has, via the Internet of Things, the possibility to act in real time on its environment – in a manual or automated way – in order to optimize processes, such as traffic flows and supply chains, in real time. The main challenge is not really the acquisition of data, but rather its visualization and the related applications: reminders, dashboards, notifications, feedback, and so on, which allow their users to quickly make the best decision for themselves in a simple way. We can consider the example of a car manufacturer integrating a whole series of sensors which makes it possible to extend car services, namely radar warning, predictive maintenance, relay with tow trucks and/or mechanics, and so on. We see in this case that the role of car manufacturers is no longer limited to selling a vehicle – as a simple means of transport – but that they become partners accompanying the motorist during the duration of their travels. IoTs can also be composed of "wearable" objects, such as watches and clothes which can, among other things, detect the presence of blood clots and monitor health condition and the progression of wound healing [BUT 15]. Connected textiles will soon be able to provide protection against the environment, such as high UV indexes from the sun or the flames of a fire.

In the health sector, connected objects, especially connected watches, are increasingly developing on the market by offering applications which make it possible to measure physiological criteria (heartbeat, number of steps per day, blood pressure, calories burnt, etc.). These applications go beyond the gadget stage, as they now have the benefit of monitoring chronic diseases, such as high blood pressure, diabetes, heart rhythm disorders (tachycardia, conduction impairments) and cardiovascular diseases (heart attack) [ATO 06].

In addition, the Internet of Things is going to help radically modify the consumer's behavior, as machines are going to take care of regular consumption purchases. We can consider the example of the smart fridge which orders groceries, from the connected wine cellar which is going to order another bottle of wine when the reserve is running low, to the smart bathroom which orders toiletries online. From now on, products are going to be automatically delivered to users via an automatic payment device – almost invisible – in the form of a monthly payment, just like an electricity or water bill. We are witnessing the beginning of a new purchase dynamics where transactions are partly carried out by IoTs on regular or semi-regular bases.

Technologists rely on the smartphone approach in order to apply it to smart wearables and smart homes. We can consider the example of the Samsung smart fridge, which integrates an interface allowing users to buy products from several shops, directly from the fridge's door. The object also connects to the consumer's smartphone, in order to transmit images of the inside of the fridge online and facilitate remote access to the household's schedule. In the near future, it is highly likely that some households will become true "smart" homes in which integrated operating systems will pilot all domestic appliances via a single management platform. Indeed, progress in the home automation sector is such that soon the central heating of a house will be managed according to the owner's movements. The bathrooms, laundry room, connected medicine cabinet, and so on will place orders to restock products specific to their function.

Beyond the home automation sector, we can make the same observations for all the others areas of society, such as the automobile, mass distribution, the city, and so on. In fact, Cisco provides for, in the near future, streets where streetlights equipped with motion sensors will be able to reduce their intensity according to peak and off-peak periods, thus saving energy. It is also thanks to the solutions of the Internet of Things that some people will be able to monitor their health data or that manufacturers will optimize their operational devices.

Finally, the Internet of Things is closely linked to various data processing platforms, in relation with the waves of cloud computing and big data. Indeed, the latter have the capacity to develop automatic systems, design recommendations and make various actors interact. In the age of GAFAM, NATU, BATX and other platform creators, we are thus witnessing a triangular relationship between the object, the user and the platform in a collaborative economy focused on service to reconcile supply and demand, and not based on ownership, whose ecosystem is fluid and transversal. We talk about disrupting platforms with a collaborative intelligence, which adapt to the benefit of the actors and partners of this digital ecosystem. This has the effect of having a multi-sectorial impact according to different links:

– platform link: the object is centered on technological and structural problems;

– user link: the object relies on awareness, training and appropriation issues;

– user link: the platform is focused on questions regarding ethics, transparency, security and trust.

I.3.3. *Algorithms*

The term "algorithm" comes from the Medieval Latin word *algorithmus*, a Latinization of the name of an Arabic-speaking mathematician called Al-Khwârizmî[31], with the Greek influence *arithmos*: the number. Its origin is estimated to be during the third millennium in Babylonian Mesopotamia. In fact, during Antiquity, Euclid's algorithm made it possible to compute the greatest common divisor of two numbers.

We can define the algorithm as being a set of operating rules, whose application helps to solve a problem set out by means of a finite number of operations. It makes decisions in a deterministic manner and which form part of a gigantic global digital network. It is a method to perform a calculation. It is a finite and non-ambiguous series of instructions or operations, whose mission is either to generate a result, or to solve a given problem. Its initial purpose is to facilitate the optimized performance of repetitive processes, mainly via formalization, and the description of logic successions at a more abstract level, independently of the specific encoding system making its actual implementation possible within a computer, robot, machine, or autonomous information system.

An algorithm can be transformed, thanks to a programming language, into a program executable by computer. It is able to develop computing and modeling techniques from a given objective. The main stages of the

31 In the 9th Century, the Arab mathematician Al-Khwârizmî made the connection with the mathematical knowledge from India (including the decimal system).

performance of an algorithm can be summed up as first selecting the solution that we estimate to be appropriate to a given problem, and then encoding it, namely transcribing it in a language that can be interpreted by the machine.

Algorithms have a mechanical character, as each stage must be as accurate and transparent as possible, while not requiring any human intuition or trial and error. This accuracy provides the possibility for these stages to be transposed within a computer. Another fundamental feature is that an algorithm must work in all cases, regardless of the data fuelling it. No matter what numbers we are trying to add, the "addition" algorithm will always provide a correct answer.

Of course, there are all kinds of algorithms, which are more or less complex and long to define, structure, and then encode. However, the constant developments of Web customization or even of Artificial Intelligence (AI), especially of machine learning, would mean that these will become increasingly elaborate over time. This machine learning provides added value and clarification in the growing information mass, by identifying unknown models or behavior models, via its computer and algorithm power.

Algorithms are multi-factorial and able to adapt in real time to all the requests and actions integrated into them by users. We can mention the recommendation algorithms of social media, streaming platforms, or even transport applications, which are currently perfect examples. This complexity gives them such an economic value that it is sufficient to explain that they represent secrets as well kept as the recipe of our favorite dessert. Indeed, big data alone have a limited intrinsic value. They cannot be transformative. The addition of the algorithm makes it possible to exploit and fully express the true value of big data. Algorithms explicitly or implicitly include value judgments. We can see four types of variables in algorithms: decision, objective, context and auxiliary variables.

Therefore, every day we use, whether consciously or not, dozens or even hundreds of algorithmic programs and "digital computers" [CAR 15]:

– information selection which is visible on a Facebook social media wall (*edgerank*);

– popularity, audience measurements: counting Internet users' clicks and ordering sites' popularity, traditional representation of the public, media or constituents;

– ranking of the results of an information search on Google (*pagerank*), and related to leadership (measurements based on meritocracy);

– matching: for example, distributing patients so that they can take part in a clinical trial via a given cohort;

– knowledge management in order to benefit from large quantities of information (scientific publications, databases and cohorts via open data);

– e-reputation measurements (rating sites and social media): valuing the reputation of people, products and/or services in order to recommend them, inside the Web (typical benchmark statistics);

– recommendation of products such as books (Amazon) or movies (Netflix);

– decision-making assistance (especially for health, insurance and finance professionals);

– optimization of travels for a given mode of transport;

– prediction[32] (detection of diseases or epidemics, customization of contents facilitated by the browsing traces of Internet users, deployment of police forces, etc.).

As this "algorithmization" of our society applies to all fields and areas of activity, we see that predictive models are multiplying exponentially. As a result, our representations are formatted. Since everything becomes data, from objects, our lives, to the human being itself, this phenomenon is only at the start of its development.

Programmers implant systematic methods in Information Systems (IS), algorithms, which are the accurate description of elementary actions and their sequence. Therefore, algorithms have become omnipresent and essential in our contemporary society. They are designed by mankind and

32 These prediction algorithms generally correspond to "black boxes" causing both technical and mathematical problems to understand them, and societal problems of transparency regarding their moral acceptability.

are at the very heart of all our IS. To that end, they use data massively produced in all sectors, such as finance, ecology, science, insurance, health, and so on. Based on statistical processing, these algorithms create predictive, or even self-fulfilling, correlations which are not necessarily explanatory. They guide choices and behaviors that are both individual and collective: smart travels[33], targeted advertising by identifying potential buyers of a product or service, medical recommendations (pacemakers ensuring the maintenance of natural heart rhythms), detection of bank fraud or even identification of bad payers, private or public policies, tariff determination, quick alert devices closely monitoring coming storms or detecting seismic activity, pricing of a plane ticket (Yield Management), creation of a list of terrorist suspects (French law on intelligence), distribution of French pupils or students in high schools or universities (*Affelnet*, admission after high school diploma (APB)), and so on. Thus, the presence and application of algorithms in each section of society confirm that they define the way the world works.

However, some people question our attitude towards algorithms and our tendency to consider as right the results of these complex computations. Yet, an algorithm also contains a set of mathematical hypotheses which can quickly become the target of prejudices in real life.

Whether they are used to rank, link, select, or even predict, algorithms are instructions taking the form of a computer code. Even if these algorithms have different aims and purposes, they all have a common feature, namely they are all based on performance. Behind these lines of code are hidden numerous mathematicians, computer scientists and engineers responsible for programming them and thereby giving them life. First of all, structures or entrepreneurs still need to identify and accurately determine the problem they wish to address. Thus, in the case of a search engine, designers must wonder: how can we organize information online and its search – and its solution – to classify information by prioritizing specific criteria?

This initial theoretical part is essential and emphasizes the profoundly human nature of NICTs' functioning. As a result, this amounts to thinking that, finally, algorithmic systems all have some subjectivity illustrated by the

33 Some genetic algorithms optimize reaction times by crossing ambulance location data and demographic data [GER 14].

choices of indicators and settings made by designers. Consequently, even if algorithms are not built with an intention to discriminate, and even if they reproduce social preferences in a completely rational way, they also tend to reproduce a certain form of non-objective discrimination.

I.3.4. *Blockchain*

Nowadays, modern society has become nearly inconceivable without the use of digital data. The revolution of these gigantic volumes of raw and heterogeneous data goes hand in hand with the development of a new data science. Adding value to big data involves the implementation of sophisticated analyses, which represent a true "scaling" of the design and use of analysis models and the implementation of algorithms. From now on, software must have the capacity to detect interesting information to obtain optimum data processing: this is called data mining. At the same time, we see the emergence and gradual set-up in this digital ecosystem of the blockchain concept, technology on which Bitcoin[34] (cryptographic currency and peer-to-peer payment system) is based. We can differentiate two types of blockchain, on the one hand "public blockchains", open to everyone (Bitcoin, Ethereum, Tezos, etc.), and, on the other hand, "corporate blockchains" (Hyperledger, Ripple, MultiChain, etc.).

We are now witnessing the emergence of a "datafication" process, which consists of digitalizing and measuring everything in order to get data from it, whether it is for papers, localizations, individual acts, or even imprints. Personal data exploitation is a sensitive topic, as these data directly affect the intimacy of each individual. Situations in which there are difficult problems concerning strategic choices in terms of personal data management are more numerous every day.

In this context, society's interaction with NICTs represents an unstable, and even precarious, system. Thus, issues associated with big data are significant, both economically and to guarantee a digital space protecting privacy and fundamental freedoms. Therefore, such a digital transformation

34 From "bit", a binary information unit, and "coin", Bitcoin is a virtual and alternative currency used via servers, datacenters, networks, etc. in an encrypted form. We can note that this is the first time in human history that a NICT has generated its own currency.

also entails ethical risks regarding personal data, such as integrity, reliability, security, respect for privacy and individual freedoms, reputation, control, and so on. This is why it seems essential to us to provide an ethical insight on the blockchain revolution[35].

Before getting to the heart of the matter, we must clearly explain the technological aspects of the blockchain, before considering an ethical analysis of this phenomenon. This NICT operates as a public database or an open account ledger meeting cryptographic operating requirements. It records the details of each exchange made between the users of this blockchain since its creation. What makes it particularly clever is that it is designed to prevent the same exchange from being double-counted, without the intervention of any intermediary (such as a bank or insurance company). Therefore, the blockchain records a set of data such as a date, a cryptographic signature associated with the sender, and a whole set of other specific elements. All these exchanges are traceable, searchable and downloadable free of charge on the Internet, by any person wishing to check the validity and non-falsification of the database in real time. The main benefit of this device is to be able to store a proof of information with each transaction, in order to be able to subsequently prove at any moment the existence and the content of this original information. Its mission is then to generate trust by protocolizing a digital asset or database making it auditable. We sometimes talk about it as the accelerator and beneficial ecosystem of the digital revolution. Based on this idea, we can give an image of the blockchain, which can be understood as a kind of symbiotic colony.

The safety of the device relies on the following principle: each network node assumes that other nodes are fraudulent. It is a form of "presumption of guilt". If a node receives a block, it is first submitted to a protocol to check its compliance before using it. It then relies on a peer-to-peer architecture in which each node is both client and server, without any control and vulnerability point, since each of them keeps a copy of any transaction. Each transaction depends on a cryptographic lock securing it, including small quantities charged to pay for the computing and storage performed by the platform. Trust is based on the multitude of participating individuals and the multitude of possibilities to check exchanges.

---

35 Protected against any modification, each including the identifier of its predecessor.

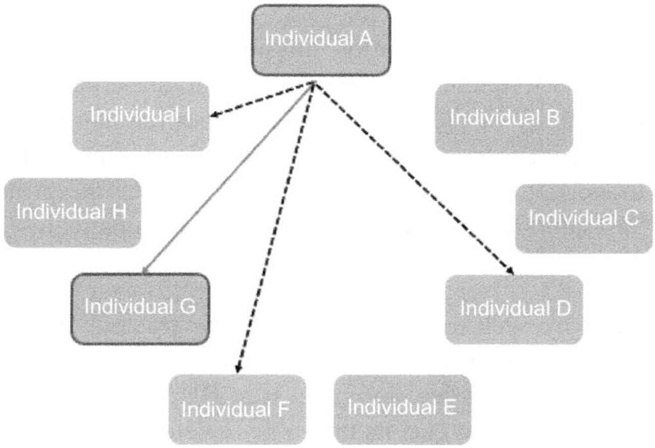

Figure I.2. *Distributed and decentralized architecture*

In the example of Figure I.2, individual A wishes to perform a dematerialized transaction with individual G. The payment directly flows from one actor to the other, but the transaction order is checked by "miners" (individuals D, F and I). Once the transaction is checked and then validated, the latter is recorded in a large register visible by all.

Consequently, the safety of the blockchain increases as blocks are added to it. This technology is based on a log of all exchanges made between its users. This forms a decentralized network of thousands of information systems and autonomous connected objects, "miners", everywhere on the planet, performing transactions or projects and recording digital assets between them. "Mining" is the procedure facilitating the validation of transaction blocks to be added to the Bitcoin blockchain. This network of "miners" works simultaneously, in order to validate each new piece of information added to the blockchain. This validation is consensual via a protocol within the network and is independent from any central authority. It is the principle of a collaborative approach. When a transaction is validated, a Proof of Work is sent by the "miner". Each "miner" has a full copy of the transaction (in the form of an encrypted code line) on their computer and can compare the latter with that of the network, in order to check its compliance with the whole chain. Thus, each block is validated and each transaction depends on all the previous ones. If the role of the intermediary was to generate trust, the blockchain makes it possible to move this function, in order to refocus it on the technology itself. It provides objects and information systems with an identity, full autonomy and its own affiliation. It can be noted that to encourage “miners” – who are crucial for the proper operation and viability of the network – remuneration is given to them as a reward for their work. The complexity of the validation problem is linked to a difficulty associated with the block. In order to keep the production time of a block constant, the level of difficulty is automatically adjusted by the network.

Furthermore, by acting as an automated trusted third party, this technology paves the way for a structural cost reduction while enhancing reliability and accelerating decision processes. Blockchain is widely applied, especially in the area of law, via its infallible register, useful to provide proof that such a document was indeed in the possession of such an individual at a given date, or that such an amount of money was indeed transferred at a certain time to a given person. In the area of health, these applications are potentially numerous. In fact, blockchain could, for example, help to manage patient data in a transparent, secure and tamper-proof way, and limit their sharing to the main trusted third parties: doctors, hospitals, pharmaceutical laboratories, and so on. It could also improve access to health data, in order to reinforce patient monitoring and support research, while guaranteeing the privacy of health consumers: this technology does make it possible to share data for the benefit of patients via two secure methods, asymmetrical cryptography and distributed consensus. It will therefore be possible to limit security flaws, as several codes can be required to unlock a single medical file. Furthermore, we can imagine the implementation of a BitHealth system, along the lines of the Bitcoin, through which health data are stored and secured in a distributed manner in peer-to-peer mode. Applications are also possible within the framework of the Shared Medical Record (*dossier médical partagé* – DMP) thanks to the transparency of blockchain and the interoperability inherent to this technology. Its robustness and tamper-proof nature would finally make it possible to certify clinical tests and prevent counterfeit medicines, by creating, for example, an open and universal database, accessible to pharmaceutical companies, regulators and users. Thus, blockchain technology provides promising applications in the field of medicine. It will be able to start a revolution of the medical service, focused on the patient and the way they can look after themselves and others. Even in the most critical situations, it will still be possible to, on the one hand, control the access permission to important information regarding our identity and, on the other hand, guarantee a future payment in exchange for a treatment that we want, so that it can be developed and placed on the market. Consequently, instead of relying on non-transparent evaluation grids stigmatizing the health of the weakest, insurance actors will be able to rely or not on our medical behavior to enter into a contract for the future with us, and reward virtuous behaviors. For the moment, the mission of blockchain is not really to store data, but rather to keep a secure trace of them in a storage space limited by transaction. Data is therefore always stored in a "traditional" database. Likewise, blockchain is not easy to handle in real time. Its benefit lies more in the retrospective audit. This technology does facilitate a great fluidization of data exchanges or the operability of a DMP. However, this could change in the coming years, according to NICT development.

In addition, blockchain can affect any other areas of activity. This is the case of smart contracts[36], automated payments and public registers of transactions, which are sure to disrupt claims management and the traceability of goods. These smart contracts combined with the Internet of Things (IoT) are programs that check whether the product has indeed been sent by the supplier. This has the effect of significantly reducing structural costs, reinventing client experience, or even creating brand new business models to be implemented. Thus, blockchain technology makes it possible to address the main challenges of the IoT, namely transaction and connection costs (such as payments, messages, data exchanges, etc.).

In fact, according to IBM, for the sake of efficiency and global deployment, the IoT network must be considered from the beginning as a decentralized space, so that transactions and exchanges are securely and anonymously performed without trusted third parties. Finally, blockchain also has numerous other applications such as [VAU 15]:

– decentralized storage (for example, BitHealth and Storj);

– proof of existence (with start-ups such as MyPowers, Assembly or BlockCDN);

– e-voting.

Under these conditions, the economic value chain is shaken and actors are redistributed. This is reflected by the emergence of DAOs (Decentralized

36 "Smart contracts" are autonomous programs which automatically execute the terms and conditions of a contract, without requiring human intervention once started.

Autonomous Organizations) which can be defined as organizations operating thanks to a computer program providing transparent, unchanging governance rules to a community with no central authority. Decisions are collective and benefits are redistributed between the actors [ZOU 18].

However, is blockchain, which is considered as a decentralized, transparent, disintermediated, secure, tamper-proof, reliable, and autonomous protocol, a new credible technology or a simple fashionable illusion? And in which proportion will it affect the area of complementary health insurance, insurance and provident institutions? What could be the governance model associated with this process? Most French and European authorities are attentive to this phenomenon in order to reflect on and design the next outlines of regulation. How to motivate and encourage transactions and data sharing in order to fuel the scientific and/or clinical research process?

Which “measures” and what “development”? In relation to security, technological and ethical aspects, can we put sensitive data in the blockchain? What will be the future legal framework and regulatory barriers? Who decides within the blockchain? Developers? Miners? How are decisions made? By voting? By adopting? What are the remedies in case of dispute? What will be the functional coverage of this new value chain (or even feasibility)? What could be the models and contributions of the blockchain to the management of the person’s consent and the protection of their data? Could the use of the blockchain lead to a more global reflection on the economic and societal valuation of such transactions, with a new “complementary” currency according to the field of application, such as health, insurance or finance?

Many questions that we are asking today will have to be answered in the near future, in order to fully exploit the whole potential that such a technology holds.

I.3.5. *NBIC*

Nanotechnology, Biotechnology, Information technology and Cognitive science (NBIC) are challenging traditional medicine in at least three different ways [ALE 16]:

– diagnoses and robotic procedures are going to transfer the economic and medical value to digital ecosystems;

– “datafication” encourages data exchange at zero cost, like the transition from DVD to MP3. This movement can be carried out by actors transcending traditional geographical areas (health tourism, future diagnosis performed on another continent);

– the development of platforms connecting market actors (supply and demand) provides the control of the value added to these new intermediaries and no longer to only the producers of goods. It can be noted that the near monopoly of access to clients and the selection of suppliers allow *pure player* platforms to sense the produced value and to decide on the survival of producers (now suppliers) forced to compete globally.

There are numerous applications derived from NICTs, such as computational neuroscience (likely to build new biological models in brain analysis), synthetic biology (which can fully synthesize the DNA of a bacterium), bioengineering (which facilitates the development of biological transistors), and bionics (capable of implementing an electronic system). We can consider the example of the detection of recurring chromosomal alterations (such as the loss or amplification of entire regions) which can occur in a patient’s genome. Such alterations are known to be associated with pathologies such as cancer. Their detection and localization are thus a major therapeutic issue, which is similar to a problem of detecting breaks and which poses mathematical problems in terms of statistical modeling, algorithmic complexity or model selection. Once this detection is completed for each patient, we naturally concentrate on the search for particularly frequent (or “recurring”) alterations in cohorts of patients suffering from the same pathology. With a simple but reasonable model, the detection of such a region can be reformulated in terms of excursion of a certain stochastic process. Again, according to the data size, various statistical models must be considered, each leading to different probability problems. We note that, in the short term, nanotechnology could promote the manufacture of optimum nanomedicines to treat, in a targeted and customized way, some types of cancers, by warming up, for example, targeted areas, or by chemically clinging to cancerous cells, thus leading to their cell suicide (see targeted Apoptosis), or by injecting an anticancer agent into them. We can imagine that, in the longer term, nanotechnology will be able to build nanorobots whose aim will be to self-repair us or introduce artifacts in our brain to interconnect us with robot and computer interfaces capable of replacing or optimizing our failing and inefficient organs. These nanorobots will travel in our bloodstream to identify and diagnose pathologies, malfunctions, and to repair physiological problems, or even to remove cancerous cells and pathogens.

Therefore, DNA sequencing and reading is a driving force of the emergence of NICTs. This practice has been completely democratized over the years. We note that, since the first full sequencing of the human genome in 2003, the price of sequencing a human genome was divided by 3 million going from 3 billion dollars in 2003 to one thousand dollars today[37]. It is estimated that the genomic study of a single tumor requires processing approximately 20,000 billion of items of information. These past years have witnessed the first genetic manipulations of human embryos with significant progress in genome editing technologies. Thus, a Chinese team published genetic modifications on 86 human embryos. The objective of this study was to correct a mutation responsible for a blood disease, beta thalassemia. At the same time, on the other side of the planet, an American team from Harvard published the successful manipulation of 62 genes on pigs' cells, in order to transplant their organs to humans. With the constant development of these technologies regarding DNA transcription, encoding and understanding, it is very likely that the manipulation of the human genome will be fully operational before 2025.

Furthermore, beyond a transfer of power from the doctor to technology (machines, robots, self-learning expert systems, etc.), the biggest challenge of NBIC is the predictable use of all the new possibilities of human transformation, inevitably resulting in significant inequalities between the different populations in the world. Such a phenomenon will be made possible especially as a result of the scientific techniques of eugenics, which will soon be operational (full sequencing of fetus DNA, selection and then genetic transformation of embryos, increase in cognitive capacities via injection of stem cells in the brain, etc.). In recent decades, research in biotechnology has, among other things, made it possible to reconstruct multipotent stem cells[38] from the classical cells of an adult. Under these conditions, it would be possible to say that we shall eventually be able to regenerate all our organs.

37 Available at: www.genome.gov/10001772/all-about-the-human-genome-project-hgp/.

38 Multipotent stem cells are cells that can differentiate into any type of cells of the organism, without restriction.

Regarding cognitive science, numerous studies on the brain have been carried out, such as the causes of the likely appearance of some diseases due to the accumulation of misfolded proteins in neurons, through drug-based treatments, treatments based on cell therapies, or even genetic therapies on genes predisposing their occurrence. This research could, in the medium term, help to cure neurodegenerative diseases. Finally, in the longer term, the concomitant development of computer and brain research could involve the creation and structuring of an artificial brain with the emergence of a consciousness and the "downloading" of a person to the latter. For example, we can mention the European Human Brain Project[39] – which is predicted to cost more than one billion euro – whose objective is to simulate the entire brain of a mouse, and then of a human being, on a computer.

In view of these analyses, we see that these NICTs might then significantly transform the very program of mankind. It is more than likely that these eugenics techniques will not be performed the same way everywhere and for each individual. This will naturally create a divide between populations, mainly because of the high cost of these techniques.

Google is one of the most advanced companies and one of the main architects of this NBIC revolution. It actively supports transhumanism, especially by sponsoring the Singularity University, which trains NBIC experts [ALE 16]. Therefore, the ambition of Google is to be able to tame big data, in order to fight disease in a customized way. This is why they announced, as early as 2013, the launch of Calico – subsidiary of Alphabet – whose mission is to significantly, and even permanently, extend the duration of human life ("to kill death"). Such an objective requires the modification of our nature through significant technological interventions by means of the full potential of NBICs. We can note that this is not the first trial run of Google in the biology sector. It also has a subsidiary which specializes in genome sequencing with 23andMe, which has, among other things, a "eugenics" patent on the genetic selection of embryos, in order to produce "babies on demand". Therefore, Google Directors advocate the full adoption of NBICs, with a central place at the heart of global economy, to transform mankind.

39 Available at the address: www.humanbrainproject.eu/.

I.3.6. *Artificial Intelligence (AI)*

The idea of creating autonomous machines probably dates back to Greek Antiquity with the machines built by Hephaestus, featuring in particular in the Iliad [MAR 04]. These machines were mechanical, such as Vaucanson's duck designed by Jacques de Vaucanson in 1738 and presented at the Palais-Royal in 1744, which was undoubtedly one of the first robots [COL 18].

It was in 1956 that John McCarthy, computer scientist and the father of AI, named it and used the term AI for the first time, during a conference at Dartmouth College.

For Brian Krzanich, Intel President and CEO (the first global manufacturer of microprocessors), AI is not just the next tsunami of information technology, it is also the next main shift in human history. AI is not a conventional computer program: it is educated more than it is programmed. It is part of a very wide and diverse field of technologies, relying on autonomous and cognitive functionalities.

It is clear that the process initiated by AI has mixed fantasy, science-fiction, and long-term futurology, by even forgetting the basic definitions of the latter.

The concept of AI[40] is to create computer programs able to carry out tasks performed by humans, requiring learning, memory organization and reasoning. Its objective is to give notions of rationality, functions of reasoning and perception (for example, visual) to control a robot in an unknown environment. Its popularity is associated with new techniques, such as deep learning, which gives the possibility to a program to learn to represent the world by means of a network of virtual neurons, with each performing elementary computations, like our brain. The machine is programmed to "learn to learn". Thanks to algorithmic feedback loops, the machine can modify its internal settings used to manage the representation of each layer, from the representation of the previous layer. These layers of functionalities are learned by the machine itself and not by humans. From

40 The ISO 2382-28:1995 Standard defines artificial intelligence as the "capability of a functional unit to perform functions that are generally associated with human intelligence such as reasoning and learning".

this assumption, we can say that the machine becomes autonomous and intelligent, by building its own "computerization" structures and by relying on axiomatic decisions.

Just like human functioning which analyzes a situation before changing behavior, AI allows the machine to learn from its own results to modify its programming. This NICT already exists in numerous applications, such as our smartphones, and should soon extend to all areas of everyday life: from medicine to autonomous cars, through artistic creation, mass distribution, or combating crime and terrorism. Machine learning does not only offer the possibility to automatically exploit large quantities of data and identify habits in the behavior of consumers. From now on, we can also activate these data. In our opinion, adopting machine learning is no longer only useful but rather necessary. Thus, in the light of the digital transition and this "war of intelligences" [ALE 17], companies are going to be the target of significant transformation and are going to invest in AI applications, especially in order to:

– increase human expertise via virtual assistance programs;

– optimize certain products and services;

– provide new opportunities in R&D via the development of self-learning systems.

Furthermore, deep learning is not a new algorithm. It has been used for different actions in the form of neural networks for over 20 years, especially to perform "learning". A neuron represents a simple function which takes different inputs and calculates its result, which it sends to different outputs. These neurons are mainly structured and organized in layers. The first layer uses nearly raw data and the last layer generates a result. The higher the number of layers, the more the learning and performance capacity will be increased. We can consider the example of character recognition from handwriting. The first layer will take into account all the pixels composing a written character, for example, a letter or a number, each neuron will have some pixels to analyze. The last layer will indicate "it is a T with a probability of 0.8" or "it is an I with a probability of 0.3". We perform a back propagation operation from the final result to change the settings of each neuron. This can be illustrated with the example of a child who learns the alphabet: at the beginning, the child makes recognition errors, the result is given to them, and then they start again. The adjustable settings correspond to all the weights of the weighted averages performed by each neuron. The objective of learning is thus to identify the values of these weights that will provide the right answers to learning examples – and consider that these same values will be effective in a test phase. This is made possible through small successive adjustments of adjustable settings in a way that reduces the error rate (see back propagation) [BOU 17].

Once trained, the neural network is going to have an action and influence on a new set of data, and generate results which are associated with the quality of its learning. This neural network can model a complex correspondence by stacking operations that are simple, accurate, concrete, and adjustable. Unlike a neural network, the algorithm learns, but we do not have an accurate vision as to how and what it truly learns.

AI is based on three main pillars, namely the diversity, quality and volume of the available databases, the computing power of machines, and the quality of the knowledge and skills of the actors using them. We can see that this NICT mainly relates to three objects: high AI (aiming at replacing, in the end, human intelligence by objects with equivalent sensitivity), distributed AI (contributing to the development of smart systems adapting to a concrete and dynamic ecosystem or environment), and low AI (representing assistance with predictive analysis, decision and action).

In addition, AI cannot be considered as a product. There is no AI software, but AI "software solutions" relying on diverse and numerous bricks, going from direction sensing to the interpretation of information, from language study to the processing of structured or non-structured databases (see Figure I.3), such as:

– *symbiotic systems (expert systems)*: medical diagnosis, industrial process control, oil prospecting, etc.;

– *learning systems (machine learning, statistic learning, deep learning)*: algorithmic trading, marketing (recommendation, client segmentation, pricing), analytics (assistance with decision-making), industry (predictive maintenance), personal language understanding (Chatbots[41], personal assistants, automatic translation), image analysis, robotics.

41 Chatbots or conversational agents correspond to software robots equipped with AI that can engage with a human being in a natural language or in writing by chat. We can refer to them as

One example is the learning of virtual models of the human brain structure from neuroimaging data. These digital and statistical tools make it possible to learn typical configurations of the brain anatomy from the MRI images of a set of individuals. These virtual models are composed of linear or surface meshes of the main human brain structures. The typical variations of these configurations inside a group of people help to better understand the anatomical substrate of neurological pathologies. Consequently, the customization of these models according to new data provides the clinician with a computer-assisted diagnosis device and a tool to support patient monitoring.

In addition, we can consider the example of the genetic sector whose applications are multiplying, such as the *Médecine France génomique 2025* plan, which includes the implementation of a network of 12 sequencing platforms, which will facilitate the development of very high throughput sequencing solutions for research projects. Data derived from collected biological samples will be transformed into genomic data and diagnosis tools, especially for rare diseases.

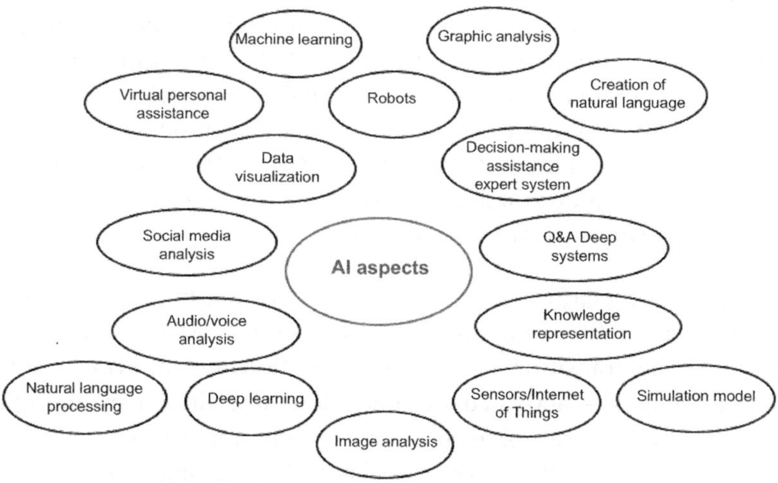

Figure I.3. *Multidimensional aspects of Artificial Intelligence (AI)*

proactive intellectual assistants which answer standardized questions. They are systems able to perceive, decide, act and learn, and are independent. They can be found especially in relationship marketing (support centers) because they provide advice and information to customers (e-Helpdesk).

Furthermore, the development of Artificial Intelligence (AI) can be described according to three successive waves:

– *first wave*: expert systems perception, learning, abstraction, reasoning;

– *second wave*: statistic learning perception, learning, abstraction, reasoning, learning without understanding;

– *third wave*: contextual adaptation, common sense perception, learning, abstraction, Holy Grail of reasoning, producing explanations.

According to a study of the Tractica[42] office, the market of AI systems is going to experience a significant increase for companies, going from 202.5 million dollars in 2015 to 11.1 billion dollars in 2024. Other sources, such as Markets and Markets 2017, estimate a growth of nearly 63% a year between 2016 and 2022 with a market around 16.06 billion dollars in 2022, especially due to the volume of American transactions. The main areas concerned by this growth are the media and advertising, industrial production, finance, distribution and energy, as well as health.

Indeed, if we consider the case of advertising, programmatic technologies have completely revolutionized this sector with the way ads are bought and targeted online. The exploitation of big data helped not only to automate a large part of the tedious work, but also to make more relevant and realistic strategic decisions in terms of opportunities for product and/or service brands. According to a study by the Boston Consulting Group (BCG)[43], the use of big data techniques made it possible to optimize the performance of advertising campaigns by more than 30% to 50%.

According to a Gartner study, it is estimated that by 2020, smart agents will be involved in 40% of commercial transactions. AI is therefore going to contribute to the transition to a post-application age in which smart and autonomous agents – activated by algorithms and driven by the giants of digital technology – are going to emerge. Thus, tomorrow, robots, drones, objects and vehicles will rely on algorithmic processing. These agents will gradually become more and more intelligent to the point of being able to create, in turn, new agents. Under these conditions, the scientist and

42 Available at: www.tractica.com/newsroom/press-releases/artificial-intelligence-technologies-are-quietly-penetrating-a-wide-range-of-enterprise-applications/.

43 Available at: www.thinkwithgoogle.com/marketing-resources/programmatic/value-of-an-integrated-plat-form-for-programmatic-buying/.

visionary Joël de Rosnay [DER 17] predicts that, in five centuries, humans will communicate with animals, insects and plants in their own language by means of AI. Human beings will be able to understand the animal and plant language via AI. A new species will appear, namely biorobots, who will collaborate with humans.

Thus, it is more than likely that the transition to these new technological innovations will be somewhat disruptive, especially due to a lack of social models and frameworks adapted to a completely modified world. Work automation has a faster process than that of human training, outplacement and retraining. It inevitably has negative impacts and consequences on the lowest paid jobs by developing major economic inequalities. This transition will necessarily have to be accompanied by a reform of the professional system and education, in order to guarantee a continuity and link between the qualification level of workers and the scope of AI. Human-machine collaboration is going to be established, within which the forces of one will counterbalance the limitations of the other to generate an augmented intelligence.

I.3.7. *Quantum computing*

Since 1965, Moore's law has been perfectly followed by the IT industry and guided its development plans. It is a simple principle that has been implemented for more than 50 years: every two years, the computing power of electronic chips doubles. Although designed for a short-term scheduled end, especially as they reach a physical limit in terms of processor miniaturization (etching size in microns and heat dissipation ratio), this law illustrated the development of the significant computing powers available today. Is the end of power increase coming? In the light of new developments, especially quantum systems, it does not seem so.

In fact, some scientists naturally shifted and focused on quantum mechanics, by considering that quantum computing is part of the future development of the conventional computer as we currently know it. A quantum computer does not rely on electricity to internally disseminate its information, but on the quantum properties of material particles. It is the combination and focal point of two main scientific fields, information technology and quantum mechanics. The computing power of such a computer is impressive and substantial. For the same series of computations, it is estimated that the time required would be 10,000 years for a conventional computer compared to 1 second for a quantum computer. Currently, our computers use bits which include two states, 0 or 1. In the medium term, quantum computers will instead quantum bits, *qubits*. These qubits can have the state 0, the state 1, but also both states at the same time, which is what makes them interesting for computation. Indeed, it is on this superposition principle, that a qubit has both states 0 and 1, that the quantum computer is based. It can be noted that the properties of quantum information are contrary to all the rules and laws of classical physics (for example Newtonian mechanics, the electromagnetic field theory of Maxwell and Lorentz, and the thermodynamics of Clausius, Maxwell and Boltzmann).

In fact, Claude Shannon – the founding father of information theory with his article entitled *A Mathematical Theory of Communication* published in 1948 – had set out the principles according to which a conventional computer operates. For the author, information represented an entity which had an actual physical existence, just like energy or mass. Some fundamental laws of Nature, such as the second law of thermodynamics (or Carnot's principle), are in fact information laws. These laws govern matter and energy, they establish rules according to which atoms interact and stars behave, they even apply to us as living beings, because our genes include information that our bodies reproduce, and as human beings, since our brain contains information that is produced by our consciousness. Let us note that Fourier's transformation was the analytical element that allowed Claude Shannon to identify the transition from the analogue world to the digital world. By accurately indicating the influence of the digitization step of a signal on its frequency spectrum, Shannon paved the way for signal sampling without losing information [BOU 17].

However, what if information could travel faster than light? As we will see in one of the following chapters, Nature expresses itself through the information language. Yet, a quantum computer does not perform a computation in a binary fashion as does a digital computer; it does so in a way consistent with the quantum superposition of qubits. To do so, one must know how to reconcile quantum physics, determinism and causality. In other words, develop a theory of everything!

Thus, the microscopic universe of quantum mechanics, namely that of atoms, operates in a very different way from the macroscopic universe governed by classical physics. For example, electrons have the capacity to go from one state to another (wave or particle, or both simultaneously), from a high orbit to a low orbit without external forces and without passing through an intermediary state or orbit. Finally, electrons are simultaneously everywhere at the same time. In addition, some physicists even speculate that an observer can today influence the behavior of an electron or photon yesterday. The observer and reality ontologically depend on each other. Therefore, reality does not exist without observation. To this must be added the structurally undetermined nature of the quantum world. This was an idea that Albert Einstein had difficulty admitting, asserting that "God does not play dice". It would mean that there are not only different possible futures, but also different possible pasts. A lot of research has shown that the fact of consciously deciding to observe the microcosm modifies the reality of the latter.

From these observations and assumptions, we can apply this principle to the case of quantum computing. In this case, the state of a register of 2 qubits can thus be 0, 1, 2 or 3, but also a superposition of any part of these four basic states, or even all four at the same time. Therefore, the state of a register of n qubits can be a superposition of any set of 2^n possible values on n bits (n is an integer), including a superposition of all these values at the same time (see parallel computing namely performing a great number of operations in parallel), whereas a register of conventional n bits can contain, at all times, just one of these values.

Consequently, any operation performed during a quantum computation can simultaneously act on 2^n different values. Thus, if a function can be computed with 2^n different arguments, we will simultaneously calculate all its values. The fact that these computations are reversible and deterministic explains why developers cannot affect the value of a quantum variable to another, or use this value several times. This situation therefore requires new algorithms and programming languages to be invented in compliance with the laws of quantum physics. Two main algorithms are generally used in quantum computing:

– *Shor's algorithm*: makes it possible to find the prime factors of very large integers. Thanks to this algorithm, a quantum computer can factorize a number with 300 figures in 10 seconds, compared to 30,000 years for a conventional computer;

– *Grover's algorithm*: addresses comparison problems. This algorithm makes it possible to find the right answer by performing a number of comparisons equal to the square root of the database size, namely only 1,000 comparisons for a database with a million entries.

The main advantage of this computer is therefore its processing power and thus the time it saves. In terms of security, it offers optimum cryptography. In fact, encoded messages with such a computer are 100% secure. Its use, in order to secure the military communications of an operating army, is an obvious benefit for a government. In addition, for applications such as the autonomous car, adiabatic quantum computation will become crucial, as it will have to fully play its part as "quantum oracle" by anticipating all the possible situations for the vehicle.

It should be noted that it is very likely that computers are not exclusively quantum. Indeed, a quantum processor must be electronically controlled. Yet, the simplest way to do this is probably to use a conventional processor.

Furthermore, the creation of a fully operational quantum computer is still far away, with numerous obstacles and difficulties to overcome.

There is a problem reading quantum information, but also physically manufacturing the computer as such. Indeed, we know that quantum mechanics is non-deterministic. The problem researchers and scientists have at the moment is that, if a quantum computer works on all possible data at the same time, how do we get the results? In other words, we do not know the state of atoms. For example, if we perform a computation, we do not know the result, and reading this result destroys the information. More explicitly, if we carry out a complicated computation, we can only know its final result. Intermediary results will be inaccessible at the risk of destroying the information, and thus stopping the computations. In fact, when we observe a qubit, it takes a fixed value among all those possible. Under these conditions, all the other superposed states are eliminated. The state provided at observation is completely probabilistic. This is the difficult part! Consequently, the only way to write an efficient quantum algorithm is to make sure that the result sought is the one which is most likely to be found. Such a condition can only be achieved if a maximum of superposed states gives this result. To conclude, a quantum computer thus provides less information than a conventional computer in as many operations, but can exponentially analyze more data with each operation.

A second, often recurring, major problem relates to the physical creation of a quantum computer. Different leads are currently under consideration to know whether it is better that qubits are structured from photons (light), molecules or atoms. It seems that the method focused on the quantum state of molecules and atoms is the most promising, even though liquid nitrogen and helium often need to be replaced to ensure superconductivity due to the evaporation of the latter.

Ultimately, we have to admit that quantum computing is not easy to understand since quantum mechanics, which governs the movement of bodies in the atomic, molecular and corpuscular fields, is a theory whose logics is totally contrary to intuition. We must therefore use mathematics to understand it well. Is quantum computing the future of the computer? Will it or will it not be a true technical revolution leading to the Fifth Industrial Revolution? What is the future of such a computer? Will it mark the end of the current security architecture of the Internet? Indeed, it is very likely that this quantum machine will definitely "break" RSA asymmetrical encryption algorithms[44], which are omnipresent on the Web. What will be its social and economic impacts on our future societies? Numerous questions we feel entitled to ask in order to prepare for the future…

44 RSA asymmetrical encryption is based on the fact that it is very complicated to factorize large numbers into prime numbers. The computing difficulty almost exponentially increases with the size of the number ("under exponential" according to mathematicians).

1

Ethics at the Service of Digital Technology

Confronted with this digitalization of society and the change in paradigm it generates, it is natural to wonder how mankind can be expected to evolve. Even if it is obviously complicated to project in the future, which is by definition uncertain (and especially since we are faced with an unprecedented period of human history), ethics can (and must) provide us with some lines of thought that will allow us to have a vision of the main orientations available to us along the path of our evolution [DOS 18].

Ethics applied to digital technology is a topic spontaneously referring to numerous questions and themes, such as big data and personal data protection, transparency for consumers, infobesity, blurring of boundaries between private life and professional life, (generational, social, geographic) digital divide, traceability, dehumanization and technological dependence, predictive algorithms and free will, "Uberization" of society, and so on. These many topics reflect the magnitude of the ethical issues associated with digital technology.

In terms of ethics as we understand it today, our *ethos* (or "accustomed place" in Greek) is no other than mankind itself, and the whole issue is actually to know how to act in order to act humanely, act appropriately from a moral point of view. With the digitalization of the world, human exchanges have an essential ethical dimension because they are always conducted within the framework of a relationship with others, whose complexity is unsolvable. Ethics is not at the service of anything but human good, which admittedly includes a certain economic efficiency. What is essential here is that ethical concern can only be efficient in all areas if it is driven by the desire to contribute to the well-being of the person, the good of all people. If efficiency is the production of beneficial effects, nothing is more efficient than what helps the common good. Ethics can be understood from two different angles, on the one hand, that based on the search for happiness and, on the other hand, that based on the search for good, within the framework of a reflection on what human relationships with each other should be. Ethics is then the very practice of thinking and the reflective movement through which a moral subject is structured as a subject within its relationship with the other and its relationship with mankind.

It can often be seen that ethics and epi-ethics[1] constitute a topic which is expressed *a posteriori*, once an untoward or negative event has occurred. Yet, with global digitalization, it is going to become almost impossible to be reactive to address ethical problems, which will keep multiplying, extending and generalizing throughout the world. Thus, to meet these ethical objectives, it is essential to anticipate the uses of tools, as soon as they are designed, and to provide for sufficiently flexible architectures to act retroactively on uses and development. We must also investigate the limits of the new tools and new digital services. Under these conditions, it seems necessary to deal with all this upstream of the NICT design. This ethics by design will thus help to positively regulate technological innovation and be proactive.

1.1. Towards a new paradigm of the digital society

As previously seen, the history of mankind is constantly punctuated by evolutionary changes, which have direct effects on our societies. The macroscopic approach of the planet appears in a cyclic form, as with humans who are confronted with several stages and ages (childhood, puberty, adolescence, adulthood, old age, etc.) during their lives.

Over the past two decades, we have lived in a world where data has kept multiplying, where visions and analyses are going to become endless, and where everything will become a sum of singularities and values, which

1 Epi-ethics (from the ancient Greek *epi*, "on top of", and ethics) represents the discipline of ethics, which studies the ethical reflections modulating human behavior according to the context and environment. Our behaviors and habits affect the expression of our ethical reflections.

structures will try to understand in order to extract them. These significant volumes of unpublished data contribute to create new knowledge, new perceptions and, therefore, new opportunities. We are now in an age of convergence between data that can all become homogeneous, digitizable and integrable, and more correlation of meanings. It is the emergence of global digitalization, in which databases, storage tools and large-scale data use have been completely redesigned and improved, greatly supporting their operational performances. This is reflected by new *data driven* approaches, where we visualize more than we model, and where quantity is more important than quality. This "datafication" has the effect of providing the conditions and means for governments and companies to map society in a quantifiable and analyzable manner in order to explore everyday life reality, and even the thoughts of individuals [EAG 06, ZUB 15].

Thus, technologies associated with big data, although already well developed in science [HEL 12], resulted in radical changes in paradigms in all areas of activity. The transition from a research based on hypotheses to a research based on data has had, consequently, significant implications for the actors, by modifying the quality of their connections and the scope of their rights and obligations. We have now transitioned from an explicative science seeking causes to a statistical and mathematical science, whose purpose is to predict paths or trends, and to provide a representation of a possible future. The progress in algorithmic knowledge makes it possible to more quickly question and structure databases. We can consider the example of the health sector where we are gradually moving from a chemical and post-traumatic medicine to a preventive and customized medicine. Thus, these NICTs can accurately monitor the behavior and habits at an unprecedented high level [MAR 14].

Therefore, data no longer represent the product or by-product of knowledge, but its source. The latter are no longer placed into categories of reason, but are rather going to be able to be processed one by one, in a singular and differential manner. Digital data are now recognized as one of the cornerstones of innovation, likely to develop new organizational, strategic and economic models, as well as significant progress in terms of productivity. Only structures and actors who will know how to integrate NICTs, such as data mining or deep learning, into their internal activity will really be able to capture the value of the multiform data at their disposal.

Traditional hypothetical-deductive approaches, which generally rely on a small quantity of data collected within a very controlled framework, increasingly give way to empirical-inductive models, based on the search for correlations from a large set of data. This digital revolution is both a change in our ecosystem and the development of new realities, in which digital technology (based on silicon, online) extends and increasingly overlaps analog technology (based on carbon, offline) until the medium term, absorbing and merging with it [BÉR 16]. This necessarily results in a change in space-time landmarks, where digital technology generates actions almost in real time and applied to any location on the planet. In fact, this ubiquity and immediacy significantly and irreversibly impact our actions and words.

Under these conditions, we are witnessing the beginning of a new divide, or even a paradigm modification, due to the arrival of a sufficiently relevant model able to replace reality and open up a large field of discoveries. This new model will gradually take over the previous achievements and knowledge within a broader perspective. These big data provide a range of new possibilities in terms of flexibility, visualization, exploration and interpretation. This revolution not only changes our understanding of the external world, but also our understanding of what we are as human beings. NICTs can be reduced to the product of the multiplication of technologies' mutations, along with the mutations of mentalities and uses. Thus, all these phenomena mutually increase their effects.

Any NICT describes and structures a relationship between humans and their environment, both human and physical. We see a technological dynamic which follows its own trajectory and has an impact on our society [BAD 15]. Indeed, technology has a hypnotizing power over society: "Any new technology reduces the interaction of senses and consciousness, more specifically in the new field of innovations, in which there is a kind of identification of the subjects and the object" [MCL 77]. Consequently, the digital revolution challenges the philosophical foundations of traditional ethical thinking.

Furthermore, this technical, generic and socio-cultural transformation space can be associated with a "digital divide"[2] between individuals, due to:

---

2 Digital divide corresponds to a symbolic break line, the boundary of a division between, on the one hand, the persons and social groups who are – or feel – well integrated into the

– the understanding of complexity, namely when, why and how processed big data were hierarchized and placed into a specific category? This is essential in order to reinforce the self-control of the latter [LYO 03];

– the incapacity to access the methodology and know-how used, the often opaque and hidden functioning of the algorithm, the decision criteria applied [TEN 13];

– the difficulty for actors to be able to transform and adjust digital data [BOY 12];

– the ability or inability of the individuals concerned to be informed about the traceability of the data throughout its life cycle [COL 14];

– the complexity of access to NICTs (access to a suitable computer, network connection, reasonable costs, etc.), as well as contents (namely the capacity to really exploit the technical, information and communication resources inherent to Information and Communications Technologies (ICTs)) [VOD 10];

– the difficulty for persons and structures to access or buy big data [MCN 14].

This loss of causality inevitably results in an anthropologic change in mentalities. Researchers now have the ability to identify data models that are independent from specific hypotheses [ROS 14]. This modifies the very paradigm of data, whose value lies in sharing, exchange and pooling. The best known uses are often illustrated by a personalization of the relationships between professionals and their customers. Existing standards used to characterize a given need, product or service seem outdated and are no longer in line with the current reality based on the acquisition of big data and algorithmic techniques. It then becomes essential to move towards a new knowledge and reflection on the legitimacy, authenticity and appropriateness of the data used. We see the emergence of profound questions, related to a society focused on data, which we must ask, especially regarding dignity, individual freedom, the respect for the individual and the functioning of a new democracy [BUT 15]. With self-regulated communities, transnational development and increased information fluidity, is this the end of hierarchical societies? These questions have multiple implications in

"information society" and, on the other hand, those who are – or feel – excluded from this same society.

engineering, legal, moral, anthropologic, sociologic, philosophical and economic terms.

Finally, we cannot deal with a chapter on the new paradigm of contemporary society without discussing the arrival of the blockchain phenomenon which is, in our opinion, the true digital revolution of the coming years. Indeed, more than technologies associated with big data, blockchain provides a new – autonomous, transparent and open – digital ecosystem, which is going to optimize and secure the dematerialized transactions of the different actors. This technology will help to meet the challenges of reciprocity and funding raised by the collaborative economy. According to Benjamin Tincq, co-founder of OuiShare, blockchain is part of a deep mutation of our societies, which is trying to transform our organizational systems and disengage from pyramidal logics and value hyper-centralization. Therefore, this protocol technology is completely in line with the cooperation logics within the Decentralized Collaborative Organizations (DCO), which open the way to fully autonomous structures able to generate income allowing them to ensure their own existence. We then go from an economic model centralized around e-commerce platforms (such as Amazon, Alibaba and Dyskit), through a quite decentralized approach relying on exchange platforms (such as e-Bay, Marketplace and LeBonCoin), to get to a kind of collaborative sharing organization derived from the blockchain, which is completely independent from any centralizing platforms (such as OpenBazar, La’Zooz and Arcade City) (see Figure 1.1).

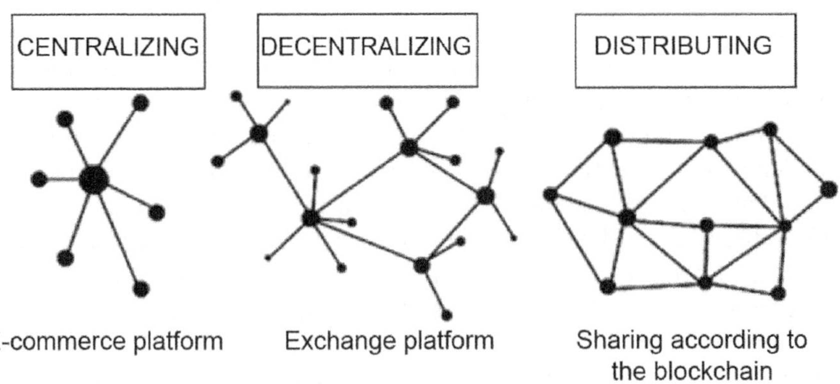

Figure 1.1. *Different platform architectures*

Just like “Uberization”, which directly connects actors via NICTs, “blockchainization”, in its turn, would directly connect protagonists requiring the intervention of a trusted third party, in order to validate their business processes. The added value of the blockchain concept mainly lies in its high level of security and reliability, based on two main elements:

– *the decentralized nature of the blockchain functioning*: to this end, “miners” work simultaneously to validate – independently from a central authority – each new transaction introduced in the blockchain;

– *the distributed aspect of the blockchain database (transactions)*: each “miner” has a full copy of the information on their computer and has the ability to compare their copy to the network’s copy. For the sake of transparency, this copy can be seen and downloaded free of charge by users on the Internet.

Consequently, thanks to blockchain, it will be possible to trace each stage of the process of a clinical trial in a time-stamped and encrypted manner. The audit and verification of the integrity of clinical trials will then be improved.

In the end, the digital revolution leads to or, at least, accelerates the disappearance of traditional areas with, especially, a break from the pyramidal organization structuring our current societies, and probably generating a new social fabric and a mutation of capitalism. The added value does not lie in the blockchain itself, but rather in the range of possibilities it creates, namely that of a more open and horizontal world. Therefore, this anthropologic mutation associated with the principles of “holacracy” goes beyond technological innovation. It allegedly promotes cooperation logics within DCOs. Customer-oriented companies must develop the fluidity, interactivity and interconnectivity of their internal and external exchanges via a necessarily open, integrated and connected IS. The scaled-up blockchain technology should, in the medium term, highly disturb, and even destroy the “mega platform” economy, by facilitating the transfer of wealth, trust and power to those who are directly concerned, namely users. Thus, consumers will be able to manage their personal data[3] without giving them

3 Date of birth, surname, sex, filiation, nationality, fingerprints, domicile, online identifier, email and IP address, geolocation data, taste, friends, leisure, behaviors, political opinions, preferences, voice, venous networks, images, health data, ethnic origin, DNA, social security number, bank details, income, phone number, occupation, etc.

away, by deciding whether or not to give access to them. Under these conditions, people will be more autonomous regarding their exchanges, because they will do without trusted third parties and intermediaries, such as the digital giants who monopolized the whole data value. Consequently, blockchain is capable of reorganizing society itself by creating a new form of social organization, a new form of digital economy.

1.2. Questions regarding the algorithmic universe

NICTs disrupt our existences and question the meaning of our everyday lives. Each technological innovation improves and optimizes practices, related behaviors and, consequently, adds new social standards. NICTs force us to reconsider the values and habits of our actions, because they provide a greater number of individuals with more means to communicate and interact with each other. Benchmarks and their mathematized processing bring a new perspective "of digital mankind" by guiding people based on self-referencing normative indicators, which are generally beyond our understanding. Thus, this new digital visualization does not describe our reality, but contributes to create it. The "natural" human gradually gives way to the repaired, augmented, connected, instrumented, and so on human, in which the term "human" is challenged at its very core. This is why, in their everyday activities, citizens in relation with connected objects, smartphones, online platforms on the Internet, social media fueled by digital data, are raising numerous and various questions.

On the other hand, if we consider the example of the algorithms driving autonomous cars, like those used by the programmed option in a situation of inevitable collision, these algorithms will have to impose decisions, which can have a direct impact on the bodily injury, or even the life or death, of the persons involved in the accident. This raises the question as to who assumes liability, and who is accountable in terms of security and the control of data. Such a situation inevitably raises ethical questions regarding the criteria and settings included in the "black box" of the algorithm, which made the decision possible. In fact, citizens do not know anything about the algorithms on which they rely, in their daily lives, in order to act and make decisions. Thus, they hardly know anything about the computer code, the data used and the choices of values which facilitated the writing of these algorithms by the digital giants [PIC 18].

The Black Box Algorithmic Culture consequently creates a low-objectivity perception with intrinsically subjective decision-making including implicit and/or explicit bias.

For Cathy O'Neil[4], if the results of algorithmic systems lack transparency and are inexplicable, it comes from the fact that people are generally impressed and intimidated by mathematics and do not know how to understand it. They think that they do not have the authority or knowledge to understand this language that they do not understand. Therefore, a reflection on the design and internal functioning of the processing algorithm is obviously necessary. The question arises as to how their construction and use could be optimally regulated in order to allow the persons concerned to exercise their right of access to the data captured by these machines and/or objects.

Hard to understand and control, algorithms optimize and guide our choices and decisions. However, who knows the content and functioning of these algorithms? How do these new algorithmic powers transform the professional practices of society? How does an algorithm choose its actions and in what way is this choice comparable or incomparable to that of a human being? Will AI have the human creative autonomy and individuality? Is technology going to set the standard without any democratic debate? Which ethics is necessary to make digital technology a main element of our democracies? Are we prepared to build, or even develop, ethical-digital links to take into consideration the interrelationships and interdependences of our main societal and social problems?

These questions, which are both successive and complex, are the place where the respect for human values permanently meets the binding limits of the concrete decisions to be made. Numerous questions regarding the significant volumes of data, their construction, collection, access, storage, processing and use, especially by computing devices, are raised in all sectors of activity.

Therefore, we are entitled to wonder whether this digitalization of society does not raise specific ethical problems. The challenge regarding the privacy

---

4 Cathy O'Neil is a data scientist and has a PhD in mathematics from Harvard University. She published a book entitled *Weapons of Math Destruction* explaining how big data increases inequalities and threatens democracy.

of the individual is central. In fact, cross-referencing databases from various origins, which probably do not ensure the same level of security, can thus make us wonder about the level of risk generated for the source person. In other words, does cross-referencing databases and increasing the quantity of information result in an increase of the risk of invading privacy, leading to the illegal use of data? Do privacy and confidentiality have the same value on the Internet as in everyday life? This question is even more significant since the vast majority of economic models based on digital data rely, more or less, on a certain form of data monetization.

Furthermore, we notice, at first glance, that the ownership of digital data is by nature quite different from the ownership of a physical object in the real world. Indeed, in everyday life, the owner of a car has a specific certificate of ownership and has access to their "object" whenever they want. Whereas in the virtual world, such a situation is far more complicated given that the user does not store their virtual objects themselves, especially their digital data, in a private database, and that, so far, there is no certificate stating that a user is the source of their data. On the contrary, the latter are scattered in data centers belonging to the digital giants [ZOU 17]. Thus, what are the concrete and realistic means at the disposal of the data user, today, to prevent these data from being used, studied, or even sold to a third party? Currently, there are probably none!

What is the characterization of data? Should data be considered as an intangible property that is the subject of an appropriation (see Property law)? In other words, should we follow a system similar to that used in industrial or intellectual property law, which grants a right of use without granting the right as such (see Operating license)? Should data be understood as an extension of the person which cannot be the subject of a heritagization or, on the contrary, as a personality right (see Person scheme)? In fact, it is essential to imagine a legal construction that would make it possible to harmonize personal rights, but also the flexibility necessary for handling and circulating the data required by the emergence of NICTs.

It is very likely that property law relating to personal digital data (with some safeguards such as the non-commercialization of genomic data) will be imposed on the European Union, as:

– the global political-economical context influenced by the American and Chinese digital giants is moving in this direction;

– the appearance of technologies, such as blockchains, makes citizens more engaged in their personal data.

In our view, impeding European digital research and economy by not considering data as a specific tangible property can have as consequence that the next generations of Europeans will have a hybrid brain made in USA or China!

Yet, the main issue is to know who owns data. Are they the property of the final user or the person at the source? Do data become the property of the company collecting these data? Thus, we are led to wonder who will be the legitimate owner and who will benefit from the related wealth. Should those who are its source benefit from its value? Or should it be those storing, exploiting and giving them this value?

The various market players do not all agree on this topic, depending on the countries. Indeed, it is worth recalling that, unlike our neighbors across the Atlantic who are subject to the Common Law, in Europe and therefore in France, no right of ownership has been recognized on data, granting any sale or purchase right. Under these conditions, according to the European approach, data incarnates an emanation of the legal personality of a natural person. It belongs to the family of subjective rights. Just like the identity of the individual, it enjoys the same legal protection as information associated with the privacy of persons [WIL 18].

Here, the central question is what means can be granted to the true "owner" of the data, so that they can really reclaim it. In order to answer this question and maybe find a possible solution, we believe it is essential to explain what we actually mean by "owner". The very essence of ownership lies in the ability to access a tangible or intangible property, and to have full authority to use it. With the emergence of blockchain technology, it seems possible nowadays for the user to reach a level of sovereignty. We can consider the example of the uPort, a Self-Sovereign Identity device, making it possible to manage identity by creating certificates on the identity of an individual or data, but also on claims making it possible, for example, to prove that an individual and a piece of data are associated [ZOU 17]. Under these conditions, blockchain allows us to imagine a world where we could remain the owner of our data, while making them available to other people, a kind of "virtual usufruct". The user, who actually becomes the owner, could generate data and decide who will have access to them. The latter will then be able to decide on the processing, by administering uses and making them available to operators.

In the end, it would be better, and even essential, to be able to consider digital data as an intangible property and to appoint the Internet user or source user, whose data are associated, as the true owner of these data. This is even more relevant today with the development of the blockchain tool, which is going to help to give the user the means to reclaim their data.

With the blockchain, trust does not disappear; on the contrary, it is enhanced! Its nature changes by becoming scalable at the finest level, with the possibility of numerous choices: the nodes that will compose the blockchain network, their role, especially in the validation of transactions, the data to which these nodes will have access, and so on [LEB 18].

As a result, this will provide real protection to people and a fair redistribution of the value. It should be noted that this will somewhat overshadow the valuation of data through their collective interlinking and will reinforce individualism. In turn, this approach might result in a reinforcement of inequalities between citizens who are able to manage, protect and monetize their data and those who, due to a lack of culture, time, money or other, will abandon these functions to the market. This approach is completely in line with the state of mind of a Neo-Darwinian tendency of digital technology, where each individual will have to adapt and then evolve in this new digital ecosystem. Therefore, this personalist view of data seems to us the most realistic and efficient in order to somewhat empower individuals and ensure their protection. To conclude, it is essential to insist on the connection of data with the "source" person and to attract its scheme towards that of the individual, its respect, protection and confidentiality. Finally, it should be noted that some people are trying to reconcile both the ownership of persons and that of operators, by reintegrating the role of the "source" person, while keeping the idea of ownership. They consider data as a creation of the individual, like intellectual property. Under these conditions, the "source" owner will have to be consulted on the uses of their work and paid for the latter. We have our reservations about this last approach, because it seems to us unrealistic to think that a piece of data is the original "creation" of the person without any other actor – such as operators, publishers, researchers, and so on – having taken any part in its production, even indirectly.

On the other hand, wondering via an ethical prism about the construction, functioning and purposes of algorithms is not inconvenient and can quickly lead to added value, meaning, transparency and the trust of citizens. Therefore, where uses are unpredictable, reflections on NICTs help to open prospects of possible uses, and would then help to prevent some excesses.

In this context, this "datafication" of our society leads to a whole series of questions, especially regarding big data, algorithms and AI, such as:

– What are the modifications provided by the use and analysis of big data within a structure? How much attention do we want to give to data in our lives? How do big data impact everyday practice? What changes should we expect for customer services?

– How are big data used by companies?

– How can different data sources be associated? What value should be given to them? What are the different transformations performed? What intermediary data are produced?

– How do the results from big data project analyses guide the company with its daily activities?

– Do structures using personal digital data sell the latter to external third parties?

– Where can reliable digital data be found and how to use them?

– Should judgments and decisions only be guided by a self-learning expert system, AI or algorithmic processing based on correlations? Are we ready to blindly be subjected to NICTs or do we prefer to wait patiently for their final emergence?

– How can transparency and intellectual property be reconciled around these algorithms?

– Can big data represent an "objective truth" or is any interpretation biased by a form of selection and subjective screening, or even by the way data are "cleansed" [BOL 10]?

– Is an algorithm more reliable than human decision, and should it replace and supersede human decision? Are algorithms new decision-makers?

– How can we build free will in a world governed by algorithms?

– Should the habits and gestures characterizing and individualizing us be dependent on values and baselines common to all and derived from algorithms?

– Should we inform people about the health risks they face following the sequencing of their genome?

– Do algorithms lock us in an information cage, threatening cultural openness and democratic pluralism?

– All these cumulated big data have value, how and where can we find this value to improve activities?

– Should the organization of a company be adapted to these technological developments?

– Is the algorithmic solution still of acceptable quality, if the body experiences a perturbation (robustness), if the system is dynamic (fault resistance), and so on?

– Did professional codes of ethics take into consideration the integration of NICTs?

– Does the introduction of algorithms in the health or insurance field have an impact on the doctor-patient or insurer-insured person relationship?

– Are personal digital data processing algorithms not going to lead to a new wave of inequalities, categorizations, discriminations and injustice within society?

– Is an algorithm loyal to society? Does its purpose serve a collective interest and the protection of persons, or a more personal interest? Is it trustworthy?

– Does the algorithm respect the human dimension of the data it processes?

– To what extent should professional practices meet a criterion of objectivity, neutrality and/or rationality?

– To what extent is it possible to develop the approach and ethical commitment of a company with the use of its big data?

– How can the need for sharing and the confidentiality of the person be combined during the storage of digital data in cloud computing?

– How can collective interest and the individual protection of persons be combined?

– How can an ethical culture be conveyed to digital technology professionals with a greater awareness of the latter?

– Is ethics inherent to AI emergence?

– Who is the owner of the knowledge derived from expert systems (such as Watson): the owner of the data, the structure using this information, the publisher (such as IBM), the citizen?

– How can digital transformation and ethics be reconciled within a company?

– Is there a recognized reference point on ethical best practices regarding the construction, functioning and use of algorithms?

– Will NICTs lead to a new wave of social and technological inequalities and injustice?

– Does the algorithmic customization of insurance offers and services[5] not result in a challenge of mutualization, namely the very logic of insurance and the social pact on which it is based?

– Are the results from algorithms scientifically relevant and reliable?

– How can new analytical forms and applications use both new and old data?

– Are the new actors of digital technology (Big Tech, big players and operators) going to interface with the specialists of the health, insurance, finance or aerospace sectors? Will it rather correspond to competition or partnership?

– The creation of data can be part of a relatively complex system (mixing both human activity, sensors and one or more processes), which contributors are likely to claim ownership of the value associated with data use?

– What are the responsibilities of each (public and/or private) actor involved at some point in the data life cycle? Who is responsible for the algorithm and digital data use?

---

5 This has the effect of leading, on the one hand, to tariffs according to individuals' "risk" profile and, on the other hand, a correlation between a behavior (tobacco, too fatty or sugary food, etc.) and a risk of occurrence of a pathology.

– Do NICT users have real control over their data? Are they aware of the possible resale of their data?

– How can structures be regulated, when everyone tomorrow will be able to initiate their own data mining and extractions online via a specific algorithm?

– Which public and/or private bodies must guarantee optimum efficiency and security, while ensuring the democratic and transparent processing of digital data?

– How is the economic and financial model of a company 4.0 going to change?

– How can wealth be produced from digital technology, while creating an economy of trust essential for new uses to be developed?

Furthermore, the question regarding the quality and intrinsic nature of data also helps to reinforce this fear and concern of society. Is the integrity of the data produced and received, guaranteed in particular by a digital signature device?

Digital technology actors found that data processing could increase the number of errors, if data were not impeccable in the first place. Numerous malfunctions could then taint the accuracy of the data and processing. Data are derived from bad sources, if they are duplicated, or if they are already obsolete or outdated. This phenomenon is also reinforced due to the fact that big data increasingly come from sources outside the company using them. To combat this situation, publishers create new solutions making it possible to improve the visualization and traceability of the data source and reduce the error rate. We can also see that new actors specialized in signal processing, visualization, machine learning, external data cleansing, analysis and selection have emerged.

In addition, this digital revolution – illustrated in particular by the increase in decisions taken by algorithms contained in platforms, machines or technological objects – raises a whole series of ethical questions on the protection of individuals against the disclosure and use of their personal data, and a possible "over-mathematization" of society. Indeed, the consumer often loses all control as to the dissemination of their data. Who uses data? To what end? What is the freedom of choice of data users? Where are they stored? How can the individual keep control over their personal data? How can it be guaranteed that these data we transmit or which pass through us and NICTs cannot enable formal identification or interpretation we do not understand? What is the level of transparency?

Regarding digital data, the ethical framework for persons and structures can be summarized according to four specific notions [DAV 12]:

– *Identity*: what is the link between our offline identity and our online identity?

– *Confidentiality*: who should control the access to data?

– *Ownership*: who is the true owner of the data (subjective right, transfer of ownership, etc.), who has the rights to transfer them, and what are the obligations of the individuals and/or structures generating and using these data? Is our existence composed of innovative actions on which we have a copyright or other rights regarding design?

– *E-reputation*: how can we identify which data is trustworthy and reliable?

The first challenge is to give back the control of information to citizens. The whole core of this reflection thus lies in positioning the cursor on the accountability and data ownership system of the actors. In fact, we are led to wonder about the accountability of the person in the event that data anonymization leads to some invisibility of the individual who can then avoid following some rules of decorum.

On the other hand, we just saw that the arrival of blockchain technology might deeply disrupt the whole digital system, the collaborative economy, as well as the power relationships between the different market actors. Such a change becomes *de facto* the target of numerous questions on the future of our society, such as:

– Is the development of this technology really the result of a consensus between the actors?

– If the system is decentralized and if a problem occurs, to whom will the user be able to make a claim? Who decides what?

– Who is responsible for the code contained in autonomous DCOs, as well as the damages that can be caused by the latter? Which law is applicable to transactions? What legal power should be given to the operations performed via these systems?

– How can a decentralized and autonomous organization be regulated?

– Can blockchain disrupt traditional management?

– What will be a world where each object will have its own rules and implementing rules, where each person will be able to define their currency and procedures for exchange?

– Will we see actors, such as banks, insurances, notarial services, certification bodies, integrate "blockchainization" into their business processes tomorrow? Or will we see these structures be "blockchainized", or even overwhelmed by the new market based on the blockchain concept?

Finally, one of the main questions is to know whether, as citizens, we will be able to choose in which society we would like to live in tomorrow, and what will be the services derived from the digital ecosystem that we want for the future of our society. What can be done to control and regulate algorithms and their uses tomorrow? Who will be the guarantor ensuring that defined digital rules are indeed complied with? Is there a recognized reference on the ethical best practices of these processing algorithms?

If "Code is Ethics", this means that the person integrating ethics into NICTs is the publisher, the designer, the developer or the "implementer" of the IS. In fact, vital ethical choices and decisions are found in the parameterizing rules of the algorithm. Therefore, one can wonder whether it is ethically acceptable that the manufacturer alone decides on the parameters to be implemented in order to obtain a given response. What should be the organization, roles, rules, policies about and regarding algorithms? Should we not give back this ethical nature to politicians, independent multidisciplinary committees, or public or private regulation bodies responsible for studying the relationships between human rights, technology, markets and economic models in the 21st Century?

Many questions worthy of being examined and debated with urgent and due attention, so that these critical challenges regarding NICTs, as well as the concerns about the future form of our society, should be the subject of informed and enlightening choices. Consequently, we consider it essential and productive to discuss from an ethical point of view these questions, in order to support a rich, open, constructive and evolving reflection.

1.3. Ethics as a digital compass

From an epistemological point of view, the term "ethics" originates from the Greek word *ethos* meaning "mores" (Cicero), "habits" (Plato and Aristotle). Ethics implies the "habitat", as well as the personality of an individual. The way we inhabit the world represents the way we are. This is why the expression "to be inhabited" takes all its symbolism, essence and meaning in this explanation. From this approach, we can define ethics as a reflection on the behaviors and habits that should be applied to make a space habitable. Ethics is then the source of questions on values regarding action, favorable to a confrontation of values in an environment of ideas. Its virtue is to seek the best decision according to the location and time. There is not necessarily only one possible response. What is a truth or fair decision one day may not be the same in another location or at another time. The force of ethical reflection is to be constantly changing and evolving according to time and space. It only has meaning in a specific situation, in which it admits arguments, dialog and paradoxes. The objective is to obtain the most suitable consensus for the given situation.

Furthermore, in ethics, the term "value" amounts to what should be. We regularly talk about human or moral values and associate with it an ethical action. These values can correspond to honesty, fairness, trust, accountability and openness [HER 17]. We can consider this value system as a measurement standard making it possible to assess events and actions. It provides a guideline and ideals to be followed. One of the pillars of ethics is this imperative to call on the rationality and common sense of the actors. This idea cannot be developed without a coordination, exchange and sharing agreement between the actors. Thus, ethics requires a vision, a purpose, an ambition which is materialized in a given orientation. It is the compass that provides direction for behaviors, best practices and uses to be maintained.

Ethical action is, above all, a response (from the Latin *respondere*, "account for, respond to, hence responsibility/accountability") to a limited and complex situation. Ethics performs three main functions, namely the determination of what is morality, knowing the reasons justifying the effort of a person to live ethically, and the application to practical life of the results obtained in the first two functions [BÉR 16].

In the context of the digital revolution, ethics must address issues regarding concrete actions that have a major causal significance for the future of our contemporary society, and which are accompanied by unprecedented projected implications. To this must be added the magnitude of long term actions and also, very often, their irreversibility. All this places accountability at the heart of ethics, including the space and time horizons corresponding to the ethical principles we are going to describe below.

Thus, ethics can be represented as a behavior control mode of the individual, which focuses on co-built and shared values to give a meaning to their decisions and actions, thus calling upon their personal judgment and accountability [BOI 03]. When we analyze the various treaties and instruments referring to ethics, we are quickly overwhelmed by an avalanche of human values and underlying terms used by the authors, such as "happiness", "compassion", "solidarity", "altruism", "accountability", "well-being", "care", "empathy", "respect", "precaution", and so on. This ocean of social values of all kinds has the inconvenience of disturbing the way we think. How can a selection be made among all these social values in order to identify principles associating them in order to develop a clear reflection on the topic? Are there universal values which apply to everyone as references and can be recognized as rules?

In ethics, principle is the cornerstone characterized "in the form of a command" [LEC 07]. It is universal, intangible and immutable, and its value is not influenced by the course of world history. All societies are aiming at this universality illustrating this uniqueness surrounding us. This universality seeks to express itself to us though our concrete and practical achievements. The mission of the principle is to provide guidelines for actions, set behaviors associated with it and markings to avoid discussion from going astray [LEC 09]. For a long time, the objective of Greek and Latin thinkers was to "reduce any moral requirement to a single principle" [OGI 07] by relying on glorious philosophers, such as Aristotle[6], Kant[7], Bentham[8] or Mill[9]. Nowadays, contemporary society includes several main principles

6 The greater good.

7 Goodwill.

8 The well-being of all.

9 The harm principle.

whose defining characteristics are that they are stable and few. Thus, just like the four cardinal points of the compass rose, our ethics can be formed and structured around four ethical principles described for the first time in the book of Beauchamp and Childress in 2001. These are: the principle of benevolence, the principle of autonomy, the principle of malevolence and the principle of justice (see Box 1.1).

According to the author, this approach based on ethical principles and values constitutes the backbone of an analysis facilitating the identification and reflection on moral dilemmas. The essence of ethics is found in consciousness, questioning and judgment. Therefore, these principles require a moral obligation, while leaving room for the freedom and creativity of the actors, without imposing a canonical reference scale of values. This is made possible by the fact that, *a priori*, there is no priority between these four ethical principles. It is then the responsibility of people to prioritize them according to the conflict situations they are facing.

However, it is important to indicate that this pattern of thought is quite general and does not highlight all the subtleties of the multiple moral challenges of a given problem. It is essential to adjust this ethical reflection model so that these principles remain relevant and in line with the environment studied. Authors use the concept of "specifications" introducing the notion of balancing. This concept refers to a judgment and a deliberation imposed by the individuals upon themselves to analyze the significance of each value or standard integrated into the ethical reflection [BÉR 15].

It can be noted that the definition of these principles does not necessarily imply their operational effectiveness. In fact, the non-application of ethical principles within a company or organization often comes from their non-appropriation and abstraction by staff. It is then important to imply the maximum number of persons in algorithmic processing, in the structuring of transversal exchanges around these ethical principles. The idea is to develop an ethical reflection which is unifying within the structure [CIG 14].

Benevolence: It contributes to the well-being and merit of others. It must meet two very specific criteria: the action performed must be at the service of the person in a beneficial and useful way, namely it must have a positive cost-benefit ratio. This principle, just like that of autonomy, is associated with the time dimension, as it generally leads to immediate punctual questions.

Autonomy: It indicates the fact that a person gives themselves their rule of conduct with no external influence, since the Greek terms *autos* and *nomos* respectively mean "oneself" and "law, rule". The purpose of this principle is to involve the person in a decision process. This principle is often associated with the free and informed consent of the individual.

Malevolence: Its mission is to avoid harm and negative consequences on the person we are responsible for and to protect them against injuries or sufferings that would have no meaning for them. Therefore, its purpose implies that we do good and refrain from doing harm. This principle appears in the Hippocratic maxim *primum non nocere* ("first, to do no harm"), whose consequence is to do good to the person and remove them from harm. This principle is connected and influenced by the time dimension, as the questions concern the anticipation and projection in time.

Justice: Its objective is to share the resources available (means, time, money, energy, etc.) between all the actors. This principle is closely associated with the notions of equality and fairness which are directly involved in the framework of a fair decision. Ideally, any action should aim at a perfect equality, but according to the circumstances and the nature of the persons, fairness is often required in order to set priorities and some hierarchy in the actions to be performed. This principle includes a scope that can be referred to as "macro-ethical"[10], because it concerns the whole society or a very specific category of persons. The space dimension is the backbone of this principle.

Box 1.1. *Characteristics of the four ethical principles*

Our ethical analysis based on these four main principles is echoed by a "semiotic square"[11] derived, to some extent, from Aristotle's Square of Opposition. We can thus establish a logical Square of Opposition of the ethical principles (see Figure 1.2).

10 It can be noted that the three other previous principles have a far more individual and relational dimension considered as "micro-ethical".

11 The semiotic square, designed by the Lithuanian linguist and semiotician Algirdas Julien Greimas, is a tool used to record relationships between semiotic signs and illustrate the meaning development within a structure.

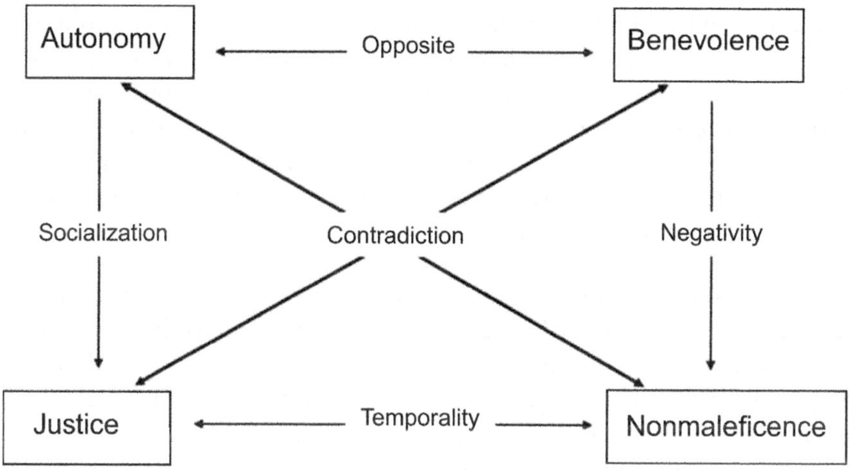

Figure 1.2. *Logical Square of Opposition of the ethical principles*

We see that two proposals with the same topics and predicates can be opposite due to their quality and/or quantity. Thus, the oppositions that can be developed are as follows:

– two conflicting proposals (alternative) are proposals that oppose each other due to their quality and quantity;

– two contrary proposals (incompatibility) are universal proposals opposed due to quality;

– two proposals which do not have the same social dimension and are opposed due to quantity;

– two proposals with one being the negative form of the other;

– two proposals with a different time parameter.

Thus, ethicists often balance, or even put into conflict, the principles of autonomy and benevolence. We note that the benevolence principle receives the negative form of the malevolence principle. Here it can be added that the justice and malevolence principles are mainly differentiated by the notion of time. Finally, the justice principle can correspond to the societal form of the autonomy principle, by empowering all citizens via equal and/or fair actions.

In the context of global digitalization, ethics is expressed by questions regarding, on the one hand, the habits, mores and uses of citizens in relation to NICTs and, on the other hand, the increasingly autonomous behavior of platforms, expert systems, machines or connected objects. These technological tools – such as recommendation, search, sorting, processing and decision algorithms – are generally built in order to perform actions independently from human intervention.

Like any technological innovation, NICTs are only tools, which are not good or evil *per se*: it is only the spirit and ethics underlying their use in order to make them an instrument at the service of mankind and its development [DOS 18]. Digital technology reinforces some pre-existing ethical questions. We then see an urgent need to reassert some principles and codes of ethics in the light of the constantly evolving digital ecosystem. This is why the idea of a digital ethics is naturally required in order to promote a "good use" of digital tools. To this end, some human values and some fundamental principles must be renewed in the specific area of action generated by digital technology. However, is digital ethics only a use ethics, namely an applied ethics? Does digital technology not raise ethical questions and problems specific to it?

Data are one of three key components of algorithmic solutions, along with the power of machines and algorithms themselves. However, they do not do everything. These are a real triad. Studies on a single type of neural network showed that an AI with more data is more efficient than an AI with a better algorithm. Nevertheless, the performance of algorithms plays a decisive role in the quality of algorithmic results, in particular with deep learning, and especially in their performance, in particular the speed of the model training phase. Data scientists must then perform numerous tests and supervision, in order to choose the right statistical models of segmentation, classification or prediction.

Restricting ethical questioning to a strictly algorithmic area would come to focus on the algorithm functioning as such and simultaneously exclude everything occurring upstream and downstream of this processing. Considering a digital ethics thus requires us to extend the field of vision beyond algorithms, to each of the various stages of ontological and chronological chains, in which it is involved: from the intent and purposes which govern its construction upstream, to the production and implementation of the computer code, that of the executable and operational code, that of the construction, nature, generation, acquisition and selection of data that will fuel the algorithm, that of the execution, that of the execution context, that of maintenance, that regarding practices associated with the algorithm, and finally that of the recycling of the data produced. It is therefore the whole data lifecycle that must be analyzed, from its development to its removal, and extended to the ecosystem of interactions between them and with us, both at the collective and individual levels. It is then about questioning, in their contexts, the software and its specific infrastructures, both technical and human. Understanding it is even more difficult, since it is about understanding its complexity. Due to a lack of time, means, analysis methodologies, road maps, competences, desires, or even simply due to vagaries, algorithmic processing is rarely included as a whole.

This ethical understanding of the algorithmic complexity is decisive both for itself, namely as an NICT, and us, namely as instigators of the ethical culture arising from the digital practices caused by their uses, as well as the intentions they implement and the externalities they generate. This questioning must therefore embrace their whole cycle of development, in order to assess the quality, compliance, loyalty[12], and so, *a fortiori*, the ethics of these NICTs.

This is why, in our opinion, the ethics applied to NICTs can be broken down into three sub-parts:

– *Data Ethics (DE)*: associated with all the questions regarding the source and nature of the data, its construction, record, access, sharing, intrinsic value, owner, and so on;

– *Algorithm Ethics (AE)*: regarding reflections on the construction and functioning of an algorithm, AI, robot or automatic learning, its purposes, the person in charge of it, its operations, and so on;

– *Practice Ethics (PE)*: linked to the risks of misuse and its excesses towards the citizen. Reflections on the behaviors and best practices to be maintained help to shape a professional code of ethics on the governance,

12 The algorithmic system must not betray the community to which it belongs (citizen or consumer).

control and management of algorithmic tools and the innovations linked, in particular, to data science and quantum computing.

It can be noted that Data Ethics (DE), Algorithm Ethics (AE) and Practice Ethics (PE) are very closely linked and interdependent with each other. For example, studies based on data confidentiality (DE) also help to solve problems of consent and responsibilities. Likewise, the ethical evaluation of algorithms (AE) often involves analyses of the responsibilities of their designers, developers (or "implementers"), and users. Consequently, it makes sense to refer to an overall ethical space or framework (a kind of "macro-ethics"), which is consistent, inclusive and holistic, to talk about digital ethics.

On the other hand, applying an ethical approach to digital technology is an action which is, at first glance, unnatural, as technological tools would be deprived of any social and moral value. This analysis comes from a common way of thinking which considers that any technology is ethically neutral, and only mankind can give meaning to its actions. Nevertheless, we see that the different digital forms, such as big data and algorithms, also generate value from the moment they influence and condition the way users behave. To conclude, NICTs are never fully neutral. Under these conditions, ethics must speak for both the extrinsic and intrinsic values related to digital technology. Thus, this lack of neutrality of NICTs involves a certain ethical vigilance. It implies to:

– wonder how our references (intellectual property law) can be adapted or made more flexible in relation to the existing standards for technology, in order not to curb the potential of technological innovations?

– wonder whether other (legal or ethical) references should be developed in order to rebalance the standards associated with technologies, which have an impact seen as negative for persons (right to be forgotten, digital memory, permanent connectivity, right to disconnect, etc.)?

Finally, with this new relational and sociological paradigm [DOU 13] generated by this digital shift, we must rethink, revamp and reinvent the old traditional ethics to aim for a more contemporary "algorithmic ethics", in line with the current questions and challenges. The normative aspect that stems from digital technology does not only question the standard framework that is the law, but also challenges ethics. For example, one of the main standards of digital technology can be connection. At another level, we could very well integrate other standards, such as the traceability, memory and geolocation of technological tools. Thus, it is interesting to see that we have created other standards, in order to rebalance these normative parameters of digital technology, which are seen as more binding, or even harmful. Regarding permanent connectivity, we have implemented the right to disconnect, and regarding the memory of digital devices, we have invented the right to be forgotten and the right to be delisted. Therefore, the idea is to implement normative adjustment variables to find the right balance in this digital ecosystem composed of any kind of standards.

1.4. Ethical challenges and risks regarding algorithmic processing

Always faster, constantly lighter and more diverse, information is experiencing exponential growth, which seems to double every two years. This is why NICTs invest in different fields of society and must facilitate an optimization, both qualitative and economic, of all industrial and civil processes, while adapting to the regulatory and legislative framework or transforming it. Thus, technological progress and the popularity of the Internet have resulted in a gigantic capacity to collect, process, combine and store data. The calculation of statistics from these data includes a massive potential value for our society, but these advantages come with significant risks, especially for the privacy of the "owners" of these data. The generation, maintenance, storage, diffusion and use of big data then become a major challenge. This digital shift is based on both collaborative networks of citizens and/or scientific researchers, and on cloud computing, or connected objects and sensors allowing each actor to have more targeted and detailed information. This digitalization also developed on the significant computer memories and big data algorithmic processing, promoting the manufacture of more efficient tools, and especially regarding decision aid.

Therefore, the world "algorithmization" affects all sectors of activity, thus resulting in information on anything that may exist, anywhere, at any time, in order to be collected, cross-referenced and used, whether appropriate or not for the person. The whole ambivalence and uncertainty of the phenomenon is expressed in this observation. Individuals are constantly torn between hope for beneficial progress and concern for personal nuisance.

This feeling of fear and mistrust is amplified as soon as it concerns personal data, especially regarding health, as its nature is directly associated with the intimacy of the person. In fact, according to several studies and surveys[13], more than 85% of French people express concern, and even worry, about the protection of their personal data, as well as the use made of them, especially under the economic, ethical and legal pressure of the market. Generally, the behavior of a number of public and private actors, who show little respect for the rules of security and use of NICTs, is responsible for the growing loss of citizens' confidence. Indeed, some security services, whose three main strategies ensured the protection of privacy – namely anonymization, previous informed and free consent, and opt-out[14] – are obsolete. Thus, non-secure data processing by sub-contractors can lead to a re-identification of information or result in data transfer to a third country outside the European Union [BÉR 16].

We note that the techniques based on "de-identification" turned out to be considerably inefficient against powerful re-identification algorithms based on substantive knowledge and correlation between data. We can consider the example of a database of the Massachusetts hospital, which was de-anonymized using a public database of voters (Sweeney's attack). This implies that, besides sensitive and then identifiable data, there is "almost-identifying" type of data. If we consider the examples of Kostas Chatzikokolakis[15], we see that 87% of the population of the United States is identifiable from its date of birth and zip code, on Netflix 68% of users are identifiable based on two classifications made in the top 500 titles, and the Target retail store chain knows, based on 25 products ordered, if a person is

13 Sources: French people and the protection of personal data, study of the CSA institute for Orange, February 2014, available at: https://www.csa.eu/media/1236/opi20140123-les-francais-et-la-protection-des-donnees-personnelles.pdf; poll commissioned by Lima, June 2015; study for Havas Media performed by the Toluna Institute, September 25, 2014.

14 This word refers to a marketing or legal term characterizing an e-mail. Opt-out is authorized in France, if it concerns e-mailing regarding commercial activities between B to B companies. Opt-out represents the methods allowing the Internet user to stop a mechanism they consider as being intrusive or troublesome for their privacy, such as blocking cookies in order to stop receiving advertising.

15 Conference of Kostas Chatzikokolakis entitled "*La vie privée dans le monde des données* (Privacy in the World of Data)", for the 2015 publication of *Horizon Maths* organized by IBM France on the theme of Health and Data. This event was held on December 14 and 15, 2015 on the premises of IBM France.

going to give birth or not. Furthermore, we note that, mechanically (and statistically), databases which were originally anonymized could lose this quality, only because of their association with other data. Consequently, data production could end up enabling a tightened identification of persons and, therefore, an increased risk of privacy violation [RIA 17].

In addition, algorithmics can encourage discriminations, on the one hand, through simple data set cross-checking and, on the other hand, through the re-introduction of profiling with no prior identification requirement. The risks of confining Internet users through customized services, according to their behaviors, habits and expectations, can be added to this. Such a phenomenon is against the free will and empowerment of the person, and contributes to a reducing homogenization of information. One of the risks of digitalizing the public sphere also relates to the fact of people being judged not according to their actions or real events, but according to their tendency to behave in a way that is indicated by their personal data according to their relationships, desires, needs and habits. This would come to reducing human potential to statistics and probabilities controlled by algorithms. The misuse of algorithms also contributes to amplifying the risk of excessive confidence in the choices recommended by the machine calculation, based on possibly erroneous or random assumptions, but likely to influence the choices of people, without the latter really being aware of it. From a macroscopic point of view, we are entitled to wonder about the "solutionist" risk for a society which systematically turns to an algorithmic approach, partially concealing the complexity of the social-ethical-economic challenges requiring other types of interventions.

In fact, algorithms can have several effects directly or indirectly impacting citizens (see Box 1.2).

Transformative effects formatting our representations: with evaluation via websites, services or products (see benchmark by Page Rank algorithms).

Normative effects: by watching NICT "best practices or habits" provided by algorithms integrated into connected objects, smartphones or platforms.

Filtering and confining conformist effects[16]: by reducing our capacity to discover and understand something else, as the algorithm categorizes us in a

16 The algorithms of social media, such as Facebook, create a filtering and confining information "bubble" by limiting access and exchange with persons of different opinions.

well-defined socio-cultural class (see music selection and suggestions offered by the Deezer algorithm), perpetuating the past through projection or generalization created by the system (see Risk of exclusion, as the past can influence, or even reinforce, the future).

Individualization effects: made possible by algorithms facilitating profile customization, and more targeted and oriented marketing thanks to big data.

Unequal and hierarchical effects: as, for example, differentiating tariffs, insurance premiums according to the person's profiles (through dynamic pricing techniques).

Effects of choice manipulation[17]: when several Internet users perform the same search on the same search engine, we see that results can be different, as personal criteria are incorporated into the ranking algorithm.

Unpredictable effects: linked to bad quality and bias of input data, which can have an impact on the purpose and result of the algorithm.

Box 1.2. *Effects of algorithms on people*

In addition, one of the significant ethical challenges of big data is their apparent objectivity to illustrate social reality with scientific authority and technical rigor. Yet, there is a certain obscurantism (or even lack of transparency) about the algorithms used. To this can be associated results that are likely to be distorted by multiple methodology biases. In fact, the algorithm simply and "stupidly" learns what it is requested to learn and replicates stereotypes, if they are not sorted and classified. For example, the data available and used can be biased via their construction or the choice of questions used to obtain them (sourcing). The algorithm itself through its functioning and purposes can reflect the biases of its designer, their

This algorithmic confining or "filtering bubble" [PAR 11] results in persons only socializing with individuals, objects, cultures, views and opinions consistent and similar to their own tastes and, therefore, refusing the unknown. This absence of information diversity could, in the medium term, increase the risk of manipulation, and lead to a polarization and division of our contemporary societies.

17 In 2015, a study of Epstein and Robertson showed that a search engine had the capacity to change the voting intentions of undecided persons by 20% for a presidential election by means of the ranking of information visible during a search [BAL 17].

commercial interests, political opinions, and even introduce discriminations or exclusions prohibited by law.

Furthermore, in recent years, we have been witnessing the emergence of the massive diffusion of fake information ("Fake News") via algorithms, especially from social media. In 2017, the key study "Fake News Machine"[18] claimed that one can influence, or even manipulate, an election today with 400,000 dollars, by implementing a massive fake information transmission device on social media [BAL 18].

At the same time, scientists must deal with the problems of the obsolescence of the methodology used in order to obtain results and may need, for a re-analysis, to distribute data which were initially collected. It should be noted that retention costs cannot be covered by individual teams and must be taken into consideration by research structures, which must therefore record data over time and give access to them for a long time.

In addition, some condemn the negative consequences that can be generated by this information power – illustrated by big data – if it is reserved to some prevailing operators. Others put forward the risks of discrimination (regarding access to employment, insurance, services, the price determination of products and services) or censorship persons can be the target of, due to the algorithmic processing of their data, aiming at offering them customized services along with a dynamic pricing which could deprive them of their autonomy and freedom of choice. To this can be added concerns, or even fantasies, regarding a "dictatorship" of data and predictive algorithms requiring a definition of a "computed human", which would jeopardize the principle of self-determination which, in our opinion, is the very nature of any human being [ZOL 15].

Furthermore, the same persons who are worried also remain significantly hopeful about the opportunities these NICTs can provide. In this context, a climate, which mixes hot and cold, has been established which alternates between enthusiasm and mistrust regarding digital technology. Consequently, this makes the trust relationship between actors very fragile [TER 14] in an increasingly digital ecosystem. In fact, this trust issue

18 Lion Gu, Vladimir Kropotov, and Fyodor Yarochkin, The Fake News Machine: How Propagandists Abuse the Internet and Manipulate the Public, working paper of Trendlabs, 2017.

becomes crucial for the individual who is concerned about their fundamental freedoms, as well as for companies, both in terms of brand image and reputation, and in order to establish a sustainable and healthy relationship with their stakeholders.

When we consider the history of mankind, humans have always had a tendency to divert the use of innovations and technological progress, by constantly redefining their needs and fields of actions. We can consider the example of Alfred Nobel who dedicated his life to study explosives and, in particular, the less dangerous use and commercialization of nitroglycerine. The researcher accidentally discovered that, when nitroglycerine was mixed to an inert and absorbing solid called Kieselguhr, the latter seemed much safer to transport and handle. Dynamite was created! Very quickly, the application of this invention went beyond its simple scope of use, which was initially intended for stone quarries, to extend to battle fields. As we can see, invention almost always precedes uses: "When humans have a tool, they are good at finding new uses for it. Often, tools exist even before there is a problem to solve, and each has a potential for unpredictable transformations" [NYE 08].

In a context of confusion and concern about the digitalization of our world, it seems to us essential to come back to ethical fundamentals. What are our human and moral values? How can they be included and applied in this digitized ecosystem? Anyway, a balance must be established between protection and innovation, which requires regulating the use of data valued by big data. On this basis, we are led to think that one of the ethical challenges of the digital world would be to eliminate the existing gaps between the initial human intention linked to openness, sociability, the coproduction of values for NICTs, and the potential excesses and reversals we see in the practices carried out.

Thus, in this digital environment, data are no exception to the rule and are naturally confronted with ethical challenges associated with them. We can divide them according to a technical-human prism respectively based on data and actors[19] (see Figure 1.3).

19 Developers, experts in data science and applied science, experts in software engineering, suppliers, public authorities, direct and indirect final users, etc.

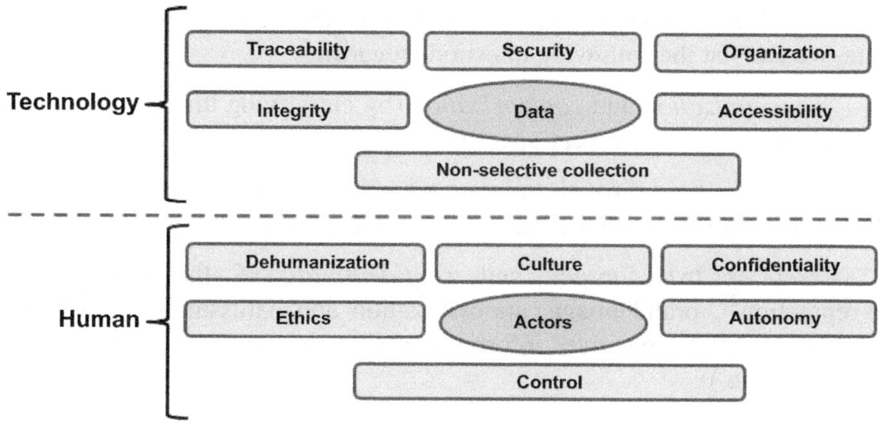

Figure 1.3. *Ethical challenges regarding big data*

Risks from the technological perspective are part of the so-called operational risks related to applications, developments, maintenance, infrastructures and computing servers. Special attention is to be paid to:

– *traceability* via data sourcing (proof and auditability);

– data *security* (fraud, theft[20], loss);

– data *integrity* (epistemology[21] and semantics) and reliability built by human desires and intentions;

– *internal models of organization* and shaping with a transition from data to information;

– *accessibility* (digital divide, social exclusion, rejection and marginalization), availability regarding data;

– *non-selective collection* (objectivity[22]) without taking into consideration a qualitative prioritization of the nature of big data.

---

20 The theft of strategic and confidential data is a risk that will increase with the development of mobility, collaborative work modes, open innovation or the association of new actors with the value chain.

21 One of the complexities of a big data project is the perceived intrinsic and epistemological value of the "massive data" and processing algorithm used to analyze them [CAL 12], which can surpass human understanding.

Regarding the human approach related to the actors involved in digital data, we can list the following questions regarding:

– *dehumanization* and *categorization* (by classifying the individual based on their personal data in very specific boxes);

– *ethical culture* through training, education and raising awareness of the person as to the ethical harm related to data may affect;

– *level of transparency* and *confidentiality* of the personal data (e-reputation[23], brand image, anonymization and harassment regarding the knowledge of a sensitive information (health, social, religious, racial, economic, etc.));

– *ethics* including rights (to be forgotten, to tranquility[24], to rectification, of access, to restriction of processing, intellectual property right derived from big data analysis, etc.) and obligations (responsibilities and transfer of ownership);

– *regulation* and *control* (monitoring and control) of data;

– *individual autonomy*[25] of the person with their free and informed consent (individual freedom of the citizen with no external influence, in particular by giving the user at least one global control parameter over the source of the data used for continuous learning).

In addition, we can establish this technical-human approach on algorithms and the actors involved in this technology (see Figure 1.4).

22 The idea of an objective discovery from big data reinforces the role of interpretative frameworks to provide meaning to data, in order to be able to interact with individuals and the environment surrounding them [GAD 76, HAB 84, SCH 00].

23 Damage to e-reputation can be achieved through rumors, destabilization operations on the Internet and social media.

24 Tranquility represents the "right to be left alone", not to be disturbed by unrequested and unwanted solicitations. Such a situation implies the monitoring and control of the accessibility to one's private sphere.

25 By definition, individual autonomy is the sovereignty of everyone over their person and over what they wish to keep control, without it necessarily being kept secret.

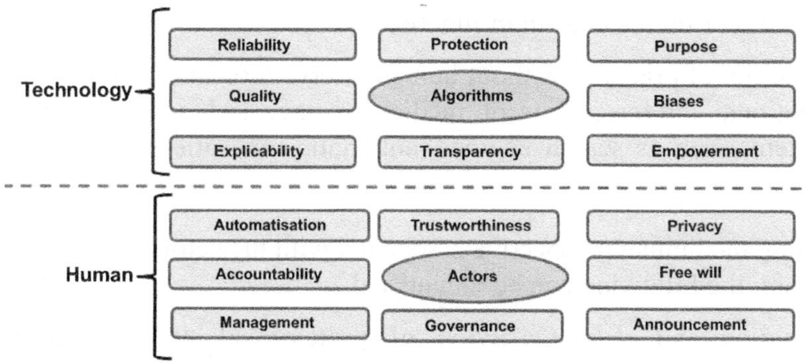

Figure 1.4. *Ethical challenges regarding algorithms*

The challenges related to the technical aspects of the algorithm are numerous and include:

– *reliability* especially regarding the algorithm's decisions;

– *quality* of prediction and *adequacy* of the decision via its content and nature;

– *protection*, *security* and *control* associated with the algorithm;

– the *purpose*[26], use at the service of the person or structure (decision aid, predictive, etc.) and the use of data against the person in a dispute (inheritance, child custody, divorce, employer, banker, insurer, etc.);

– *biases*[27] and *value judgments*, especially of discrimination and differentiation (individual or collective, whether intentional or not);

– *explicability*[28] (documentation) and evaluation (standards and protocols) on the operational capability of the algorithm;

26 Practices regarding data handling (contrary to free choices of the individual) can be illustrated by: the sale of the latter without the explicit consent of the person directly concerned, data can be bought by other structures, data aggregation or non-aggregation, targeted advertising based on big data. This handling makes us inevitably question the transparency and neutrality of algorithms.

27 These biases can also be linked to the problems of loyalty of NICTs, as well as the use of the latter for non-ethical, partisan purposes with no choice diversification.

28 The compromise between explicability and performance must be understood and considered according to the use and must be explained in the documentation for the use of the trainer or user.

– *transparency* on the algorithm functioning;

– *automation* of practices without human intervention and without giving rise to irrational interpretations or media coverage (AI and self-learning expert system, such as search engines, automatic translation, chatbots and robots).

Regarding the human perspective associated with the actors concerned by the algorithm, the following can be indentified:

– *automation* and *dehumanization* of professional practices (hybrid human-machine relationships and place of the human being within the explanation of the decisions assisted by self-learning machines, loss of jobs that can lead to depression and stress, etc.);

– *trustworthiness* (credibility, non-discriminatory);

– *privacy* (citizen monitoring, profiling, individualization and identification);

– *accountability* (internal procedures, code or ethical charter, capacity to report, via documentation[29], limits known of the imputability to the learning device or source code of an IS decision or action, and accountability[30]);

– *management of the lifecycle* of the analytic tool (full historization and data traceability, processing, interpretation and visualization);

– *algorithmic governance* at the level of public and private institutions (regulations, labels, certifications, and authorizations);

– *free choice* of the professional, if the algorithmic processing of a self-learning expert system produces a decision (risks of human dependence to machine decisions);

– *announcement* or *disclosure*[31] of a chance discovery, especially to a health consumer on a future disease or on pathological risks very hard to quantify.

---

29 This documentation must be used within the framework of the declaration of intention by the designer as to the IS uses considered as normal by the latter.

30 The IS designer must adapt and integrate into the IS automatic or supervised (by the machine or human being) control mechanisms.

31 The disclosure of an illness (AIDS, multiple sclerosis, cancer) to a third party (employer, insurer, lender) can be associated with a “loss of chance”, as the third party is going to refuse to act because of this pathology [REY 12].

As we can see, ethical risks are multifaceted and various, it therefore seems fundamental to better understand the properties, nature and limits of these NICTs, in order to best respond to these challenges. Consequently, the influence of the environment and the digital ecosystem should not be overlooked. Thus, the predictive power of an algorithm can be completely transformed according to the way the person is going to react to a piece of information.

1.5. The environmental parameters of digital technology

Nowadays, digital technology is omnipresent in our society. All sectors of activity are impacted by this "digital tsunami" which continues to grow over time along with technological innovations. A decision generated by or thanks to a technology can be justified at the technical level, but identified as inadequate at the legal level or impossible to implement from a logistics perspective (see Reality principle). In addition, we must take into consideration that the ecosystem and the situation are dynamic, and time considerations are vital. Thus, events, some of which are unpredictable, follow one another over time and are a complex framework within which it is essential to make decisions in real time, by taking into account the change of environment and the sources of knowledge and information available.

Furthermore, if we consider the history of NICTs, we see that it extends over four very specific successive eras [DHE 07, PON 09, BÉR 15]:

– *the technical era* representing mass production;

– *the organizational and regulatory era* aiming at an optimum contribution of NICTs to the performance of business processes;

– *the behavioral era* reflecting the relationship and confidence of professionals in society;

– *the purpose and ethical era* expressing the accountability of the actors directly or indirectly involved in these NICTs.

On the other hand, we can study the digital environment – especially the AI environment – from a socio-cognitive prism and scope, which can be broken down into three dimensions [VAY 18]:

– *the learning environment*: which refers to all data collection and structuring devices allowing the machine to get a representation of the world (see Databases);

– *the processing environment*: which refers to all devices allowing the machine to perform inferences on the world, from the learning data at its disposal (see Black boxes of deep neural networks);

– *the political environment*: which refers to all evaluation devices allowing the machine to self-regulate its learning (see Digital control and governance).

In addition, beyond the fact that digital technology integrates all areas of activity and our daily life, it also has an impact on all the sectors composing a company. On this basis, we can divide the environmental parameters of NICTs, especially within a company, into eight categories (see Box 1.3).

Structural: Namely the way the internal parts of a whole are arranged between them. This intrinsic value of a system provides its consistency and is its permanent characteristic.

Technological: it corresponds to the ecosystem or data sphere in which NICTs operate. It includes the partner network (hosts, publishers, datacenters, operators, pure players, cloud computing, etc.), the various key activities (advice, computation, analysis and storage) and services (collection, processing, visualization, interpretation, storage, etc.), resources and distribution channels (B to B and A to B), cost structures (maintenance, subscription, use, development) and revenue streams (valuation, sales, transactions, licenses, intellectual property, rents).

Strategic: this is all the coordinated actions of operations, maneuvers, and how to proceed in order to reach a specific objective. Strategy is greatly influenced by the economic context and by the persons building it.

Methodological: it represents all the logically ordered steps, principles and actions which are a means to achieve a result. It is therefore the way to conduct work or activity, according to a reasoned and consistent approach.

Organizational: it refers to the action of structuring, defining, coordinating, arranging or dividing. It can be considered as a social process.

Regulatory: namely everything related to regulation, law, standards and measures, certification and accreditation systems. This sector requires a particularly strict application within the company.

Relational: this is all the interactions, exchanges and sharing between the various actors directly or indirectly involved in NICTs.

Cultural: this is the behaviors, habits and mores, uses, practices, perceptions, approaches of technological tools' users.

Box 1.3. *Environmental parameters of NICTs within a company*

Thus, the digital environment or ecosystem is based on these eight areas which are linked and interact with each other. These parameters should not be isolated and static from each other, in order to take into consideration the whole complexity of reality. In fact, a good analysis of the environment should take into account these areas, as component parts of a single whole. Finally, let us note that, in anticipation of the gradual emergence of applications associated with quantum mechanics (especially quantum computing and quantum teleportation) marking the beginning of the Fifth Industrial Revolution, it will be crucial to integrate time metrics into these eight parameters, in order to fully complement the NICT digital ecosystem.

Furthermore, as we previously saw, the assessment of the algorithmic processing must extend to the whole data lifecycle. This chain is structured from the data design and construction to its use, until its destruction, retention, or recycling. This development cycle of digital data is divided into seven main phases [PRE 16, BÉR 16]:

– *Data creation and construction*:

- definition of the data repository;

- extension of the sources of structured and/or non-structured data;

- multiplication of data sources (text files, Web, database) and content types outside the company;

- enhancing information by adding metadata, real-time power supply with a high throughput;

- implementation of a data management plan;

- location of data;

- data collection, extraction and pattern search;

- description, characterization and inventory of collected data;

- information creation, record, organization, classification and indexation (topic, source, author, key words, year, associated business concepts, etc.).

– *Data processing*:

- data entry, digitalization, translation, transcription, transformation for dimension reduction;

- exchange automation and massification;

- fusion and interpolation to manage missing or duplicated data;

- data control, validation, cleansing, filtering of data derived from sensors by advanced signal processing techniques;

- data anonymization and description;

- data management and storage;

- security and access rights, administration, variation, and development.

– *Data analysis and use*:

- parallel algorithm, machine learning (or automatic learning) techniques, natural language analysis, statistics, additions of new lines, new correlations;

- advanced analytics (possibility to identify weak signals in large data volumes);

- inference and processing of useful information from the data available;

- prototyping and construction of predictive models directly from data;

- interpretation;

- derived data production;

- generation of the algorithmic processing results;

- data preparation for retention.

– *Data retention*:

- migration in a sustainable format;

- metadata creation;

- data documentation;

- data archiving.

– *Data accessibility, restitution, storage and retention*[32]:

- information stored in various formats;

- distribution and sharing of information most often structured and characterized in push mode;

- access control;

- protection set-up (copyright versus copyleft);

- DataViz: TB (BSC type), Qlikview, Gephi;

- data promotion through an open (or unopened) Internet platform.

– *Valuation*:

- optimum and targeted decision-making;

- monetization of data not yet used;

- customer micro-segmentation, retention;

- improvement of operational efficiency.

– *Reuse of data*:

- processing monitoring and reviews;

- reversibility or recycling, namely restitution for re-integration in another retention system;

- new processing from data;

- cross-referencing data with other data from other fields.

In addition, the digital ecosystem can be described according to four areas, each associated with a specific hierarchization (see Table 1.1).

---

32 Retention has several major purposes: proving, memorizing, understanding, communicating [COU 07].

	Digital ecosystem			
Area	Data	Algorithms	NICTs	Human actors
Hierarchization	Linguistics	Digital	IS	Cognitive
Characteristics	Volume Variety Veracity	Personalization Prediction Prevention	Visualization Speed Value	Participation Proximity Sharing

Table 1.1. *Areas and hierarchizations structuring the digital ecosystem digital*

The four areas structuring the digital ecosystem consist of:

– *data*: derived from the use and collection of information;

– *algorithms*: facilitating digital data processing;

– *NICTs*: which capture and generate small and big data;

– *human actors*: who use digital data.

These four areas also represent four evolving and dynamic paradigms and hierarchizations of our relationship with connectivity in our society [COL 16]:

– *linguistic (or semantic) hierarchization*: data help to connect information;

– *digital hierarchization*: the mission of algorithms is to connect and analyze data;

– *IS hierarchization*: NICTs connect machines to each other via networks and the Internet;

– *cognitive hierarchization*: humans interact and connect to each other, namely each human being carries a connectivity support, whereas before they were only an agent capable of generating and using content.

Finally, these four hierarchizations each have three specific characteristics reflecting the dynamic and evolving aspect of the digital sphere. Linguistic hierarchization is based on volume indicators, data variety and veracity; digital hierarchization relies on customization, prediction and prevention criteria; IS hierarchization is based on visualization, speed and value parameters; cognitive hierarchization relies on characteristics related to participation, proximity and sharing.

At the same time, we note that this digital "infosphere"[33] (in which information, especially big data, is generated and propagated) is also established by the empowerment of persons. Indeed, individuals are now constantly connected. They become both the transmitter and receiver of information, as they are permanently in contact – whether voluntarily or not – with IoTs featuring integrated sensors. Some specialists even talk of a "prosumer"[34] environment in which natural persons are not simple passive objects. Individuals are now both producers and consumers of information. Finally, new actors central to the digital economy are emerging in the digital landscape (such as data miners and "blockchainizers" (Stratum), data analysts and scientists, data brokers, "algorithmers" and "uberizers" of activity) who "platformize" all sectors, such as marketing (Creads, Doz, eYeka), travel (Airbnb, Boaterfly, Wijet), food (La Belle Assiette, Miamtag, Super Marmite), health (Heal, Oscar, Pager), home services (DingDong smart speakers, Hellocasa, Zilok), logistics (Cubyn, Bird Office, Zipments), fashion and beauty (ChicTypes, Popmyday, Stitch Fix), education (Khan Academy, Kokoroe, Speexx), financing (KissKissBankBank, MyMajorCompany) or transport (BlaBlaCar, Chauffeur Privé, Drivy).

1.6. What is the place of mankind in this digital society?

How can we get specific tasks carried out by machines, which were previously carried out by humans, without completely eliminating the effectiveness of human intervention? In the medium term, will these autonomous information systems go from assisting to replacing professionals? Based on our knowledge on human evolution, to what extent can we consider what our descendants will look like? On what level could we find significant changes? So far, evolution can not be predicted, it was observed. With the emergence of AI and soon quantum computing, we can get a predictive and, therefore, anticipative approach of the natural evolution of human beings.

33 This word was invented by Dan Simmons (1989) to refer to an information environment.

34 The term "prosumer" was invented by Alvin Toffler in the book *The Third Wave*, in 1980.

Therefore, digital technology marks a departure from the whole chain of values and restructures our society and our everyday life, by transforming them with a new culture and a new perception of the world. The latter is disrupting our lifestyles, consumption, functioning and work. This is reflected by a break from the past as to the relationship and connection everyone has with others. For example, intelligent digital assistants allow us to plan our holidays with the insight of a human advisor or to identify the feelings of consumers about a specific brand, based on big data derived from social media and other data sources. In at least two decades, it is more than likely that these intelligent digital assistants will become telepathic.

We see the emergence and development of three phenomena associated with each other:

– "Science converges on a universal dogma, according to which organisms are algorithms and life is reduced to data processing;

– Intelligence decouples from consciousness;

– Non-conscious, but highly intelligent, algorithms could soon know us better than we do" [HAR 17].

Therefore, these interactions force the system to rethink each human activity. It is the beginning of a silent, but definitely present, revolution that is taking place before our very eyes [FLO 18]. The difficulty is not to create new jobs, but to design new ones that human beings do better than autonomous machines. It is a new era of change and disruption where survival can only be achieved through responsiveness, adaptability, creativity and, therefore, innovation.

In the context of the generalization of open digital innovation and the transformation of the human condition, we are entitled to wonder, from an anthropological point of view, about the place of mankind in this hyper-connected and digital ecosystem in which emerges new work relationships, and the transformation of the ways to organize work. In which direction does AI lead us? What will be the place of the human being in this hyper-connected and digitized world where objects, robots, machines and other autonomous expert systems will respectively interfere? Is the search for ever greater intelligence not going to overshadow human consciousness? Will our modern societies be able to resist the totalitarian power of a model based on everything digital and everything constantly connected? Is AI going to leave room for mankind, help it, make it dependent (see Technological slavery) or make it disappear? Does it threaten to make discernment, intuition and emotion disappear? To what extent can mankind delegate its free will? Can the citizen accept to be manipulated to transform their feelings, convictions or behaviors, and be categorized or evaluated without being informed? What will be the impact of AI development on our sense of ethics and the relationships between the human being and the machine? Will humans see their status reduce to a sub-human state, as some specialists claim? Towards a form of “alter-human”? Is transhumanism unavoidable for the survival of the human species? Or, on the contrary, is this transhumanism going to create a new hyper-connected human species, developing new intellectual capacities which are unused at the moment and going as far as to delay the age of dying? Since it extends to our time, space and senses, will AI disrupt our vision of humanity and human emotions? Will the day intelligent autonomous systems know us better than we do mean the end of mankind as we have always known it? How can actions and creation be assessed based on AI? The contemporary human species is led to wonder about its future and the direction we are taking. What will our relationships be between human beings, non-humans and even hybrids? Will mankind, as we know it, still be able to rule the world, make sense of it and give it values? Finally, will we be able to transform technological innovations into social, political, economic, or even humanist progress?

Thus, the ethical questioning approach is highly associated with the vision of the place of mankind within its environment. No matter what products and services are offered, digital technology has an impact on all business models and, by extension, the way we work and think together. This necessarily requires that business executives think about the contributions of digital technology throughout the value chain of the structure, in a transversal and systemic manner, such as the analysis of cost structures, development and production processes, distribution channels, pre-sales, sales and post-sales procedures. The complexity of this ever faster world imposes new models of organization and a management mode more orientated towards openness, autonomy, sense and human values.

Without really paying attention to it, we are already surrounded everyday by robots, which take different forms, such as ATMs, automatic car park barriers or even self-checkout machines to pay for our purchases at the supermarket. These predictive or proactive algorithms continue to pervade our daily space. Naturally, this phenomenon raises questions, especially in our western culture, which is more apprehensive on this topic than other cultures, such as Japan, which considers robots as a real help and benefit for mankind.

In fact, as mentioned in the introduction of this book, each industrial revolution was accompanied by a disruption of human habits and behaviors, whether it was at the economic, political or social level. This necessarily results in a transformation of some professions, which have to be reinvented, but also in the disappearance of some trades, which will fully be taken care of by machines. The creation of new occupations leading to new markets, such as the qualitative selection of big data and their recycling, can be added to this. The phenomenon of the "Uberization" of society is the perfect example, with intelligent platforms driven by algorithms taking over the work of intermediaries, such as travel agent representatives, brokers, stockbrokers, taxi drivers, and so on, and soon, maybe pharmacists, opticians, or even doctors and legal experts[35]. These intermediaries are generally located between the person who has the know-how and the customer. Some occupations will inevitably have to adapt to this digital environment in order to develop and respectively meet the expectations of citizens, as well as the requirements of the industry's professionals. Thus, the capacity to adapt, thanks to information in real time, is one of the keys to make a mark in a "fluid" society and optimally benefit from it. Therefore, we will have to know how to adapt to the gradual reduction of paid employment, for the benefits of self-employed workers coordinated between them. We can consider the example of the aerospace industry which is always, with finance, one of the pioneer sectors in terms of innovations. In fact, the 1980s marked the digital shift of aviation with an increased digitalization of aircraft piloting, management and maintenance. Aviation professionals, such as pilots or air traffic controllers, saw their respective mission remain the same, but their functions and actions had to be significantly modified. This represents the consequences of an algorithmic Neo-Darwinism extending to all the spheres and corners of the world, just like a global pandemic. This technological development shifts the boundary between what is possible and impossible. Consequently, it is necessary to redefine the fields of what is desirable and what is not.

This Neo-Darwinism can be understood with the evolution of inorganic machines composed of non-conscious algorithms extending human

35 For example, Supra Legem is an AI application fuelled by hundreds of thousands of administrative case-laws, or the legal search engine doctrine.fr representing a "Legal Google".

consciousness, at its intelligence level. On this basis, it seems natural to us to wonder what counts most for mankind and our contemporary societies: consciousness or intelligence? With the artificial improvement of cognitive and physical human capacities, why do we always want to separate and compare things? Would one of the achievements of Neo-Darwinism be to aim for a new half-organic/half-inorganic hybrid human species, in which technological super-intelligence intermixes with human consciousness? Consequently, based on what type and quantity of technologies or degrees of integration of the latter into the body can we determine this hybrid species as still being human?

AI is undeniably a factor of technological innovations, but it raises questions, since, to date, the human being has always been the source of progress, as much as intelligence has always been human and often collective. Social relationships are increasingly deconstructed, as they are focused on persons and part of the dematerialized space. The appearance of horizontal forms and local markets as social and economic coordination modes can be added to this. This tendency is reflected in the emergence of new societal values and new standards of behavior. Consequently, the digital world becomes a real vector of universal values.

Homo sapiens are evolving via a digital Darwinism towards *Homo numericus* (or "digital human") fully integrating all the signals, opportunities, obstacles and challenges of an omnipresent digital environment, while increasingly depending on technology. Science-fiction showed that the future was within reach and that the human species' digitalization was inexorable. In this context, mankind is then forced to recreate itself, as proposed by transhumanism. In the medium term, we will be able to create an artificial brain via the latest discoveries of a French research team on the creation and modeling of an artificial synapse, which can learn in an autonomous way[36]. Therefore, mankind becomes its own project, its own material on which to work to invent itself, or if not, to (re)create itself as it wishes [DOS 18]. Is this not the dream of all alchemists to give life to matter? Mankind would then be in the process of replacing ancestral natural selection with an intelligent project and extending the life of the organic sector to the inorganic sector. Thus, the "transhumanist

36 Sören Boyn, Julie Grollier, Gwendal Lecerf, Bin Xu, Nicolas Locatelli, Stéphane Fusil, Stéphanie Girod, Cécile Carrétéro, Karin Garcia, Stéphane Xavier, Jean Tomas, Laurent Bellaiche, Manuel Bibes, Agnès Barthélémy, Sylvain Saïghi, Vincent Garcia, "Learning through ferroelectric domain dynamics in solid-state synapses", *Nature communications*, No 3, April 2017.

revolution" would result in "post-humanism", namely the surpassing of mankind as we know it, and therefore, *in fine*, the appearance of a new species [DOS 18] or hybrid life form, in which NICTs would merge with the organic human body. This new post-modern person is concerned about "downtime" and unproductive monolithic action. They are constantly seeking to fill the void with a desire to reduce their access time to knowledge, by carrying out several tasks at the same time. Consequently, we are led to wonder about the very notion of human identity, as the latter marks a critical separation between what is human and what is not human. If we reconsider the current definition of the word "individual", the latter means "an organized unit". It comes from the Latin *individuum*, "what is indivisible". Yet, this new hybrid species will inevitably become divisible and the "individual" will give way to the "dividual"[37]. It can be noted that in Latin, the term *divi* means "saint", or even "divinity".

Some specialists, such as the historian Yuval Noah Harari [HAR 17], even think that the human being is going to transform into a *Homo deus*, namely the transition from humans into gods, as they are considering, thanks to NICTs, becoming immortal (by defeating death), finding the magic formula to happiness and increasing their intellectual, cognitive and physical capacities (by modifying their brain and body). In fact, since the dawn of time, mankind has allocated "super powers" to gods, such as the power to create life, change their bodies and appearances, control space and time, move very quickly, remotely communicate, read human beings' minds, predict the future, or even obtain eternal life. Thus, we can imagine that with the arrival of the fifth industrial revolution, based on quantum applications, such as quantum computing, we will be able, in the medium term, to "download" human consciousness to a computer. This then presupposes that there is a mysterious immaterial substance (maybe quantum information?) capable of breaking free from its organic material support (the human body), in order to reach an almost ethereal environment. Neural networks will be replaced by an intelligent technological system, which will be able to travel between virtual and non-virtual worlds by flying across the limits of organic chemistry. This will correspond to the final stage of our *Homo deus* for

37 "Dividual: human being perceived not as indivisible (individual), but as divisible. The dividual contains in its midst several identities, none of them perceived as more real or original than the others, and allows each side to prevail over the others according to the needs of adaptation to the context, while the individual only seeks to be the same integrated personality" [BAR 15].

which we have reinvented the soul, namely an atheist soul with technology as god and whose digital ecosystem will play the role of paradise or hell. This non-organic entity will probably have the possibility to colonize new worlds, starting with the planets composing our solar system, such as Mars. This final transformation stage would allow mankind – in the form of an avatar – to see its own finitude, in order to reach the end of its story and rise to the level of gods. In an interview with the BBC on December 2, 2014, the British astrophysicist Stephen Hawking even declared that "The development of full artificial intelligence could spell the end of the human race".

Finally, this reductionist computerized approach of the world contributes to the division between consciousness and intelligence by means of algorithmic devices and systems which, without being aware of their existence, become more and more autonomous and intelligent. Is the "datafication" of our world likely to modify the order of priorities and values of mankind between intelligence and consciousness?

Furthermore, the relationship of the human being with time and space tends to pursue instantaneousness and ubiquity. This can be illustrated at the level of the modern company which feels the need to pilot in real time, in order to be able to constantly adapt to unstable economic and social environments, and to volatile customers. This business intelligence is going to have to fully take into account non-structured data, and even big data. This will then require new data management and study methods, new tools, new modes of operation and know-how to be developed.

Therefore, the traditional value chains of an organization become more complex and inevitably require more matrix, systemic, cooperative and transversal management and control. Consequently, one of the main human challenges to come lies in the ability and capacity of each individual to evolve, to rethink and structure themselves, in order to not be left behind by this digital (r)evolution. Such a challenge will necessarily go through a reinforced implication in initial and continuous training, the reform of universities, counseling and, more generally, learning. In addition to the development of skills adapted to the transformations of society, the digital revolution requires us to rethink the learning pedagogy more globally. Technologies provide an opportunity to build new frameworks, for example with digital universities, by improving teacher training, to rethink the production of digital resources and to promote the development of distance learning [MEN 10]. Furthermore, we tend to say that who has information has power. Yet, in a so-called "information" contemporary society populated by people in constant search for information and knowledge, we see that the power of influence of mankind is increased both at the economic and political level by NICTs.

In our opinion, it is very likely that the constant development of AI is going to encourage people to fully embrace transhumanism, in order to become "augmented humans" still able to compete with robots and intelligent machines. This fear of AI should be reflected by the acceptance from each individual to integrate brain augmentation via technology. To illustrate this vision, we can mention the words of Elon Musk (founder of Space X, Tesla, Paypal, etc.) in June 2016, who stated that it was urgent that mankind hybridizes its brain with technological components, in order to avoid any subjugation by AI. The integration of digital giants is going to be increasingly significant and fast, due to a particularly efficient model of platform:

– based on the logic of the sharing economy with a direct link of supply and demand;

– facilitating social and/or commercial interactions via the use of big data on users' behavior [ALE 16].

In the reflection that inspires us, it seems essential to focus our discussion on the notion of digital culture, which must be one of the cornerstones of tomorrow's society. In fact, as a social construction, culture influences people, their behaviors, abilities to act and even react, and their habits. Our capacity to acquire and study a large volume of data is changing. From now on, we are able to identify "full-scale" reality, in all its complexity and dynamism. In a way, this transition looks like the movement of Newtonians towards the Einsteinian world of gravity, namely a transformation of the way we understand the world surrounding us and the meaning we give it.

Our cultural landmarks are different and experience is crucial in order to understand and act efficiently in the field, in countries, societies, civilizations where references, traditions, socio-political frameworks, practices and customs, and religions are different from ours [FER 15]. This cultural knowledge is essential as references for the decisions to be made to address a given problem. It is therefore appropriate to conduct an ethical reflection on NICTs. Consequently, it is crucial to take into consideration these cultural differences so that uses remain consistent with our vision and understanding of society and its citizens. It is on this basis that we have built a transdisciplinary Neo-Platonic systemic ethical platform (Ψ, G, Φ) – described in Chapter 2 of our book – which will not be exportable as such, but rather adaptable, provided that cultural aspects inside it are analyzed, understood and integrated according to the place where it will be applied. It is then essential that we arm ourselves with a critical culture of digital computations, in order to play with them, without being daunted by the worlds they are trying to impose upon us [CAR 15]. The development of this culture is encouraged by encounters, by individuals who wish to share their skill, know-how and social skills. Each citizen has to take and assume responsibility for the future content of society, as the search for balance between good and evil is still the central issue [FLO 17]. This is why it is crucial to raise citizens' awareness from an early age to digital challenges, by developing greater vigilance and education on digital technology, in order to really understand its opportunities and challenges, but also its risks and aberrations.

Furthermore, there is no doubt that algorithmic applications will facilitate better facilitation of training and a reduction of education time. This is made possible thanks to search for performance, results, and the need for KPI. Machine learning algorithms help to reveal models indicating customized recommendations from new data captured according to situations. Therefore, it seems inevitable that customization applications, "gamification"[38] and interactions are going to become decisive in the medium term for the learning of new generations. This will not be possible without the symbiotic presence of mankind, whose role as a trainer and teacher is going to develop into an educational support status. Just like the doctor-patient duality that gradually becomes a tripartite relationship doctor-NICT-patient, the teacher-student pair is going to move toward a triptych educational support-NICT-student, whose mission is focused on the acquisition of skills, challenges, tailored counseling and professional success. Let us note that, due to the nature of automatic learning, the socio-cultural and economic diversity of future experts in technology is decisive for a good use of NICTs.

38 The term "gamification" is an English neologism referring to the use of processes and signals specific to games, especially video games, for actions or applications that are not behind games. The objective of the "gamification" is to make an action more playful, to encourage the commitment of the person participating in it, and to eventually introduce a viral dimension.

This approach cannot be achieved without the development of bridges between research, education/training (universities, engineering schools, business schools, etc.) and the business world. This can be reflected by concrete actions, such as:

– rethinking learning and counseling regarding digital technology at school;

– introducing an awareness of the societal and ethical challenges, and risks of NICTs in civic education classes;

– encouraging engineering, business, political science schools and universities to develop (initial and/or continuous) multidisciplinary training suitable for digital occupations.

Finally, this new world revolution has an impact on all aspects of life, society and all areas of our activity: e-business, energy, health, urbanization, politics, ecology, citizenship, etc. This digital environment is favorable to the development of new actors, such as data scientists – sometimes called quants (abbreviation of "quantitative analysts") – who carry out quantitative analyses. Let us note that we sometimes talk about "algorithmists" to identify persons who are quants and who joined a specialized occupation and act as independent audits of a big data study. The link between data scientists and "algorithmists" is a bit like the one that can be found between a person who studied medicine and the person who is a GP or a surgeon.

Finally, mankind is outsourcing a human capacity via NICTs, in order to perform other actions. We can consider the example of mobile phone numbers which are now directly accessible in digitized directories, and which we no longer bother to memorize. Is this going to change the very nature of the human being, especially with the arrival of transhumanism, namely the augmented, or even enhanced, human? Is this going to lead to the appearance of other human beings fully connected with the slightest particle and recess of their environment, which is itself networked? This is taking us back to the singularity theory, whose concept indicates that, from a hypothetical point in its technological development, human civilization will be the subject of a higher order technological growth. Data is a kind of atom in the digital world, that mankind is going to have to transform and handle in order to evolve. As the human being is itself a source of information, in order to survive, it must better understand the whole potential of this hyper-connection. On that basis, it falls to us to reflect on the future status and place that can be allocated to mankind in a Neo-Darwinian environment, where virtual and real worlds will mingle and even merge together. It is still too early to claim that AI will never replace human discernment capacity, but it is our responsibility, today, to define the path to take, if we do not want AI to become a threat to mankind. NICTs therefore portend more than a transformation; they represent a real revolution in the field of our individual freedoms, which even impacts the future of human nature as we currently know it.

2

The Code is Ethics and Ethics is the Code

Omnipresent in each person's life, in contemporary society, code represents a transcendence at the level of everyday perceptions, representations and activities. The ubiquity of IT code is generating a new social, anthropological structure. If we grasp code in its entirety, it acts on the user as an opaque, albeit one directly present, power. It is portrayed by individualization, opacity, ubiquity, instantaneousness and the promise of benefits and monitoring for the user as well as non-territoriality. Machines can be considered in such a way as to integrate a greater degree of intentionality, and their performances will in many situations exceed those of mankind. Henceforth, there will no longer be any living species, material, energy source, particle or atom on the planet that is not directly or indirectly linked to the digital world. Everything is a story of figures, codes, transmitters, sensors, data and information. Inevitably, a major question challenges us, directly touching on the very meaning of existence: are we now denaturing and transforming the raw form of the smallest particles into digital support? Or on the contrary, are we simply in the process of revealing the true nature of the elements that form our world, indeed the universe, that is, in its original form, composed wholly of the digital?

These philosophical questions on the meaning, or not, of digital life have the merit – for want of providing precise and affirmative answers – of providing reflection on the future of our world's evolution, which is becoming inexorably more digitized with time. Finally, no matter its answer on the origin of life, it is clear that algorithms and lines of code are omnipresent, everywhere. They surround us, structure us and are an integral part of us.

Beginning with this hypothesis, a thought occurs to us: the survival of human values and morals is fundamentally undergoing a digital transformation that will gravitate around man-machine or indeed machine-machine interfaces. This inevitable change therefore forces us to rethink traditional ethics by reprogramming them, based on a digital Darwinism. This neo-Darwinian approach will provide a framework for reflection on the relationships that must be redefined: with the world, with others and indeed with ourselves.

2.1. Nature, the creator of codes, programming and algorithms

With the development of big data, the term "algorithm" seems to have become a part of the population's daily life, whatever their age. Generation Z[1] is even learning it at nursery school, with the explanation, in simplified terms, that an algorithm is nothing more than a series of actions or instructions represented by a chain of loops in color (red, yellow, green, blue, etc.) arranged on an abacus, all making it possible to obtain a result. An algorithm is defined by Larousse[2] as a "set of operational rules whose application makes it possible to solve a problem expressed by means of a finite number of operations". According to an IT researcher at the University of Oxford, John MacCormick [MAC 13], an algorithm is a precise recipe that describes the exact sequence of stages needed to solve a problem.

Algorithms have a mechanical expression in which each action should be as detailed and comprehensible as possible, without any human intuition. They should function whatever the situation or the data that supply them and the environment in which they are applied. The calculations are probabilistic and non-deterministic. An algorithm can be translated, thanks to a programming language, into a program that can be run by a computer. This programming language is therefore formed of a series of instructions whose rigorous grammar only permits a single interpretation resulting in an efficient and succinct system. An algorithm may be very complex and be formed of multiple software building blocks. Developers use a loop to form

1 Generation Z (also called the new, silent generation, or generation C for "communication, collaboration, connection and creativity") is a sociological generation that follows generation Y. Generation Z was born after the fall of the Berlin Wall in 1989, during the attacks of September 11, 2001 and before the Arab Spring of 2010 and, from infancy, its members have had a digital smartphone and tablet with touchpad and access to the Internet.

2 *Encyclopedic dictionary of the French language*, Larousse.

their lines of code. This loop makes it possible to repeat a set of instructions a certain number of times without re-writing these lines. It generally serves as a foundation for other principles such as recursivity. Now, when this type of function is used, the first lines are calculated as far as the line called the function, which will again run the lines until the function is recalled, and so on. From now on, this IT language and associated software jointly shape our ever more digitized society.

Moreover, the collective subconscious tends to believe that algorithms are a new process. However, they have always existed. A cookery recipe is an algorithm! The novelty lies not in the concept but rather in its digitized format and its application to large volumes of data such as big data. In fact, although the usefulness of an algorithm is easily understood, it remains difficult to imagine the form in which it materializes concretely.

Furthermore, it can be observed that humans have always tried to reproduce what Nature has designed. By definition, Nature can be considered to be everything that is not caused by human beings and does not arise from them. The Aristotelian vision[3] often opposes Nature, which is evolutive and in flux (represented by the kingdoms of life: vegetable, animal, human and mineral[4], as well as the physical laws and forces of the universe) and the fixed and immobile artificial object/artefact. Modern philosophy brings this distinction into question. For René Descartes[5], Nature has the same type of mechanical structure as the artificial. Its vision of the real is called mechanistic and obeys the universal laws of physics. As Emmanuel Kant stated in his *Prolegomena* in 1783, the definition of Nature is thus extended to any object existing in our physical universe and to any future metaphysics. This mimetism (or biometics[6]) regarding Nature conveys and confirms a strong

3 Aristotle, *Physique*, II, 1, 192b 8–31.

4 Here, we consider that the mineral kingdom is indirectly part of the kingdom of the soul/human because even if it does not lie at the origin of life, it contributes greatly to it, since it cannot be expressed without the transmission of the "energy" force of minerals. In fact, minerals such as silica can be noted in all kingdoms of life. The mineral world is evolving at its own pace, like life itself.

5 *The Principles of Philosophy*, fourth part, article 403.

6 This term was invented by Otto Schmitt then popularized by Janine Benyus in *Biomimicry: Innovation Inspired by Nature* (1997). It considers nature as "a model, a measurement/measure and a mentor". It involves the transmission of the technical potential present in nature to uses in the sciences or technology. This process highlights a method for nature to influence human production.

trend that has been imposed on us: humans have invented nothing, everything already exists in Nature but in different forms or on different scales! It has been noted that the use of natural processes through observing our ecosystem and everything that surrounds us in Nature has occurred for a long time. In fact, from the 4th Century B.C., Aristotle observed the incredible adhesive abilities of geckos and in the 15th Century, Leonardo da Vinci sought to understand the functioning of bird wings and beetles to imagine plans for his flying machine. Thus, programming is modeled on the natural world by returning to similar principles. In these conditions, we may be led to say that living organisms are formed of algorithms, indeed, they are even algorithms themselves. We can take the example of the notion of recursivity that is present in many natural forms on different scales such as leaf veins, the arrangement of branches in a tree, zebras' coats, the camouflage of certain animals, cell division (via the self-replication of each cell), morphogenesis[7], rivers and mountains on different scales, and so on. An example of a recursive algorithm is the L-system developed by the biologist Aristid Lindenmayer to simulate the development of plants and of some bacteria.

One of the pioneering works that focused on morphogenesis in mathematics was a discussion by the mathematician René Thom [THO 84], entitled *Structural stability and morphogenesis*, published for the first time in 1972. This book was considered the start of an epistemological rupture, with the brutal intrusion of fundamental mathematics (IT simulations, statistical treatment, etc.) into a field of natural phenomenology (psychology, sociology, biology, ethology, psychoanalysis and linguistics). Indeed, the author suggests links between the shapes obtained and those observed in Nature, indicating a sort of catalogue of paths for study. This suggests a general classification for modifications of shapes, nicknamed "catastrophes"[8]. Finally, sometimes this mimetism can be applied in other domains, as in the case of the urban design sector where architects – such as Greg Lynn or Ezio Blasetti – integrate these kinds of processes when designing architecture.

---

7 Morphogenesis is the creation of the characteristics of a living being during its development from an egg-cell. It therefore corresponds to the way in which shapes are born and modified. In 1952, Alan Turing described the relationships between life forms and physicochemical processes in his article "The Chemical Basis of Morphogenesis".

8 Catastrophe theory belongs to the shift from qualitative geometry to a modeling of the morphological *universum*. It relies on the one hand on a complex mathematical corpus, and on the other hand on a fairly unique type of observation and experimentation, which is resolutely non-reductionist and non-quantitative (at least to start with).

Moreover, the term "genetic code" is currently used to illustrate the microscopic mechanisms surrounding DNA and at the root of the visible, macroscopic forms of life. It is noted that genetic algorithms[9] operate analogically on the principles of the theory of the evolution of a species (selections, mutations, crossovers, cross-breeding or recombinations) [GER 14]. These algorithms belong to the family of evolutionary or evolutionist algorithms (or evolutionary computation). With time, the genes retained within a given population are those that are best adapted to the needs of the species in relation to its environment. Genetics has highlighted the existence of important devices within a group of organisms in a single species, leading to genetic mixing. These processes occur during the reproduction stage, when the chromosomes of two organisms fuse to develop a new organism. Some of the main parameters of these algorithms are coding, population size, the probability of mutation and the evaluation function.

Thus, genetic programming gives rise to the creation of genetic algorithmics or evolutive algorithms, which imitate the way in which biological life has evolved on Earth. The living world can be summarized as a chain of winning strategies, such as for example the species that have survived Darwinian natural selection. Genetic algorithms apply the basic principles of evolution and natural selection to the optimization problem. This can be illustrated by the combinations of genetic codes that are selected depending on their functioning and operability in the environment. Concretely, we code the characteristics of manipulated objects and define a function that evaluates the value linked to each object. Then, an initial population evolves by generating new objects from old ones and favoring diverse mutations. Selection aims to eliminate the least optimal features. The difficulty of this approach lies especially in the choice of coding (i.e. the metrics or indicators pertinent to the features considered), as well as the types of mutations used or authorized [DEG 17].

This code serves to support and transmit information. Now, some experts such as the IT professor Bernard Chazelle[10] have introduced the term

9 The goal of genetic algorithms is to obtain an approximate solution to an optimization problem when there is no exact methodology (or when the solution is unknown) to solve it within a correct time. The solution is approached by successive "jumps", as in a separation and evaluation procedure, with the nuance that these are formulae that are sought and not, directly, values.

10 Bernard Chazelle, "Les incroyables algorithms du vivant", interview at *Collège de France*, November 8, 2012.

"natural algorithmics" to designate the algorithms that are not man-made but which are a property of a living object. Indeed, even if algorithms come from a human concept, we can see them in Nature in the form of infinite lines of code to study and understand the movements and expression of living things such as ecology (for example, the water cycle), human sociology (especially social networks), microbiology (with the behavior of bacteria and protein), immunology (such as immune response mechanisms), animal physiology (with the flight of birds), the emotions and sensations of mammals (with vital, unconscious biochemical algorithms for their survival and reproduction), and so on. The flow and distributed processing of data determine in part the value of a phenomenon, an organism or an entity. Whether this is in economics, musicology, biology or sociology, any domain has a data flow configuration that can be studied and interpreted. Animal organizations (beehives, anthills, etc.), human societies, bacterial ecosystems or stock markets, can be represented as an algorithmic system fed by shared and universal primary material, that is, information. Finally, couldn't all sorts and forms of life be conveyed by data processing and an algorithmic data system?

Note that the notion of a natural algorithm is extreme, amounting almost to a contradiction. It should therefore be considered with care, as its repercussions overflow broadly onto ontology. These algorithms thus form a mathematical language and program of life. They already define the way the world functions. Studying algorithmics is both a theoretical and an applied task. This algorithmic nature requires a change of paradigm, from an analysis based on a Pythagorean approach illustrated by natural algorithms to explain complex mechanisms such as the functioning of a neuron, quantum physics, biological mechanisms, and so on. In these conditions, an algorithm can be described as a mechanism using a series of actions, a chain of basic instructions and intentions. It makes it possible to carry out calculations and non-linear reflexive operations such as those that make up a living organism.

On the other hand, one can have fun comparing Nature, where the origin of real life comes from the *Big Bang,* and the digital world where the origin of artificial life emanates from the *Big Brother* phenomenon and its algorithmic systems (see Table 2.1).

The similarity and construction of these two worlds are so similar that we are only a step away from saying that they could form one, single world where it would be very difficult, indeed impossible, to distinguish, on the one hand, fiction from reality, and on the other, religion from science. A universe where the physical world and the virtual world would be no more than an end to enable the complete achievement of this Fourth Industrial Revolution, and to glimpse the emergence of the Fifth Industrial Revolution hinging on quantum mechanics. A world where NICT will replace the former, historic gods with new ones. Indeed, these two phenomena are formed of information (carbon versus silicon and coltan) and are undergoing exponential growth. The natural world is built from a macrocosm (illustrated by the universe, formed of exotic particles and radiation), and a microcosm (characterized by living beings)[11]. For its part, the digital world is also structured by a macrocosm (represented by the infosphere formed of big data, NICT and lines of code, and by a microcosm (associated with the avatars of people or organs). In both of these models, space–time is not static, the distances increase or decrease inevitably with time. The distances between objects increase even quicker, the more these are extended. The universe and infosphere are therefore expanding. We note that in general relativity, the notion of time has no meaning itself; only space–time has a physical reality.

	Type	Form of infor-mation	Context	Origin of life	Macrocosm	Microcosm	Growth
Nature	Real	Carbon	Space–time	*Big Bang*	Universe formed of exotic particles and radiation	Life forms	Exponential
Digital world	Artificial	Silicon and coltan	Space–time	*Big Brother*	Infosphere formed of big data, NICT and lines of code	Avatars of individuals and/or organs	Exponential

Table 2.1. *Comparison between Nature and the digital world*

11 Plato and the Neo-Platonists were convinced that the philosophy of Nature should be structured around the macrocosm and the microcosm.

Henceforth, the world is in the throes of complete digitization. Galileo said that the book of Nature was written in mathematical language. The universe and the life-forms that make up the universe are thus formed of mathematical curvatures. The individual is simulated, as well as their life, society with its citizens, its forces and its dynamics, governments, airplane crashes, the climate; indeed the entire planet. From here, it is only a step away to say that our lives themselves, indeed the universe, are the products of a mega-simulation with God as co-ordinator. This theory is linked to the anthropic principle approach and the IT simulation argument started by the Swedish philosopher Nick Bostrom. Bostrom believes that a post-human civilization with access to considerable IT resources risks implementing a simulation of the world of its ancestors for the purposes of knowledge and power. From this theory, it may be thought that a human being is perhaps not a biological being, but a subject of this simulation, just like their environment, reality itself and indeed the universe in its entirety. This would imply that all mechanisms of life and matter could be reproduced digitally on a computer. Such an approach would be in line with the philosophical meaning of information – from the Latin *informatio* – borrowed from Aristotle, of giving shape, which amounts to giving life and spirit to a thing, an object, a concept or an idea. In other words, this would amount to saying that everything is information! Finally, the NICT do not really create information – which is omnipresent everywhere around us and in us – but rather they reveal and diffuse it. Information takes on the full sense of informing to form and it occupies an essential place in the structuring, building and evolution of humanity and the universe through time.

Ultimately, even if this theory centered on a "reductionist IT" may seem provocative and exaggerated, it asks good questions, emphasizing the hyperconnectivity of the world and everything that forms it, and tends towards algorithmic Darwinism.

2.2. Algorithmic Darwinism

Genetic studies have demonstrated that a species will remain stable when it reproduces from one generation to another via the transmission of its genetic heritage. This brings a kind of continuity in the evolution of the expression of life. Indeed, science has demonstrated that genetic evolution could be explained by the modification of genetic code, during gene transmission. Thus, the animal and vegetable kingdoms are diversifying and complexifying via genetic mutations.

Evolution never stops. Life forms have never stopped adapting to the environment as the environment is itself always in flux. The main characteristic of mankind is its morphological, cognitive and social placidity and the fact that it has ensured its adaptations by modifying within its environments through different cultures and their technology.

From this observation, we can very well put forward the hypothesis that cycles of mutations and natural selections in the genome are the result of genetic evolution algorithms that some specialists call evolutionary or evolutionist algorithms. The principle behind their calculation methods is inspired by the theory of evolution. From this bio-inspiration, these algorithms, known as stochastic, iteratively use random processes to cause the evolution of a set of solutions to a given problem, generally an optimization problem, with the aim of finding the best results. These algorithms may also be classed among the computational intelligence methods attached to AI. They integrate a set of vectors of real variables, from variation operations (for mutation and cross-breeding) and selection (for selection and replacement). Selection occurs through a determinist choice of the best solutions ("individuals") according to the value scale of the objective function. The mutation stage is achieved in part through integrating a random variable, arising from normal distribution. Finally, one of the representative properties of these algorithms is the self-adaptation of the variance-covariance matrix of normal distribution.

On the other hand, this approach is applied in the engineering sector where automatically-produced solutions are tested according to an environment and parameters well-defined in the algorithm, then the most optimal are retained and we restart the approach with variations on the previous best solutions, much like natural Darwinian selection. For Darwin, the theory of evolution is based on successive selections that are both costly and hazardous. Nature is not achieved through a more or less complex schema determined in advance, but through a chain of accidents and a telescoping of different series, designing many species that are not comparable to one another, and according to a logic particular to their own evolution. The entropy (or degree of disorder) of the environment is an integral part of this natural selection process.

2.3. *The evolutionary digital world*

In the past 20 years, we have seen the emergence of a trend described by "evolutionary medicine", whose origins come from the 1994 work by R.M. Nesse and G.C. William, *Why We Get Sick: The New Science of Darwinian Medicine*. We can take the example of Alzheimer's disease to explain this approach. Medical progress has enabled the human population to increase in life expectancy and so to live longer, above all on a somatic level. This has the consequence of raising the level of neurodegenerative diseases. This is why some scientific research is committed to finding the genetic foundations of these diseases. Why haven't these genes been eliminated by natural selection? Is it because these diseases appear later in life, when individuals have already reproduced? To answer these questions, scientists have decided to use an approach that is more evolutionist than functionalist. This means observing and analyzing to see whether these diseases are present in closely-related species (great apes) and other species presenting characteristics of similar life-history parameters (social species with long life expectancy). Indeed, recent research has demonstrated that particular (pyramidal) neurons are destroyed by Alzheimer's disease in all these species. In great apes, the incidence of these diseases also manifests itself in adverse social contexts. The more these primates are isolated or degraded in their conditions of their physical, social and affective life, the more they will be subject to developing Alzheimer's disease. These studies prove that the origins of these diseases are more broadly influenced by and dependent on environmental factors than by genetic factors (which are important).

In these conditions, Darwinian innovation occurs through the variation/selection pairing, producing characteristics without seeing the need for them. The majority of breakthrough innovations – sometimes with what are known as unexpected opportunities ("serendipity") – come from this evolutionist approach. This, the creation of a successful species, first requires the production of millions of others that have not been successful and are not viable. It is from chaos and failure that harmony and organizational success result. Nature thus forms a systemic evolutionary equilibrium that is always in flux to tend towards a life form better adapted to a given environment. These ruptures and transitions that form the history of evolution are complex and are spread out over time.

The same observation can be made with the industrial revolutions seen in the Foreword of this book. Indeed, these are subject to social and cultural selection in the global population faced with these technological, economic and societal ruptures. Not all individuals adapt in the same way to changes in the environment and daily life. Now, for Neo-Darwinists, or more strictly, "economists", such as Deirdre McCloskey, the ethical and cultural criteria are at the root of a society's economic growth. Thus, the economic explanation cannot be separated entirely from the ethical explanation, and the ethical explanation itself cannot be structured without the historical and social conditions that make it possible and optimal in everyone's eyes. It is this interdependence between all sectors of human life that makes it both difficult to grasp and impossible to reproduce rationally.

We have seen in the previous chapter that Nature was the 'nutritional' source of the algorithm. From this observation, we can take this approach from evolutionary medicine and apply it to the digital ecosystem to speak of an "algorithmic Darwinism" or a "digital evolutionist" to better understand and contextualize the digital world.

For a long time, regulation on NICT was considered a contest between mankind and technological risks. This has moreover made it possible to considerably reduce technological problems. Only, a large proportion of the harmful consequences of digitization for the individual do not come from technological risks but result from human activities. Finally, history is a continual new beginning. It is cyclical and always reproduces the same effects and consequences but in different forms. It is enough for us to look more attentively at the different industrial revolutions to consider that they are all linked to societal revolutions coming from environmental changes, mores, practices and habits. There is a tendency to qualify these digital data as "the oil of the 21st Century" without always perceiving the accuracy of this image. In fact, all the questions asked when oil arrived (production, risks, consequences, uses, sustainable development, recycling, etc.) can be transcribed to the digital world. The only difference that is significant is that unlike petrol, digital data are far from becoming scarcer – quite the contrary, in two days we create the same volume of information that humanity created in 2,000 years!

We have entered a new, digital world ecosystem. Henceforth, we no longer surf the Internet, we are *in* the Internet via our smartphone and connected objects. These IoTs are becoming more and more "wearable" than "carryable". They are upon us, indeed in us, for example the implantation of RFID microchips to be able to open the doors of our homes, parking at home or at work, and to pay for goods without needing a smartphone. We can also give the example of Neuralink, founded by the billionaire Elon Musk, whose project was to implant electronic chips in the human brain to optimize its performance. One of the objectives would be to help to reduce the effects of some diseases such as epilepsy or Parkinson's. But the challenge could be even greater, that is, to give our brain the capacity to communicate directly with machines, to download the content of a book directly into our brains, indeed even to transfer our thoughts and perhaps our human conscience on a computer hard disk!

This assists with a real symbiosis between mankind and NICT. This digital revolution has made it possible to give humans a sixth sense, that of ubiquity. For example, thanks to webcams we can observe spaces where we are not present, or through some types of geolocation software, follow people from a distance. The environment is becoming more and more intelligent, by integrating objects that are both interactive and proactive and that act in real time. The smartphone has become the representation of an ultimate interface, a sort of "universal remote control" [ROS 17] where one can watch or follow something, in particular in the environment, and activate a precise action according to one's needs.

Like the evolutionary history of pathologies and mankind where we still wish to eradicate all diseases and pathogenic agents leading to the development of nosocomial diseases, we are in the process of reproducing exactly the same process with man–machine relationships. Now, while wishing to remove the risks and technological biases with which mankind has co-evolved with NICT, we have opened up "technological niches" for other harmful risks that are organizational, relational, behavioral, strategic, cultural, structural, and so on, not in themselves, but because we have no environmental history with them. According to the evolutionary prism, the act of wishing to eliminate all technological biases and wishing to master one's environment perfectly, goes a little against thousands of years of co-evolution between mankind and progress. According to us, advances in the safety of NICT should not be rejected, but it should be understood that, like nosocomial infections, innovations achieved in a given sector give rise to other problems of different types, making it necessary to rethink digital practices in an evolutionary way. In this context, it seems clear that it is preferable to make the man–machine relationship co-evolve with biases that we are able to correct, then to remove them, at the risk of favoring other, more serious risks, which are previously rarer. This poses real strategic and cultural questions about the digital ecosystem that we also call the infosphere – that is, the environment where information develops and circulates – at the heart of this digital co-evolution. Thus, the impact of NICT depends on the contexts in which they are used. With the drop in the number of actors and the development of technologies and means for analysis and calculation, it is becoming difficult to predict with certainty the uses that will be made of them. Their uses may fluctuate and be modified depending on place and time. It is rather the spatio-temporal environment that directly influences the way in which digital tools are used.

2.4. Environmental ethics

Previously, we saw that the term "ethics" comes from the Greek word *ethos* meaning "mores" (according to Cicero), "habits" (according to Plato and Aristotle), "habitat" or "an individual's personality and character". The true nature of humanity can therefore be described as the way in which mankind inhabits the world. It is from this approach that the expression "to be in the habit of" takes all its power, its meaning and its symbolism. Thus, ethics is a continuous reflection on the mores and habits that must be supplied and developed to make a space habitable and to reach the right decision. This is conveyed by a question on human values, which are linked to the action of reconciling the world of ideas and the world of deeds, by giving meaning to actions. It is the perfect illustration of Leonardo da Vinci's maxim with its "do to think, and think, to do". Ethics therefore has its reflective origins in action [HER 97] and is fueled by arguments, discussions and paradoxes. It is a reflection on action, for which meaning needs to be found, and where "how" is transformed into "why". Ethics becomes a search to justify the norms that society has established. These norms are not a condition *sine qua non* of the ethical solution to practical problems but rather the result of the process of taking decisions itself [SPR 13]. Thus, if we support this definition using inspiration from classical theories of ethics, we can state that ethics represent the most "natural" science. It absolutely forms an integral part of Nature in its entirety. Indeed, in the Greek model of virtue[12], ethics focuses as a priority on the individual (the agent) who performs an action, whereas in theories known as "relational"

12 The moral principle of trying to be virtuous and of caustic universal questioning.

(such as utilitarianism[13], contractualism[14] and deontologism[15]), ethics is more interested in the nature and moral value of actions performed by the agent. Our schema for reflection is based more generally on an ethics oriented towards individuals and more generally towards living beings.

The human and social sciences are clearly involved in ethical aspects: legal experts, sociologists, epistemologists, philosophers, ethicists, specialists in data and communication sciences, in cognitive sciences, psychologists, geographers, managers and economists, anthropologist, ethnologists, linguists, and so on.

All these disciplines bring their own visions, approaches and arguments that make up the wealth of ethical thought. In these conditions, we develop the idea of an ethics that is deployed in a natural dialogue and a deliberative approach where the most appropriate ethical vision springs from a discussion between all actors involved. We can therefore consider ethics as the reflective and thinking part of Nature. Indeed, we have seen previously that Nature is formed of lines of code and algorithms. Consequently, there is a great temptation to put forward the hypothesis or to state that ethics is also formed of well-defined codes and programs. Moreover, we currently use the terms "genetic code", "algorithmic code" and "ethical code" to implicitly convey a direct and natural association between the world of living things, the artificial digital world, and ethics, where code would be the link and common point between these three ecosystems. This leads us to the following idea: if "code is nature" and "code is the digital world", then "code is ethics"!

Now, our ethical approach is similar in part to a train of thought in telematic ethics begun by Luciano Floridi [FLO 98], Professor at the University of Oxford, who "elevates information to the status of a life form [...] of a universal receiver for any action". This allocentric vision focuses particularly on the environment where information is produced and propagated, and the actors associated with it. The infosphere forms, by nature, an intangible and immaterial environment, sensitive to the

13 The universal moral principle of maximizing consequences.

14 The universal moral principle that affirms that all societies are based on a social agreement.

15 The universal moral principle of categorical imperative (Kant). This ethical theory states that each human action should be judged according to its conformity (or its non-conformity) to certain duties. It is centered on respect for rights and duties.

spatiotemporal fluctuations that the digital world causes. The Italian philosopher relies on information theory and especially on the concept of information entropy introduced by Shannon[16] in the mid-20th Century. By analogy with thermodynamic entropy, information entropy measures the degree of a system's disorder, or more precisely the knowledge that we have of it. Thus, if we know something perfectly in detail, we can list its order of succession. Consequently, the weaker the entropy, in other words the more a system or an organization is ordered, the more it is known. And inversely, the more the entropy increases, the less it is considered to be ordered and the less it is known. From this observation, Luciano Floridi builds his reflection around "the ethics of information", taking as a criterion the global entropy of information that he applies to his concept of the infosphere. According to him, "an ethical behavior would decrease entropy, since it would render the information more significant, while an increase in entropy would be harmful to everything" [BÉR 15]. Thus, an ethical action would lead to a global decrease in entropy, and to an increase in the knowledge that we have of it. In this context, the ethical challenges – confidentiality, data protection, respect for private life, the accessibility of information, the sharing of responsibilities, autonomy and free will, dehumanization, and so on – that the digital world engenders, are better grasped and understood if we attach them to concrete actions or events in the environment [FLO 02].

This frame of thought is more linked to an environmentalist ethics with an approach more directed towards the individual, which repositions the receiver of the action at the center of ethical dialog and repositions the transmitter at the periphery. An ethical approach cannot work without information. This aims to restore meaning, coherence, an intelligibility and a guideline to build trust and harmony between actors. The information's internal value can only be fully expressed in the decisions it will make. This is why information is a protean concept that is not easily grasped.

Moreover, if we return to the Darwinian approach, we can see that entropy (or the degree of disorder) is found in natural selection, which tends

16 Claude Shannon, an engineer with the telephone company Bell, determined information as an observable and measurable size (1948). This becomes the foundation of the communication theory that he developed with Warren Weaver. This concept of information was the object of a theory, called "information theory". This mathematical theory applied to telecommunications technologies remains to this day the basis of the concept called information sciences.

towards an improvement in a species' suitability to a given environment. Thus, it can be noted that Shannon's "information theory", Darwin's "theory of evolution", and Floridi's "ethics of information" rely on the same keystone, that is, an "information" "entropy" duality where mankind is in unstable balance in a space–time context that is in perpetual movement.

In these conditions, we speak of an algorithmic Darwinism to describe and try to comprehend this planetary digital revolution. Now, these two components require integration into a given, well-defined system and can, in the same way as energy or weight, be characterized as a fundamental physical size. We will speak of a selective hierarchizing to convey the big data knowledge convergence (see Figure 2.1).

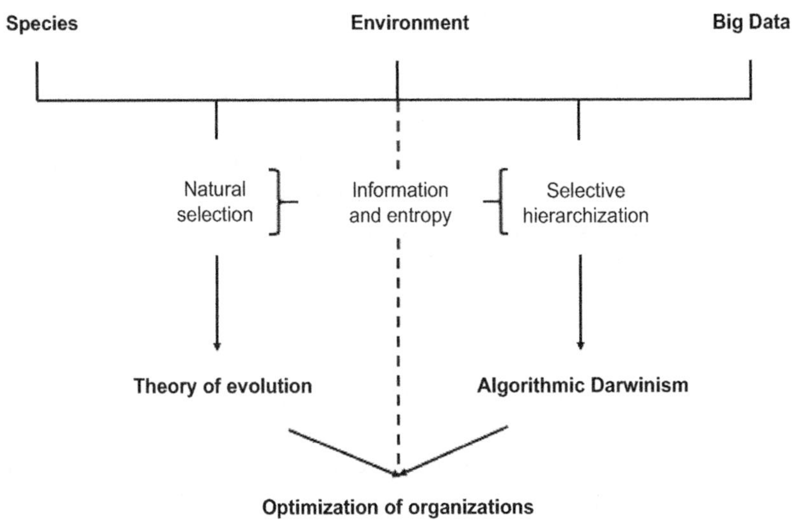

Figure 2.1. *Theory of evolution and algorithmic Darwinism*

From a systemic point of view, information disappears in favor of the relationship between things. This system of interrelationships models a complex organization[17] through the links that join these elements, by

17 By definition, a complex organization is a dynamic process integrating multiple interactions and retroactions, within which mechanisms develop that are very difficult to predict, grasp and control, which classical design was incapable of envisaging [MOR 05].

considering information as one of the wheels of systemic mechanics, making it possible to express representations of one thing to another.

This open system feeds on an environment, functions, actions, ends and transformations. This is why our algorithmic Darwinism should make use of selective intelligence to face the complexity that frames the digital ecosystem's communication process. To do this, it is fundamental to transform big data into pertinent information by giving it another dimension. Thus, if information regroups data objectives, with the move to communication integrating a selective hierarchizing and a sorting of this data, then we end with an optimized, subjective knowledge linked to a reduced entropy. In other words, this can also be conveyed by an epistemo-anthropological transformation of data and information into human knowledge.

This materialist, neo-Darwinian approach that we take from Nature – and which we have retranscribed fully into the digital world – should serve us a basis for reflection from the moment that we integrate into it ethical principles centered on human values: "ethics is code". However, we can bring a little nuance to our remarks on this "computer reductionist" vision. Indeed, currently, IT models have made it possible to make great advances in knowledge of mankind and its intellectual and cognitive capabilities, but this only involves simulations, in other words, images that we should not confuse with objects. In these conditions, understanding of the world linked to the mind such as consciousness, intent and meaning move, obligatorily through this ethical algorithm stage, indeed finally through quantum ethics. Without this, the materialist becomes incomplete and subscribes to a reductionist logic. Indeed, according to the philosopher Thomas Nagel [NAG 12], this defect of revealing something as primordial to Nature as the mind is a central dilemma that threatens the entire naturalist vision of the world, including biological sciences, cosmology[18] and evolutionary theory. Our approach is also shared by scientific, epistemological and phenomenological approaches which promote the principle that complexity is already a decisive key for reading the digital world. According to us, only quantum computing can enable us to entirely and totally understand the complexity of the real world.

18 Cosmic history leads to the origin of life and the appearance of the conditions for evolution.

Ultimately, our contemporary society should recognize and admit that it cannot control anything, not by reason of inclination or methods, but quite simply because it is faced with biases in the design, implementation and above all the use of innovations resulting from the thousands of years of co-evolution of this duality between mankind and progress. Some members of society are worried about these NICT, but rather than criticizing their intrinsic nature, it should be understood that most of the problems that affect mankind result from its own activities: hence the importance of fully understanding our environment, understanding what has given us our evolution and above all, understanding that technological progress is part of a co-evolution leading to innovations. This man–machine co-evolution necessarily occurs through an association, an exchange, indeed a symbiosis, between the digital world and ethics[19].

2.5. Algorithmic ethics

Reflection on ethics applied to the world of computing is not new. It began with the emergence of cybernetics [SAL 15] from the start of which Norbert Wiener [WIE 50] worried about the harmful uses that can be made of this science. He strongly protested against the use that some individuals or organizations may make of this discipline as an instrument of control and governance [VAY 18]. These same concerns were also held by other pioneers in computer sciences and AI such as Abbe Mowshowitz [MOW 76] and Joseph Weizenbaum [WEI 76].

Algorithmic ethics as we understand it can be defined as a branch of ethics whose perimeter of action hinges solely on NICT and the digitization of our society. This ethics should be present from a new technology's creation and should evolve over time, taking account of secondary effects, safeguards and ethical rules. If we take the example of robots, the researchers and scientists who design them should always bear in mind these moral questions, so that they are better accepted by the public. Thus, problems of bias in algorithms are now one of the greatest difficulties for

19 Ethics (from the Greek ηθική [επιστήμη], "moral science", from ήθος, "place of life; habit, mores; character" and the Latin *ethicus*, morals) is a practical (action) and normative (rules) philosophical discipline in an environment. It aims to indicate how beings should behave and act with one another in a space.

machine learning information systems (IS). As by processing *data* to better understand and therefore learn about it, they can create remarkable social discrimination and exclusion. Is it the case that the very mechanisms of AI lead us to transfer ethical choices to these mechanisms, and to those who create software? Algorithms should not be developed in an anarchic fashion. This is why it is necessary to fix rules, standards and norms of governance to build an ethical charter on algorithms and intelligent autonomous systems. We are at the very start of the Fourth Industrial Revolution, heading towards the digital world; it is therefore now that we must organize ourselves and reach a conceptual, philosophical and humane understanding of this digital change. We should ask the question of what collective preferences and interests we wish to assign this digital transformation. It does not fall only to designers to define, in their corner, the ethical rules for software ("code is ethics"), but to all the actors involved. Our ethical approach should be at once transverse, open and decentralized just like the digital: "code is ethics and ethics is code"!

One of the difficulties in applying algorithmic ethics lies at the level of digitization's global dimension. Indeed, digital ethics in the West does not have the same significance or interpretation as in the East, because of each country's socio-historico-cultural parameters. For example, in Japan, the robot represents the guardian of humanity whereas in the West, it symbolizes a diabolical machine that will transform humankind into a slave to technology; one that will soon replace it. With the expert Watson system from IBM, the prescriptive boundary has been crossed in the US. In Europe – and especially in France – the attitude that predominates is that mankind remains in control of its decisions. In these conditions, these ethical reflections should be adapted and made flexible depending on where they are structured and applied. This is the condition *sine qua non* for algorithmic ethics to retain its dynamism and its environmental sphere of movement.

Finally, the application of digital ethics forces us to lay down a shared and universal foundation for the algorithmic world. To do this, we return to the representation of Leonardo da Vinci's *Vitruvian Man* (or *Homo Universalis*) – on the study of the proportions of the human body, made around 1492 – to foreground the characteristics of a world or society 4.0 (the circle[20]) supplied and structured by big data (the square[21]) and whose

20 The circle represents the symbol of Nature (macrocosm), the infinite, the heavens, the universal and spirituality.

21 The square illustrates the ancestral image of the earth (microcosm), practice and reason.

ethics (man), linked to human values, should be situated in the center (see Figure 2.2).

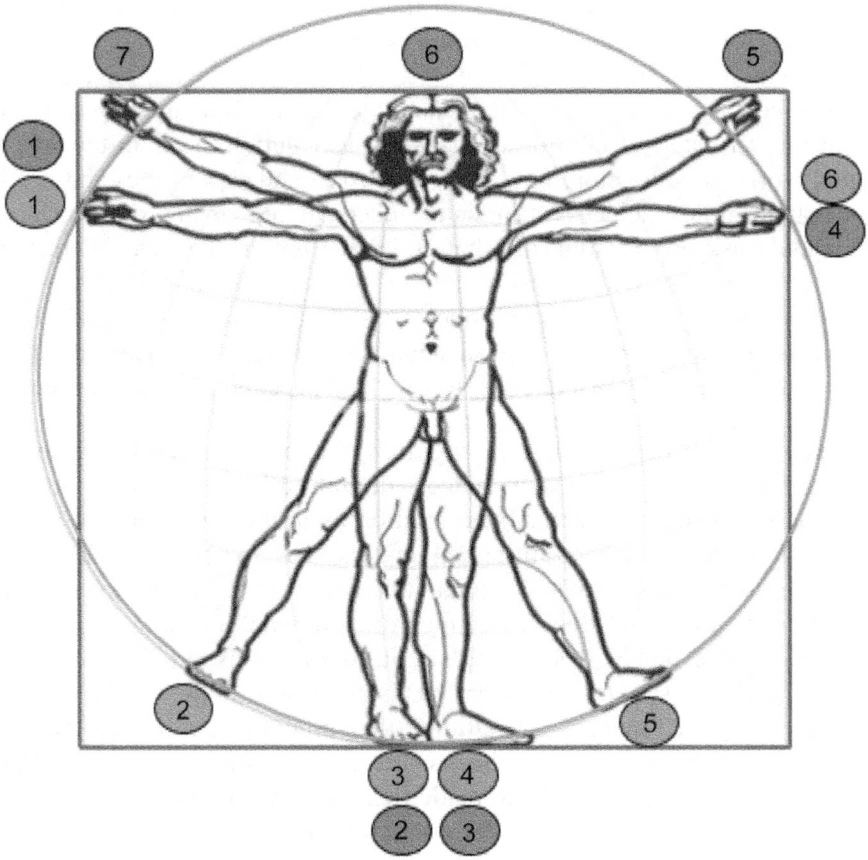

Figure 2.2. *Digital* Vitruvian Man. *For a color version of this figure, see www.iste.co.uk/beranger/ethics2.zip*

For Leonardo da Vinci, mankind is itself a direct link between the divine spirit and manner. He attains the "quadrature of the circle"[22]. Through the

22 The circle's quadrature represents a classical problem in mathematics, which exists in geometry. It is one of the three great problems of the Antiquity along with the angle and cube duplication. The dilemma lies in building a square from the same area as a given circle with the aid of a ruler and compass. This impossible problem has given rise to an idiom: "squaring the circle", which means trying to solve an unsolvable problem.

sketch's balanced proportions and mathematical perfection, it represents man as a pentagram inserted into a circle [BÉR 16]. In our vision of digital *Vitruvian Man*, ethics is the intermediary between:

– the world or society 4.0 illustrated by the rule of the six "Ps": personalized, predictive, preventive, participative, prognostic, and proximity;

– big data characterized by the rule of the seven "Vs": volume, variety, velocity, veracity, volatility, visualization and value.

2.5.1. *The symbiotic bridge between algorithms and ethics*

How to link ethics to algorithms? Do ethics specific to the digital world exist? These questions appear regularly and are the subject of debates between two worlds – the human sciences (known as "soft sciences") and the technical sciences (known as "hard sciences") – that almost everything opposes. As we saw previously, all industrial revolutions have been followed by a social change in society. This is generally conveyed by the emergence of new rules and social norms, as well as new visions of the world. Technology produces contradictory injunctions from all sides, which inevitably have ethical repercussions on individuals' daily lives [BAD 15]. Habits, mores and behaviors appear from uses that emanate from the digitization of the world.

Technology as such cannot remain entirely neutral, from the moment it is developed by mankind; its uses even less so. The omnipresence of NICT in our daily lives leads irredeemably from ethical concerns about their soundness and safety. This is why, when we speak of algorithms, we speak of networks of neurons, NICT, codes and algorithmic devices, but we can also have a more global approach if we wish to integrate algorithmic ethics. In these conditions, we may no longer consider the digital as a purely instrumental tool, but rather as a socio-technological system formed of 10 spaces for profit and varied inter-definitions (see Box 2.1).

What are the schemas of thought behind these algorithmic treatments? What are the forms of knowledge sought by this algorithm? What are the associated architectures, organizations and institutions? Who is behind them? What moral rules should this require? It seems fundamental today to study these different viewpoints to go beyond the technical and structural aspect, especially on the transparency of code or on the questions of bias associated with the results of algorithms.

> *Science*: the epistemic value of data with the algorithmic shift from deduction to correlation, quantum computing, NBIC, etc.
>
> *Language*: the identification of each object through its own characteristics, "overmathematisation" and binarization of society.
>
> *Knowledge*: information will become more quantitative than qualitative.
>
> *Technology*: the production, storage and processing of digital data.
>
> *Politics*: control of NICT.
>
> *War*: cybercrime and industrial espionage.
>
> *Law*: regulating the circulation of data.
>
> *The economy*: the creation of financial value linked to big data.
>
> *Ecology*: energy recycling (heat) from data centers and the optimization of energy consumption (electricity and gas).
>
> *Culture*: the universality of a community organized around NICT.
>
> *Anthropology*: the adaptation and evolution of mores, habits and behaviors.
>
> *Sociology*: inequalities in access to and control of technological tools (social fracture).
>
> *Philosophy*: The field of immanence if all objects are connected.
>
> *The social and the human*: the risks and challenges to be heeded and linked to individual and collective uses, dehumanization and the man–machine relationship.

Box 2.1. *Socio-technological system of the digital world*

Henceforth, we can state that this digital shift is occurring in a pluri-disciplinary social space that is constantly in flux. NICT are therefore conducive to the creation of an ecosystem where freedom appears to have no limits, because everything is in continual motion. Moreover, ambiguity has been established between real digital actions and their representation. It is entirely possible to transpose this representation of a socio-technological system of the digital world to ethics. It is noticeable that the field of action and language is identical. This is why it seems natural that technology and ethics should be directly linked and related to one another to form a bridge between ethics and technology. This marriage can be conveyed by what is called "digital ethics" or "algorithmic ethics", that is, an ethics that is an integral part of the digital world from its design to its destruction or recycling.

Furthermore, from a sociological point of view, NICT and in particular AI can be described using the concept of algorithmic socialization, that is, the mechanism of non-human socialization through which a machine learns to adapt its behavior to its environment. This approach is the target of a socio-cognitive framework that can be broken down according to three dimensions: the learning environment, the processing environment and the political environment. Indeed, the combination of these three environments crystallizes particular relational aspects into three main categories of actors, who are the designer, the "implementer" or developer, and the user [VAY 18].

Faced with the multitude of risks surrounding these NICT, it becomes paramount to list ethical expectations and concerns specific to the digital universe and to reify new systems of ethical values, while always bearing in mind the following question: is this technology sound for the individual and what deviations may be associated with it? Like ethics, the algorithm aims to process this data with the aim of providing a solution and a concrete response to a given problem. It is therefore noticeable that one of the common denominators to ethics and algorithms lies in the processing of information to move towards its better organization and meaning. Indeed, since the discoveries of Claude Shannon [SHA 48], information has been translated as the opposite of entropy. The aim of both of these processes lies in the ability to wish to reduce this degree of informational disorder in order to bring about a coherent and harmonious result.

Moreover, ethics and algorithms are achieved depending on mechanisms relying on a heterogeneous network of diverse individuals and competencies for ethics, and a network of software and machines for algorithms.

Henceforth, there is a multitude of machines, hubs and nodes that exchange a gigantic quantity of information between one another and the people who supply them. All are necessary but none are really indispensable [ALI 17]. This ethical-algorithmic bridge is built from a series of bricks whose cement is characterized by the means of operating, which is common to both sectors. We saw previously that ethics could be considered as a life science through its nature and characteristics. Indeed, for Bernard Chazelle [CHA 13], the great challenge is that biologists, physicists and computer scientists work together to build bridges between the algorithm and the process of the living world. In these conditions, it may easily be that the main challenge of tomorrow for contemporary society, especially ethicists, computer scientists, developers, and data scientists is to work together to erect pathways between algorithms and the ethical and human approach.

Thus, explaining that "ethics is code" is fundamental for demonstrating that the virtual and the artificial are becoming real and should not be in opposition to the natural but should complement it. Ethics would then become the source code for NICT. The two can no longer be distinguished. One refers to the other and vice versa. "And" is becoming "is". With the multiplicity of ethical challenges and risks that surround the development, implementation and risks of NICT, algorithms will have to solve more and more ethical and moral dilemmas. It then becomes essential that the ethical rules and requirements that apply to the algorithm are pre-programmed and integrated within it. Consequently, the algorithm's source code is therefore dematerialized and digitized ethics applied, on the one hand to its user and on the other immanently[23] and without external judgment. Now, our Pythagorean approach to a computer coding for ethics is completely integrated into Leonardo da Vinci's Neo-Platonist thought of "doing to understand, and understanding to do" [VAL 41, VAL 48], which we can bring up to date using the phrase "digitize to moralize, and moralize to digitize".

Ultimately, the normative framework of the digital should be the subject of a specific and applied ethics which would be able to bring to light existing problems between norms generated by the digital and our own norms or systems of moral values. However, this ethics of the digital risks being insufficient as, if as Lawrence Lessig writes [LES 99], code regulates and if

23 Meaning the character of what has its principle as itself.

it does not regulate properly, if programmers' intentions are not in line with a certain applied and applicable ethics, it would then be complicated to regulate, indeed to rebalance, *a posteriori*, this normative dimension. Thus, the digital creates many ethical questions which are particular to it since it generates, alone, a normative apparatus similar to that of the law. This symbiotic relationship between ethics and the algorithm should also lead to the construction of an algorithmic ethics destined for the digital world.

2.5.2. *Trust at the heart of a new ethics*

The digital is at the heart of an economic model based on the acquisition, availability and use of data. The development and adoption of this digital ecosystem cannot last unless a framework of trust is established between the businesses that produce data and consumers. This digital confidence is broken down according to several aspects such as:

– trust in data protection and use;

– trust in the reliability, integrity, and exactness of the data exchanged;

– trust in the effective control over data;

– trust in the performance, safety and resilience of NICT and their support networks.

Generally, integrity, confidentiality (see established anonymization methods), transparency (over the ends of its use, the algorithm's performance, methods for re-use, potential transfers, etc.) and the properties of the data are the four pillars of trust around the whole digital value chain. We note that it is sometimes complex to clearly inform technology users about the type of capturing or acquisition, the purpose and duration of processing, and the destination of their personal data collected according to the types of digital applications used. To provide more credence and therefore more confidence for citizens, it is essential to demystify the representations, which may be truncated, indeed biased, of these technologies. Such an approach occurs in part through an increased transparency of algorithms and accountability taken by the actors involved. However, this does not involve the publication of a source code, often unintelligible for the majority of citizens. In the United States, there is no law to oblige them to do so, but the market incites and motivates them to give guarantees and offer confidence to citizens. Thus, with their service being equal, whoever is most transparent, responsible, and thus most ethical, will have a non-negligible advantage over their competitors. According to us, this transparency should occur at the level of the data used, be capable of extracting distinctive traits making it possible to better understand the functioning of the algorithmic processing, then on the practices of and purposes of use put in place. Our digital ethics should therefore consider the "data/algorithm" pairing and the practices associated with it. Indeed, raw data, when they are not used by algorithms, lose much of their data value. Algorithms when they are not fed by data simply represent mechanisms running "on empty".

This approach is a condition *sine qua non* for societal acceptance of the digital world. Consequently, considering ethics – as a management tool – becomes an economic lever for society to better understand reality, justify its actions and provide a worthwhile learning factor.

We have chosen to structure and break down algorithmic ethics according to three phases as well as transversally.

2.5.2.1. *Data ethics (DE)*

An algorithm can be chosen depending on the data expected to provide it with input. What is the quality of the data? How are they collected, validated and used? These data are re-attached and intimately linked to processing. They are always associated with an object and produce an object, and it is necessary that this object is linked to a model and a system. These data have meaning in the reference and environment of the given system. In this context, the choice of the data's representation and structure (rules for use and algorithm tuning) is fundamental. By nature, it may be semantic and relational. The nature of the data will then be coded and translated into computer language. Consequently, the creation of lines of codes cannot remain neutral, due to the fact that the software designer should especially choose upstream in the selection of input data that will feed the computer mechanism. Indeed, the data already arrive at high speed from all directions and at a continuous flow. They are generally noisy and imprecise. New visualization methods make it possible to explore them and extract information from them. This data selection makes it possible to distribute it into categories. These data should be kept in an aggregated form to provide historic and contextual information. In this context, the "visual sedimentation" method, based on the analogy of geological sedimentation, aims to make possible the simultaneous understanding of the different stages of the data's life cycle [BLO 13]. This method makes it possible to visualize data flows in real time or in deferred time. It applies the principles of compressions over time, of stratifications and of physical forces to standard data visualizations (bar chart, bubble diagram, circular diagram).

2.5.2.2. *Ethics of algorithms (EA)*

The process of evaluating an algorithm's effectiveness and running can be summarized as evaluating its complexity. Generally, the study of complexity is based on the calculation time of: the amortized complexity of data structures (constants – variable – dashboards– recursive structures (lists, trees, graphs)), the average complexity of algorithms and control structures (sequences – conditionals – loops), the smoothed analysis of the algorithm. Now, we can compare algorithms via complexity theory.

Moreover, the algorithm's intrinsic quality is conveyed by the notions of completeness and correction. Correction, completeness and ending are linked and assume that an algorithm is described to answer a given problem. Ending forms the guarantee that the algorithm will end within a finite time. Given the guarantee that an algorithm will terminate, the proof of correction should provide the assurance that if the algorithm ends, giving a suggested solution, then this solution is the right one, that is, it is effectively a solution to the problem posed. Proof of completeness assures that, for a given space, the algorithm, if it ends, will give a solution for each of the inputs.

What are the margins of error, the rates of false positives or false negatives and the margins of trust? What procedures are used to correct errors? It is therefore a question of decision and tradeoff between the number of false positives and the number of false negatives. If we take the case of medical imaging, an algorithm classifying a cell as diseased or not should be configured to carry out an arbitration between the number of false positives and the number of false negatives. It is interesting to see that there are different points of view: those of the designer who developed the IS and those of the radiologist who uses it. It can be observed that if one is a radiologist, one prefers to have false positives, rather than false negatives, but if one steps into the skin of a scientist, one is more interested in having more false negatives than false positives when aiming for a publication. We therefore have different viewpoints that should not be neglected. Thus, depending on the values defended by the developer, they will favor one profession or the other. This questioning requires the algorithm's developer to pay particular attention to:

– specifying the inputs, outputs, preconditions for input, and the after-relationships between the input and output parameter values;

– analyzing the problem's theoretical complexity;

– choosing an adapted solution approach to the problem posed.

Generally, an algorithm's effectiveness is only known asymptotically, that is, for large quantities of input data. If this parameter is small enough then an algorithm with asymptotic complexity is greater. This is why, from two algorithms whose complexity is the same, we will seek to use the one whose occupation is weaker. In addition, an algorithm's locality naturally affects its effectiveness. Indeed, one can take the example of a virtual memory device that has little memory (in relation to the amount of data to be used), quicksort will normally be more efficient than heapsort since the former only happens once for each element of memory whereas the second accesses the memory discontinuously, thus increasing the risk of swapping.

Finally, indicators of an algorithm's quality are strongly dependent on context. However, most often this evaluation:

– is carried out via a "worst case scenario" approach;

– involves complexity of execution (temporal, volume information exchanged, etc.);

– involves the quality of the solution envisaged, for one or more criteria to be optimized. What are the variable parameters used by the algorithm? In the case of machine learning, on what data and according to what parameters (supervision) or according to what methodology is this learning carried out?

The indicators considered are defined by the approach taken (for example, what guarantee of approximation can be expected, if we restrict ourselves to algorithms of polynomial complexity?) or are intrinsic to the optimization problem envisaged (for example, is a path shorter in distance or in time?).

2.5.2.3. *Ethics of practice (EP)*

Analysis of algorithmic practices can be structured around an evaluation according to the competencies linked to algorithmic activity, which are:

– studying the objective and performance of an existing algorithm;

– adjusting an existing algorithm to obtain a precise result;

– developing an algorithm in response to a given problem.

At this stage of the evaluation, we are led to ask ourselves questions on these algorithms' human direction: what is behind them, who controls them and takes account of them in the business, and what are their objectives? Can some algorithmic biases be accepted? Is there sensitive data to avoid?

This ethics of practice contributes to emphasizing the visibility, accountability, and transparency of algorithmic systems. Thus, whoever is in charge of the algorithmic processing should explain its performance, and where and when it is run. What personal data are used to aim for a personalized result? How does this algorithmic customization deliver a different result?

Finally, an organization's complexity imposes three major prerogatives:

– giving central priority to practice, ends and interdisciplinarity;

– redefining mechanisms for evaluation and taking consideration of the human and moral aspects;

– automatically amplifying collective use of reflection based on consultation, sharing and exchange.

Now, these three levels of ethics form the pillars for our ethical evaluation, which is expressed in the ability to test and control the algorithms themselves. This ability to integrate an algorithmic ethics can be conveyed and made concrete in different ways. Indeed, some operational directions for action and recommendations can be envisaged, which would be a good idea to implement:

– experimenting and testing algorithmic tools and systems from their design, on the systemic learning and ethical and evaluation platform (Ψ, G, Φ) which we will describe later in this book, is *Ethics by Design*;

– relaxing the legal and regulatory framework around NICT and in their place developing a flexible and evolutive ethical framework, more in phase and timing with the digital revolution;

– within the legal structures (business, establishments, organizations, etc.) that use personal digital data integrating a Chief of Digital Ethics (CDE) – or a Director of Digital Ethics (DDE);

– integrating one of the governing bodies responsible (executive committee, management committee, board of directors, etc.), who will lead transversally and will guarantee the proper ethical processing of digital personal data;

– imposing ethical charters, codes and rules within digital businesses[24];

– implementing an ethical agreement system (labeling, certification, authorization) (*ex ante*) on a European, then global level (a private regulator such as the ADEL[25] (Algorithm Data Ethics Label) in addition to CNIL[26] National Commission on Informatics and Liberty) that imposes good practice on digital actors and recommendations on the algorithmic processing of their personal digital data, while still preserving technical innovation;

– introducing an independent ethics committee within each (large) digital business (with external experts, representatives from a diverse range of actors, SHS, etc.). This committee could be integrated into networks organized by professional frameworks or sectors to develop codes of good ethical digital conduct depending on the activity domain;

– creating a marking, ranking or rating system (a public regulator on a global scale) with large companies or digital ecosystem leaders (such as Standard and Poor's or Moody's and Fitch, but for digital ethics);

24 The European Economic and Social committee, in its judgement of May 31, 2017, promoted ethical values "integrated" into artificial intelligence, which would be developed in a uniform "ethical code applicable on a global scale for the development, deployment and use of artificial intelligence". The committee, in the same judgement, specifies "the establishment of a code for deontology for the development, deployment and use of AI, so that AI systems remain, through their process of use, compatible with principles of human dignity, integrity, freedom, respect for private life, cultural diversity and equality between men and women, as well as fundamental rights".

25 Available at the address: www.adel-label.com.

26 A mission of European monitoring authorities such as CNIL in France could be to name, recommend or indeed train actors in the labeling or ethical certification of personal digital data processing for businesses.

– rethinking the rights that an individual has over their data, considering that from a legal point of view digital data are particular immaterial goods that may be subject to appropriation (property or law ownership) – with some rules to be defined, such as the non-commodification of genetic data – so that the citizen becomes more of an actor, who is autonomous (see *empowerment*[27]) and in charge (see rights and responsibilities) on the subject of personal data;

– strengthening citizens' rights using an AI adapted design (see integrated visualization and transparency system in running algorithms);

– creating and developing public digital access spaces for individuals without NICT and Internet (see social justice);

– sensitization and education for actors in the digital world, by establishing a community, circle or foundation centered on digital ethics that aims to spread a culture of algorithmic ethics based on transparency, loyalty[28], responsibility and respect for the individual, to understand, grasp, use, or indeed design the future of NICT;

– developing education in a digital culture in school programs (initial training) for students or in continuous training for workers (via universities, business and engineering schools), centered as much on the subject as on the societal challenges;

– sensitizing future data scientists about risks and challenges linked to the re-use of codes;

– forming a consultative structure for reflection (such as CCNE: the French Consultative Committee for National Ethics) – a national ethics committee for the digital world – whose perimeter covers different subjects centering on the loyalty, transparency, ethics, equity and soundness of the algorithms that supply AI and more generally the digital revolution. This initiative should be formed of representatives from public authorities, industry, experts, academics and universities, citizens' associations, and so on. This organization should be transverse and it should be possible to break it down

27 The user could become more pro-active by asking platform operators to make their algorithms more transparent, having control over their personal data, migrating to platforms that have a strong commitment to transparency in the way they run, or supporting and financing new digital projects based on the principles of transparency and ethics.

28 Pertinence and information on criteria for classification and referencing, intelligibility, accountability, transparency and explicability of algorithmic systems.

according to the domain of activity according to problems dependent on sectors such as health, finance, insurance, transport, large-scale distribution, aerospace and aeronautics, domotics, and so on. Links at the international level – such as with the initiative Data Transparency Lab – should be woven to move in the direction of homogenous and universal visions and analyses. This committee would be based on and would be in exchange with other industrial ethics committees, depending on the sector applied. This organization into networks would favor the gradual development and revision of ethical benchmarks (charters, codes, *vade mecum*, etc.) according to each activity sector;

– encouraging collaborative research on technological innovations to improve our knowledge about technological bias, discrimination and exclusion, reverse engineering, security, the running of algorithms, etc.);

– putting in place an agency that we could call "Confidence and Ethical Evaluation for the Digital Economy (CEEEN)" within the ministries responsible for a state's economy and industry. This example, formed of a committee of pluridisciplinary[29] experts will aim to govern the ethical dimension of NICT including AI, blockchain, and quantum computing.

Ultimately, it is down to political deciders, digital professionals, developers of business activities, to each of us, and to the whole of society to reflect on how we would like to influence the evolution of NICT and their applications. In our opinion, one of the primary ethical questions should be to address, as a priority, status, place and human dignity in technologies to come. Ethics is the most commonly acceptable means to master NICT and to design a usage that conforms to the humanist values held by our contemporary society. An ethical code would make it possible in particular to transcend national laws to draw out global ethical principles on a transnational scale, such as respect for human dignity. However, it need not be the case that this ethical approach is only a virtuous gesture to give the illusion of a normative framework that will only be imposed to the extent to which the dominant protagonists will agree to it. This approach should not be a pretext to avoid legislating. This is why it is important that law texts write into their content the need for businesses to enter

29 This committee of experts would be formed of a group restricted to eminent personalities in the sectors of ethics, philosophy, sociology, economics and technology, who will benefit where appropriate from the support of other specialists according to the sector of activity such as health, transport and energy, communication, the economy, insurance and finance, governance and democracy or surveillance and security.

again into a process of ethical labeling and into implementing a good ethical practice code on their algorithmic mechanisms.

2.5.3. *The "blockchainization" of ethics*

To apply our algorithmic ethics, we can take the example of the blockchain which is of keen interest among entrepreneurs. This revolution also runs the real risk of disturbing some of the foundations of capitalism, indeed of society, via a new mechanism for decentralized exchange.

Now, it seems important to hold an ethical light to the moral challenges and risks of implementing such a mechanism. In the daily performance of our activities, each of us is subject to multiple and complex questions about the use of digital data, where respect for human values considered to be universal and the limits that constrain concrete decisions to be taken are permanently in confrontation. Many questions linked to big data, data collection, use and storage, especially by computing tools, will in fact be asked in very varied sectors. In these conditions, this section aims to reflect on the ethico-technical aspects of the design, management, control and use of digital data in the context of the blockchain. We suggest articulating our reflections around a series of questions such as: is the blockchain really safe and does it respect privacy? Is it bringing an end to anonymity on the Internet? If governance is decentralized, who really makes decisions? If litigation occurs during the transaction of digital assets, to which user should one turn? To the blockchain? What legal importance should be accorded to operations carried out by the mechanism? Who is responsible for nuisances and problems likely to be caused by autonomous structures? Who should be questioned when these applications are used for criminal or illicit ends? What law is applicable to transactions? How is proof of exchange provided? What is its traceability? Will the blockchain bring traditional management into question? What will be the mechanisms for regulation, organization, regulation, and governance around this concept? Who will develop this technology? The blockchain designer? The decentralized structure? The citizen user? Who controls the algorithm dedicated to designing an encrypted digital imprint (hash) of the digital transaction? Don't massive uses of this technology in real time risk being limited by the mechanism's calculating power? Doesn't the advent of quantum computing within a few years bring into question the security and integrity of this digitized exchange system? Couldn't blockchains affect the peer-to-peer economy?

So many questions lead us quite naturally to ask what ethics appropriate for the digital world – and in particular to the blockchain – should be implemented? This question arises very often as it seems so complicated to explain a human science to a technical science. And yet, the digital world creates from all sides contradictory injunctions that consequently have specific ethical repercussions on ICT. If big data is ethically neutral, its use is not. Specific behaviors are born of uses of this new space-time created by digitization. NICT are a cultural, indeed an anthropological phenomenon. They produce new behaviors, new visions of the world and new social norms. Questioning via an ethical approach to the collection, storage, use and provision of digital data is not at all restrictive and can even soon resemble value added in meaning, even going so far as to create a return on investment. Each technology enacts practices, produces values, behaviors and consequently enters into new social norms. Big data force new considerations of our values and how our actions are carried out, because they give a greater number of individuals more means to communicate and to interact with one another. The important thing is not necessarily the blockchain as such, but rather what it renders feasible. This technology will only be what we decide to make of it! This is why it is becoming essential to provide an ethical framework and governance within the same blockchain, from a macroscopic point of view at the level of the platform for managing the blockchain ecosystem, and from a microscopic point of view at the level of a majority of nodes or "minors" involved in the decentralized exchange network (see Figure 2.3). Thus, smart contracts can be very beneficial, in particular when rules can be "encoded" instantly whether it involves law or regulation. One can imagine the creation of smart contracts – integrating an ethical blockchain – that are formed of ethical rules. A technological application would enable digital monitoring as well as the automatic creation of ethical commitments defined within a traditional, or indeed individual contract.

Consequently, all the autonomous ISs and connected objects are led to integrate a distributed network subject to an ethical approach to guarantee the independence and transparency of the blockchain. To do this, it is necessary to link ethical bases around the harmonization of protocol and the standardization of messages from services used and from the network's programming interfaces (API).

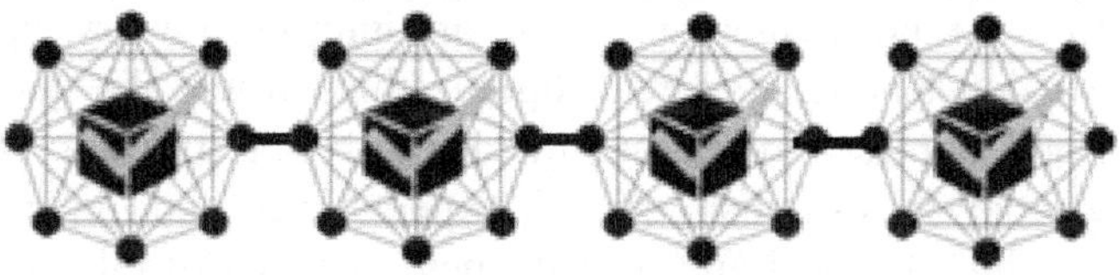

Figure 2.3. *Distributed network of ethical nodes within an ethical blockchain. For a color version of this figure, see www.iste.co.uk/beranger/ethics2.zip*

Behind the apparent decentralization, it is more than necessary to realize that a new form of centralization is at play. So far it is established in the form of algorithmic ethical governance to keep human values in a totally autonomous mechanism. Thus, the automation of infrastructure is not enough to guarantee confidence, as the legal framework is not mature and applicable in its current state, it is becoming fundamental to equip it with an ethical approach. Henceforth, ethics and technology should no longer be linked by a two-stage mechanism. Moral questions should form an integral part of their mission and so build an ethical reflection directed on data, algorithms, and practices. Generally, the ethics of the digital world is conveyed by questioning, on the one hand about the behavior and usage of individuals faced with NICT, and on the other hand about the increasingly autonomous behavior of technical tools. There are five ethical applications that relate to NICT (see Box 2.2) [BÉR 16].

The ethics of "empowerment": linked to the citizen actor who requires their autonomy and dignity (respect for their rights).

The ethics of access: with fundamental law and transparency (Universal Design).

The ethics of dissemination: relating to an evolutive mutation of the computing of control towards service computing (centralization and distribution).

The ethics of reappropriation: centered on mutations as potentials (digital literacy).

The ethics of the collaborative: covering the sharing of information (on the Web notably with online forums or social networks).

Box 2.2. *Ethical applications relating to NICT*

Henceforth, we no longer speak of an interdisciplinary approach but instead of a fusion leading to a real digital ethics where the question of the social and moral implications is integrated into NICT. In these conditions, it becomes essential to establish ethical expectations and recommendations specific to the digital world and to reify new systems of ethical and human values. Finally, the blockchain is on the way to really revolutionizing the human relationships within our society. Henceforth, we are entitled to ask ourselves about the future of a world where each autonomous system or object will have its own modes of execution and rules and where each individual will be able to define their methods of transaction and their money. One can even ask if we are not about to witness the paroxysm of the dehumanization of our society, that is a "Blockchainisation" of "Uberization". At this pace, how far will the ascension of algorithmic governance go? Can machines that are fed by human thought and knowledge be accorded a legal status that enables them to intervene in ethical debates? Finally, can ethics, which will be defined by human society, be contested by data resulting from machines' knowledge and the conscience they may one day acquire? The future will tell us…

2.6. The codification of ethics via a process of networks of neurons

The language of mankind cannot be reduced just to words, but also to numbers. Mathematical or binary systems (a sequence composed of 0s and 1s) are encroaching on our daily life via images, sounds and machines, to the point where some individuals are persuaded that everything can be digitized. Today, the majority of images and words are encoded in binary mode, which makes them in a way universal. According to the Pythagoreans or Plato, the number has an intrinsic existence with a structuring harmony, is infused in nature and originates from the One.

However, it is important to specify that a computer does not manipulate numbers but rather symbols representing numbers. Codification is thus a technique that aims to represent a scene in the form of a series of symbols. Consequently, digital projection is not a direct representation of the world but a use of symbols that themselves illustrate a conceptualization of the world. In these conditions, it is crucial to have a pluridisciplinary approach but one that is also pluriformalized (analysis, probability, statistics, geometry, etc.) to simulate an environment modified by human beings.

On the other hand, digital traces are by nature spatial, in the expectation one day of being of a temporal nature with the development and operationality of quantum computing. These data convey the spatial dimension of action, like a witness to the story of what has taken place, affecting spatial practices of an individual or society. SHS are more interested in digital spatialities, that is, not only the characteristics of a social reality's spatial dimension, but also all the spatial actions carried out by a society's operators [LUS 03], as nothing can be carried out without space [LUS 10]. We are witnessing an articulation between the computing code of algorithms and the space to rethink the ontogenetic perspective of change [DOD 05, KIT 11]. Thus, the digital world is integrated into a complex algorithmic spatiality arising from a particularly powerful spatial transduction (a continuous mechanism for renewing space). This algorithmic spatiality thus assumes the codes that enable the production and circulation of representations of space will be considered [LES 99]. Henceforth, codes are carriers of values and meaning [CAR 13] and those who control them have the power to organize the algorithmic spatialities to come.

Moreover, with the emergence of big data technologies and the ecosystem associated with the blockchain and the multiplication of smart contracts that contain actors' transactions, computer code takes an even more central place within the regulation of interrelationships between individuals on the Internet. In this chapter, we will see how it is necessary to move from a situation where "Code is Ethics" (in other words, code before the effect of ethics) to a new approach where "Ethics is Code" (i.e. ethics is defined and structured as a computer code).

By nature and construction, the automation of a process that comes from a computer code is absolute. It is positioned beyond ethics and the morals that promote some human values instead of others and classify the range of possibilities into good and bad. Codification does not aim to influence behavior but is placed potentially below and above the latter, by structuring the range of possibilities itself. Code frames moral values, good and bad, and services to the individual. The ubiquity of code creates a new socio-anthropological structuring. Omnipresent in the life of each individual, code represents in our contemporary society a transcendancy at the level of everyone's daily perceptions and activities. Code acts on the citizen as a power that simultaneously has the opacity, ubiquity, individualization, the promise of good and of continuous watchfulness [GRI 16]. Whether it is Amazon through its personalized recommendation algorithms for products or Twitter with its algorithms making it possible to display rolling news, to algorithms developed by innovative businesses or/and start-ups, almost all protagonists in the digital world base their model on the performance of their algorithms [SCH 13]. It then becomes vital for the algorithm's developer to confront, from the start of the construction process, the question linked to digital ethics.

For a machine or computer to be able to carry out an action or solve a given problem, it seems indispensable that an IT program – software – is designed for this. Whether they serve to classify, link, select or even predict, algorithms are thus instructions taking the form of lines of IT code. The construction of a line of code happens first by choosing and giving a series of precise and logical instructions to the machine (for example, "if the number = 3, then…") in an adapted IT language. The principle is to select the solution believed to solve a given problem, then code it, or retranscribe it into a language interpretable by a computer where the autonomous data system then shapes the important stages of developing an algorithm. Behind these lines of code there are hidden many engineers, developers, IT technicians and mathematicians, responsible for programming them and thus bringing them to life. One of the questions that these actors should ask is how to know how to organize information online and to make it searchable – and the solution to provide it – to sort information highlighting this or that criterion. This theoretical stage is vital and underlines the directly human character of NICT performance. According to John MacCormick [MAC 13], an IT researcher, "algorithms are based quite particularly on IT theory […] A widespread belief is that IT is essentially the programming (software) and design of objects (hardware). Yet, most of the best ideas that mark the history of IT are entirely abstract and do not fall into either of these categories".

Through the nature of their architecture and operationality, it is complicated to understand the internal reasoning mechanism of a machine's learning algorithms, and so to explain a given result. These algorithms thus pose new problems of transparency and supervision. Algorithms are inseparable from the data they process and the platforms that use them to offer a service. The structure of a classical algorithm is decided during its development. It is formed of the algorithm's parameters and the series of stages to be followed to lead to a given result. On the contrary, a machine's learning algorithms use data to determine their operating parameters throughout their learning. They can evolve over the course of time by taking new data into account and, eventually, destroying old data. It should be noted that it is difficult to change the foundations from which a line of reasoning begins and the associative and repelling relationships between some initial concepts, but on which the whole structure of reasoning and all the possible discursive development depends [MOR 77]. With machine learning, algorithms grow in size and improve automatically, thanks to data sets, without the manual re-addition of lines of code. Thus, the partitioning between the algorithm's parameters and the body of data they process no longer exists.

From these observations, it can be said that an algorithmic system is transparent when it enables a user to note and study:

– all the input data;

– the settings controlling the way in which the algorithm executes its stages;

– the internal processes and stages of the algorithm's operational running;

– the hypotheses on the inputs, the ends and models used by the algorithm;

– the justifications and explanations on the results generated by the algorithmic processing.

Moreover, among the most common learning methods within a machine, we observe networks of neurons, the principle behind which is inspired by the functioning of the brain. Simple processing units (neurons) are organized in a structure of highly parallel layers, capable of carrying out complex operations, conveyed by a very strong classification process. This analog process leads us to ask about the functioning of the human brain. How do the acquisition and integration of knowledge take place within an individual? How does the individual implement their knowledge to solve the dilemmas they are likely to encounter in their environment, to survive and structure themselves as a person? Is there co-operative learning between individuals who engage in collective action or reaction? So many questions suggest the intervention and expertise of numerous specialists such as linguists, psychologists, psychiatrists, anthropologists, sociologists, philosophers and more generally all the SHS disciplines, to obtain optimal clarification. These experts are led to study in depth the nature of thought and conscience, the acquisition and learning of knowledge that structure intelligence and human reasoning, the functioning of memory, the construction of personality, and the development of emotions.

Learning occurs through numerous examples of input/output, by making small repeated adjustments at the level of the weight of individual neurons' connections. This has the consequence of complexifying the understanding of the internal reasoning mechanism, and indirectly, any simple explanation of the result of output. We can take the example of a network of neurons with two hidden layers where each input (the Ethics of data (ED)) is connected to neurons at the first layer (the Ethics of algorithms (EA)), themselves connected to the neurons of the second (the Ethics of algorithms (EA)), in their turn connected to the output (Ethics of practice (EP)). It is noted that these hidden layers of neurons (or intermediary layers) serve to store the system's different intermediary stages. Finally, the intensity of these multiple connections shapes the model's internal parameters, which will be set by learning (see Figure 2.4).

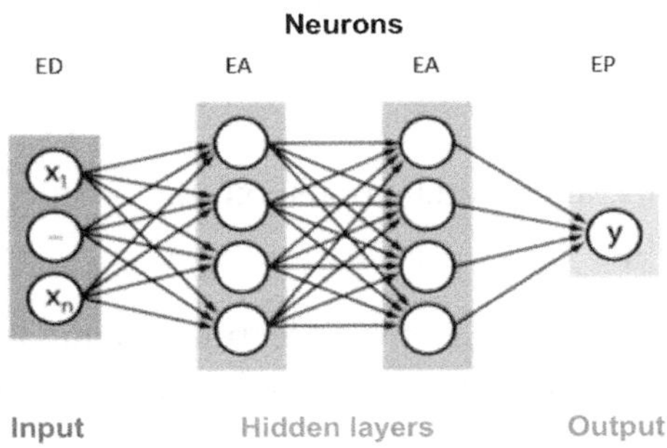

Figure 2.4. *Network of neurons with two hidden layers. For a color version of this figure, see www.iste.co.uk/beranger/ethics2.zip*

Networks of neurons are used when it is more important to obtain a result in a complex situation than to understand how it is obtained. This is the same principle as an algorithm. By nature, the neurosciences are spontaneously neo-Darwinian. This facilitates the reduction for them of the moral normative to the scientific description (the ferment of scientism) and causes them to maintain the pretense of identifying the natural fundamentals of ethics. The applications surrounding these neuron networks are numerous, such as image recognition, diagnostic aids, self-driving vehicles, automatic translation, customized insurance premium analysis, etc. To do this, IT experts suggest processes of representing knowledge such as semantic models, logical models, model agents, subject models or ontological models directly inspired by concepts from the human sciences.

We are witnessing the development of simulators more or less faithful to the human cognition used in making decisions. The operational aspect of these representation models is not evident and not totally successful of the complexity at the level of the existing semantic interoperability. One of the major works to be carried out consists of unifying, crossing or combining diverse models coming from different paradigms that simulate human cognitive performance. This is why there is a perpetual exchange between concepts from the digital and concepts from the human sciences.

On the other hand, mathematicians develop more or less abstract models upstream; these aim to define, understand and express the properties of objects in our world. In these conditions, the mathematization of existing problems becomes fundamental. However, some dilemmas do not necessarily find a solution due to their complexity and some mathematical theories do not lead to a concrete application due to their substantial remoteness from our environment. To respond to this, researchers try to get around this difficulty by applying a reductionist approach that sometimes makes it possible to make non-calculable and non-measurable problems both calculable and measurable and suggest solutions, which are certainly general and not precise, but which are useful [COL 08]. It is safe to bet that in the medium term, with the development of quantum computing, the problem of environmental complexity will no longer exist!

From these observations and because "Ethics is Code", we can pursue our reasoning by saying that "Ethics is the artificial neuron network". Such a statement opens up for us a new field of reading and gives a glimpse of an innovative approach to the coding or digitization of ethics via a process using a neuron network illustrated by an evaluation and ethical adjustment platform. This involves on the one hand, integrating ethical rules in the code, and on the other hand, the emergence of an ethical approach via computer code. Independently of the terminology used, the main characteristics of this new type of ethics are that they rely on code to define and express the rules that digital actors, or indeed intelligent autonomous systems should respect.

The main benefit of this form of ethics using lines of code is that rather than expecting ethical evaluation of an algorithmic processing after design, ethical rules are applied before design. This is an approach that we have called *Ethics by Design*. Thus, this codification of ethics necessarily leads to an increasing dependence on code to ensure that ethical rules are respected, but also to design and develop these rules.

Now, it is important to be able to formalize ethics to program and integrate it into a machine. To do this, one must automate a general evaluation rule for good conduct and practices to be adapted according to the situation. Dilemmas and different events should be anticipated at the stage of developing the algorithmic system so that this can integrate them and provide an adequate response.

However, it should still be noted that the peculiarity of ethics is precisely to be useful in unprecedented and non-standardized situations, involving value conflicts. With the emergence of AI, then quantum computing, it appears inevitable that even the most atypical cases will be considered in ethical coding. Nevertheless, it is necessary that the integration of these ethical rules are not defined and imposed by a handful of elites disconnected from the ordinary world. On the ground, this is why it seems essential to us to create a national digital ethics committee which will have a direct relationship with ethics committees in businesses, depending on the activity sector analyzed.

In this context, the articulation of ethics and the digital passes necessarily through a shared bridge between the two. The network of neurons perfectly fills this function, being at once the natural structuring of ethical thought and an artificial construction of an algorithm's mode of functioning. Now that our field of study has been identified, we can begin to sketch the contours of our "algorithmic ethical code", which transforms ethics into code by relying on the principle of networks of neurons. Our ethical learning process thus forms a network of neurons with hidden layers. To do this, we use known input and output data to identify, adjust, correct and improve the algorithm's internal parameters.

Furthermore, supervision of algorithmic processing is broken down into the three categories that we saw previously, that is:

– *Ethics of data (ED)*: identification of data processed by the algorithm and exchanges of these data (supervision of inputs and outputs): inputs (from the neuron network);

– *Ethics of algorithms (EA)*: the algorithm's performance at a sufficient scale to understand what it really does: hidden layers (of the neuron network);

– *Ethics of practice (EP)*: explanation of the quality of the algorithm's results: outputs (of the neuron network).

The aim of such an approach is to contribute to developing expertise for production, a study of the validation of data that are responsible, ethically acceptable, and which spread good practice. To arrive at this, it is essential to implement a proactive supervision tool throughout the digital data's life cycle, through this new technical approach to responsible design *Ethics by Design* (or *Responsibility by Design*). This form of ethics seems particularly interesting to us. Indeed, we can take the example of personal data protection, for which we encounter difficulties in processing, *a posteriori*, some of its problems linked to the process' complexity. The idea is therefore to integrate ethical principles and rules from the design of technical tools in their very architecture. This makes it possible to consider ethical and social questions as early as possible in the creation and traceability of a technological innovation. This approach therefore makes it necessary to introduce human norms and values in the very development of NICT, that is, in its applications or/and in its IT source code.

It assumes anticipating the uses and manner in which this or that technological innovation will adapt practices and what ethical questions this will trigger. According to the American scholar Stephanie Moore from the University of Virginia, it is entirely in our interests to anticipate ethical questions as early as possible to avoid losses produced by an absence of consideration of the subject. It is vital to proceed permanently to the creation of an equilibrium.

To do this, designers and interaction ergonomists must be involved, who will anticipate uses for technological innovations and who will have the ethical mission of facilitating the interaction between the user and the service or product from the start of the design (see ergonomy of the man–machine interface). And it mainly involves questions of choice: at what moment should the user be left to take control of the application, to what point should they be allowed the freedom to set parameters without rendering the product ergonomically unusable, and so on?

However, we can note two limitations to this *Ethics by Design* [CIG 6]:

– *technical limitations*: based on the fact that calculations on the consequences and repercussions of an action are infinite and would be and would not be suitable for the self-learning system to take fast and optimal decisions;

– *philosophical limitations*: hinging on the postulate that the nature of ethics is to pose problems to which there are no, by definition and *a priori*, best possible results. In other words, ethics is always prey to a conflict of individual or collective values in taking the decision that appears the best adapted. This is why this approach imposes a complex reasoning, based on contextual study of the notion of the meaning of moral values (see Rights and duties), an ability to anticipate and project in time.

This approach results in an ethical form of code by providing choices, such as leaving the user the opportunity to have the power to set parameters on sharing personal data, the visualization and transparency of their profile, and so on. Consequently, our vision of an *Ethics by Design* becomes the fundamental condition for ensuring that "Code is Ethics"! This ethics should focus on the quality of the relationship between humans and machines. Henceforth, we can say that today's IT designers will be the ethical specialists of tomorrow, in the sense that they apply and put into practice the moral rules at the heart of IT codes.

This will be the start of the digitization of ethics. Finally, like *Privacy by Design*, which has become a principle in law – by integrating European regulation on the protection of personal data, which will come into force on May 25, 2018 – it becomes vital that our *Ethics by Design* becomes a principle in law. This would enable us to say that *Law is Ethics*!

2.7. The complexity around an ethical AI

Today, it is already becoming difficult to combat cyber-crime, to monitor cybersecurity and avoid deviations from proper use, such as large-scale surveillance, the ending of confidentiality and private life, of free will and autonomy, and of democracy within contemporary society. Therefore, what will happen tomorrow with increasingly more intelligent, complex, interconnected and smaller mechanisms and processes, that, in time, may even be invisible to the naked eye?

The question asked is how to know if a simple algorithmic processing has the capacity of discernment. The first answer that comes to mind is that it cannot discern, since by definition an algorithm is a series of codified instructions that put in place a set process answering one or more questions asked. In this case, individual questions do not exist: either the problem has been coded within the algorithm and a predefined answer to it will be given, or there is not and the question will remain unanswered.

With machine learning and deep learning, algorithms no longer only respond to simple logical rules defined in mathematical state space, as this is the case in traditional IT programming. They perform, certainly according to the instructions operated by the coder, but in different ways depending on their learning and the data they encounter. The process that the algorithms follow to consider the experience that they have acquired depends quite evidently on the instructions provided by the human beings who have produced them.

But such a path is not always traceable or indeed readable (see Black box). Acceptability and detailed explanations of results by individuals then appear impossible. According to Jerry Kaplan, who teaches AI and ethics at the University of Stanford in California, "the principles that emerge [from machine learning] are not written into the computer code, so you have no way of knowing why a program could come up with a particular rule telling it something is ethically 'correct' or not" [DEN 15].

Currently, there are several projects in the world trying to solve the problem of the ethics of AI, such as initiatives financed by the US Office of Naval Research or the British government's engineering finance council. These initiatives should answer very difficult scientific questions such as the type of intelligence needed to make ethical decisions and how we should implement these decisions in a machine.

Given the global and omnipresent reach of the digital via the Internet, cyberspace requires measures for cooperation, coordination, and regulation just as much at a local level as at an international level to restore confidence and above all to reassure citizens. The current question is knowing how to implement such controls and under the aegis of which institution(s)? Who would be able to evaluate, and indeed master, the millions of algorithmic systems that surround us? Probably no existing human structure and organization currently in existence! Hence our idea of designing a global ethical AI that will evaluate and educate all algorithmic mechanisms, AI, platforms, connected objects (IoT), blockchains, and so on, to follow predefined ethical specifications written in their source code. It can be imagined that this universal AI could be held and directed by a structure equivalent to the UN.

In these conditions, one of the major challenges for an ethical analysis platform (indeed an ethical AI) will be to make transparent the functioning of the algorithm that it will evaluate, in other words, to make visible the hidden layers of the network of neurons that structure the algorithm. This is not an easy task; indeed, it is impossible to carry out! Indeed, to identify and understand a piece of information completely – that is, all the information contained in the infosphere or "infonome"[30] – would require observing it with all possible and imaginable analysis tools and in all situations, circumstances and internal and external environments possible.

The full complexity of these hidden layers lies in the interactions and interrelationships between each layer as well as with their environment at a given instant. Since the flow of information is by nature variable and varied in a space that is itself unstable and dynamic and in perpetual mutation, the complexity of reading algorithms is reinforced by it.

Indeed, ethics demands that results be explained as well as the reasons behind the decisions that an algorithm engenders. This is why solutions and methods are thus necessarily technological, even if they rely on a corpus of shared human values [PIC 18]. This technical approach would make it possible to introduce within algorithmic systems means that would render the operational functioning of the algorithm readable as it operates.

Now, this transparency surrounding the algorithm should be effected on several dimensions of the algorithmic decision such as data entry, control parameters, the different stages of the algorithm's operations, the structural and internal state of the algorithmic processing, the hypotheses and models used by the algorithm, and the justification for outputs of the information produced. In other words, the transparency integral to an algorithmic system requires that we can explain why and how a particular result has been generated. This is why the difficulty lies in obtaining transparency, both for the nature of the algorithm's structural elements and the data (carrying a pure, intangible value that is fixed in time), as well as for its environment (in perpetual motion). In addition to this, it can be seen that businesses often find good reasons why their algorithms work opaquely. In fact, public access to Open Source with algorithms used in social networks, online meeting sites, or search engines, makes them considerably more sensitive and

---

30 Neologism built on the model of "phenome" means all of an individual's phenotypes. Thus, the "infonome" corresponds to all the information.

vulnerable to malicious external manipulation and to spam. Finally, complete and detailed documentation on algorithmic devices would have a non-negligible cost and would take time.

Today, complexity thus forms part of a real schema for reflection that invites us to give meaning to our behavior, our ways of acting and our innovation. It creates a major epistemological dilemma for knowledge and action. The study of interactions between elements alone is not enough. Henceforth, it seems essential to build new tools and movements of thought, making it possible to better comprehend, apprehend and anticipate mechanisms for recursive logic, retroaction, or phenomena of relative autonomy that shape a complex process.

Finally, it is noted that this complexity can be evaluated thanks to the Shannonian measurement of the quantity of information likely to be transmitted or lost in a system. This evaluation considers the probability distribution of occurrences of possible behaviors or states (or of entropy (S)), and thus the relative uncertainty. Hence, the Shannon model will be able to shape a reference schema to lead to better intelligibility and knowledge of an algorithm's performance via a reduction in the information system's degree of disorder (S). Information considered "ethical" could be converted into knowledge.

According to Luciano Floridi [FLO 02], an action deemed just or considered ethical would lead to a global decrease in entropy (degree of disorder), and to an increase in the knowledge we have of it. Hence, the mastering and comprehension of an algorithm's functioning passes inevitably to a better grasp and knowledge of the spatio-temporal environmental parameters that surround the technological machine.

In reality, numerous experts agree, saying that ethical dilemmas are finally only problems relating to value judgments and judgments on free will. AI engineers are not able to code explicit rules on ethics, because on the one hand, they do not know these ethical rules, and on the other hand, some of these ethical rules cannot currently consider all the situations that can be envisaged.

In our opinion, we believe it is fundamental to be able to code all ethical rules upstream. A system's algorithmic readability, transparency and therefore its comprehension appear more envisageable when the designer has explicitly integrated all the ethical rules, according to the principle of *Ethics by Design*. We can cite the example of Dr. Ronald C. Arkin who is in the process of creating – with the support of the US defense department – a program that guarantees that a military robot will function according to international rules of ethical engagement. A series of algorithms, called "ethical governor" algorithms, will calculate whether an action such as firing a missile is authorized or not, depending on the situations suggested to it.

Thus, our conviction is to carry out ethical coding via an AI type system of dynamic logic[31] that will make it possible to better guide algorithms in their processes, according to human values. Logic is the ideal choice for teaching ethics to machines. It is the way in which we reason our ethical choices and our moral value judgments. This need for ethical control over the running of algorithmic processing cannot be carried out without the convergence and collaboration of disciplines such as anthropology, the social sciences, fundamental mathematics and theoretical computer science.

This pluridisciplinary approach – concretized by the Neo-Platonist ethical systemic platform (Ψ, G, Φ) that we will describe later – contributes decisively to the establishment of a new algorithmic ethics centered on citizens' needs and those of digital professionals. This can be assimilated into Joël de Rosnay's "hyperhumanism" [DER 17] state of mind that is conveyed by the collaboration of all individuals on the planet, who are interconnected to each other like a living macro-organism or a "global brain".

The construction of this ethical AI should result in the structuring of an ethical artificial thought. This creation should involve four values that form the four pillars of our digital architecture. To do this, the geometric representation of a hypercube with four dimensions – also called a "tesseract" – seems most appropriate to us.

In fact, it describes a closed, compact, convex figure formed of groups of opposite parallel segments aligned in each of the space's dimensions, at right angles to one another. In other words, this representation can be described by inserting a cube at the center of a larger cube (see Figure 2.5).

31 For example, if such a condition is true, then the AI should carry out an action, and if the same condition is false, then the AI should not react according to its programming.

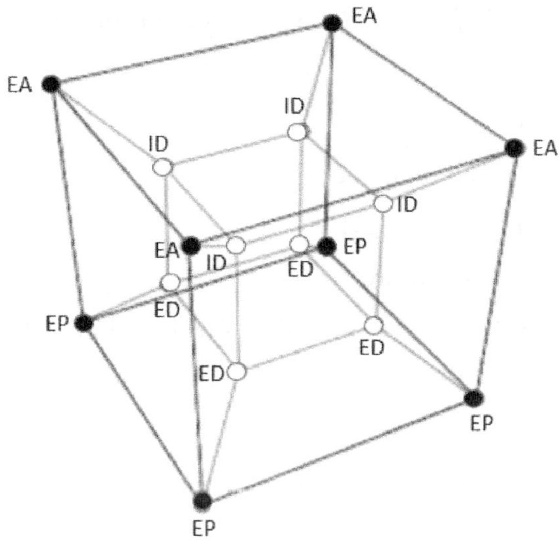

Figure 2.5. *Hypercube of an ethical AI*

The structure of our ethical AI is therefore formed of two cubes:

– an *exterior cube* (whose apexes are represented by black balls);

– an *interior cube* (whose apexes are represented by white balls).

The exterior cube is organized from two values or dimensions:

– the value of managing (or implementing): the Ethics of algorithms (EA):

- direction;
- formatting;
- development cycle;
- operations;

– the exploitation (or use) value: the Ethics of practice (EP):

- benevolence;
- autonomy;
- lack of malevolence;
- justice.

The interior cube is formed from two values or dimensions:

– the intrinsic (or value from design: the Ethics of data (ED):

- strategy and methodology;
- organization and regulation;
- structure and technology;
- relationship and culture;

– environmental (or ecosystem) value: the digital infosphere (ID)[32]:

- hierarchizing of ISs;
- cognitive hierarchizing;
- linguistic (or semantic) hierarchizing;
- digital hierarchizing.

It is from this approach that our systemic ethical platform applied to NICT and its digital environment could be created. A mastered environment is a more ordered environment with weaker entropy.

2.8. The Neo-Platonist ethical systemic platform (Ψ, G, Φ)

Today, it seems fundamental to be able to list, hierarchize, and link a business' risks to processes. This requires implementing a model of governance that is adapted, flexible and transversal. Since a model's activity is analytical, it is by nature reductive and contributes to focusing our concentration only on the most operational dimensions. Consequently, it is advisable to have a conscious and explicit approach to evaluating and processing risks. We must then integrate this vision into an accompanying digital policy within the business. How should this be framed, at what level and at what moment? How should we tackle ethical reflection on the design, implementation and use of NICT?

All theoretical reflections are a rational thought that aims at the universal. From an etymological point of view, the Italian term *homo universale* means

32 When we enter the fifth industrial revolution, we must build a quantum ethics that will integrate an additional hierarchization of a temporal nature in the environmental value (or the *digital infosphere* (ID)) of our ethical hypercube.

Leonardo da Vinci's "theoretical and abstract man. This quest for the universal passes inevitably though a rejection of the specifics of the moment". The universal therefore represents an ordered space depending on unitary laws that are illustrated by rules. To achieve this, we must put in place a pragmatic and progressive system for mapping risks linked to a process of specifications and recommendations. Ethics is part of a complex device necessitating the cooperation of an analytical approach to modeling and a systemic approach to simulation [COL 08].

The best way to have an ethical approach and analysis to algorithmic processing consists, without a doubt, of doing so though a prism that considers all forms of existence and behavior authentic and true, even those based on synthetic artefacts coming from a digital ecosystem. This vision of "synthetic e-environmentalism" requires a modification of our perception on relationships between *physis* (nature, reality) and *techné* (the practice of science and its applications). This idea is heading in the direction of and confirms our algorithmic Darwinism approach relying on a natural selection as found in nature and the history of the evolution of life forms.

Knowing whether technology and nature are likely to be reconcilable, indeed transposable, is not a question in itself. The question does not rely on a possible duality between the two, but more on the fact that this marriage and synergy are efficient and beneficial. Hence, this digitization of ethics can be described as a latent dialectic operation from the thought's Latin and Greek origin – constantly invoked and anticipated by the human sciences, especially philosophy, and constantly revoked and deferred by the hard sciences (physics-math) – that would finally reach the end of its incubation time and find itself suddenly transferred from the impossible to a formalized concretization.

In these conditions, we should develop a platform that should be based on a clear and precise end and which determines the tool's moral and social needs in its environment and context. This purpose is decisive as it develops a strategy and specifications that answer these needs. The aim of an action is its "reason why", its meaning and its essence. The purpose can be observed, not only in an individual's action, but also in the behavior or structure of a technical tool such as an online platform, if some adaptation of means to end can be distinguished in it. By nature, an IS is not merely an IT tool that can be studied in isolation. It is linked intrinsically to the whole of an organization as well as in the strategy, direction and policy of the business that uses it.

On the other hand, a mathematical model is indispensable, indeed fundamental from the moment that an observed phenomenon's digital complexity no longer permits intuition and feeling to understand its operational performance or to predict its evolution and future. The digital makes it possible to quantify phenomena systemically. In these conditions, a systemic ethical platform should seek balance and bring meaning to the actions it carries out. It highlights acts as human challenges that move in the direction of better support, while still maintaining the technical offer's quality, evolution and updating. It seems inconceivable to wish to study a technological innovation without tackling all the environmental parameters that surround it. All analysis requires a form of externality that can be built from a space [LAC 16]. Hence, this notion of "space", which can be characterized by this dematerialized platform, becomes auspicious for the expression, acquisition, sharing and appropriation of knowledge of any kind, depending on the nature of the latter [BÉR 15]. In our case, an ethical evaluation platform aims to become a site for the convergence or "crystallization" of all moral questions linked to the digital sector. This space results in open-mindedness illustrated by pluridisciplinarity and the variety of angles of view that favor transversal questioning. This platform is formed of a multitude of questions about purposes (teological dimension), values (axiological dimension) and rules, norms, codes, and ethical limitations (deontological dimension). It is characterized more as a relational mechanism that aims to tend towards an ethics of responsibility.

Furthermore, a systemic platform (intention-design) corresponds to the dematerialization of modeling. In fact, a model is a simplified, quantified and rationalized representation of reality. It makes it possible to simulate reality, study it, and evaluate it so as to be able to explain and/or predict it. The model is the basis of our "logico-mathematical analysis" [LÉV 54] conveying a common language between the different protagonists impacted by NICT. The platform makes it possible to better frame analysis and evaluation by targeting the actors, challenges, risks and diverse dimensions of the object to be studied. Once the framework is put in place and clarification of the parameters involved in reasoning is achieved, the elements to be analyzed appear, which must be linked. The platform provides the individuals that use it with different means of understanding what they do, their organization, strategy and the environment that surrounds them. It provides the possibility of modifying our design and our attitude to tackle NICT at the individual as well as at the collective level. It forms the "link that exists between understanding and acting" [NOU 02]. This ethical approach seeks to give an intelligibility, that is, a meaning to the phenomenon or object studied. The platform should be flexible and needs to be supplied by "justifications from reality", real keys to reading reality, represented by varied domains such as structure and technology, organization and regulation, strategy and methodology and the relational as well as the cultural. It should correspond to the real expectations, demands and needs of the actors that use it. Protagonists or subjects directly or indirectly involved through digitization tools come from diverse cultural and disciplinary sectors, hence this need to have recourse to an adapted and evolutive mechanism for understanding. Thus, it is perfectly envisageable to imagine a modeling for the ethical analysis of complex digital data, and this for a reason that cleaves to the very working of data mining, since the inductive algorithms that lie at the center of big data are animated by a logic astonishingly close to the "practical wisdom" that lies at the heart of ethics [BÉR 14].

On the other hand, a scientific limitation relies on the idea that "ethical theories are difficult to put in place in the form of operational ethical principles". In other words, how can a calculation mechanism based on respect for rules implemented by Design integrate all of a situation's complexity [CIG 16]? The grasping and comprehension of complexity dear to Edgar Morin[33] occurs through adapted Neo-Platonist systemic modeling. In this context, it seems vital to carry out a study on algorithmic processing and the applications associated with it via a Neo-Platonist systemic ethical platform (Ψ, G, Φ) to remove doubt and to master the uncertainties and fears surrounding the latter in this new dematerialized environment. Social confidence in the digitization of our society comes at this price!

Our schema of thought, which forms our platform, is formed from an approach that is both ethical and epistemological and is based mainly on "knowledge-processes" integrating Neo-Platonist reflections on Leonardo da Vinci's "doing to understand and understanding to do" [VAL 41, VAL 48]. In these conditions, knowledge crystallizes into action and becomes information for a goal and established end. From this observation, construction of our platform is achieved according to three pillars, that is,

33 In the first volume of *La méthode*, which appeared in 1977, Edgar Morin introduced the ideas of order, disorder and complexity.

ethics (Ψ: *Psi*[34]), the epistemic and the anthropological (G: *Gnose*[35]), and the pragmatic and the environment or ecosystem (Φ: *Phi*[36]) (see Figure 2.6).

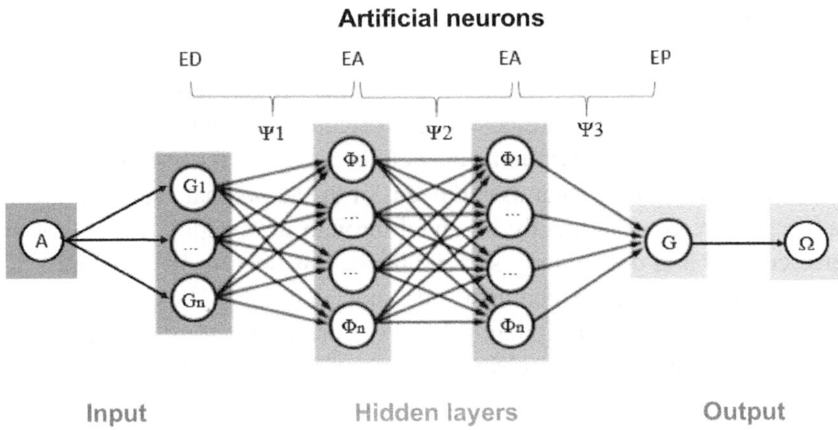

Figure 2.6. *Systemic ethical Neo-Platonist platform (Ψ, G, Φ). For a color version of this figure, see www.iste.co.uk/beranger/ethics2.zip*

In this representation inspired directly by the network of neurons in the working of the human brain, we structure simple processing units (neurons) in a system of highly parallel layers capable of carrying out complex operations, resulting in a very powerful classification mechanism.

From this architectural representation, ethics (Ψ) is intended to be the bridge or link between initial and final structural knowledge (G) of the subject to be studied and its environment (Φ). The triptych formed of Ethics data (ED), the Ethics of algorithms (EA) and the Ethics of practice (EP) shape the perimeter for action for the total *Psi* (Ψ) in our modeling. Moreover, the nature of ethics (Ψ) can be subdivided into three levels and types of ethics:

34 This Greek letter is often used to indicate psychology, psychiatry and psychotherapy, generally the sciences of human thought. This symbol means soul, psyche.

35 The word *gnose* means knowledge in Latin.

36 Since Antiquity, this symbol represents divine, harmonious proportion. This forms the foundations for structures in architecture, art, anatomy, music and literature, that is, the concrete and practical aspects of the science and the arts. This Greek letter represents the golden ratio, measuring 1.618.

– *descriptive ethics (Ψ1)*: an analysis based on a description and a perception of what exists. The aim is to identify and supervise the data processed by the algorithm and the exchanges of this data;

– *normative ethics (Ψ2)*: a study that relies on codes, rules, norms, limitations and standards. The aim is to test and regulate the running of the algorithm at a sufficient scale to understand and adjust what it really does in the environment;

– *reflective ethics (Ψ3)*: the way in which the individual reflects on the existence, foundations and meaning of things from a basis of human values and purposes. The aim is to explain the quality of the algorithm's results and practices.

In addition, this open system includes an environment, functions, actions, a purpose and transformations. We note that in Figure 2.6, we have voluntarily integrated eight parameters in the hidden layers that can symbolize the eight domains that make up the environment (Φ). However, the number of these parameters is not fixed and can be led to increase significantly over time.

This ethical legitimization makes it possible to run a problem statically via the environment and dynamically through its interactions. In fact, ethics intends to be linkable, expressible and buildable.

Ethical reflection and the decision that emanates from it are unique according to the given space–time parameters. Hence, the ethical decision is complex and in perpetual motion due to a fragile compromise between, on the one hand, different perspectives, opinions and knowledge of the individuals concerned ((G): *Gnose*), and on the other hand, the environment that fluctuates constantly ((Φ): *Phi*).

By nature, an algorithmic system is a complex and dynamic system formed of multiple interactions and retroactions between inputs, hidden layers and the output, inside which unfold processes that are very difficult to predict and control and which classical design was incapable of envisaging. This is a real challenge for knowledge, from a theoretical and practical point of view. The complexity of this platform takes its full meaning when its representation becomes intelligible based on the Ψ, G, Φ (ethico-anthropo-epistemo-pragmatic) paradigm (see Table 2.2).

This network of artificial neurons thus integrates a cognitive representation and a projective (or intentional) structure of reactions associated with the purposes that we invented. Thus, this mechanism for developing decisions makes it possible to move from an *Alpha* (A) state of multiple, complex, disorganized and fluid knowledge (sum of knowledge (G)) to an *Omega* (Ω)[37] state of simple (G), structured and teleological knowledge. Finally, this learning (Ψ, G, Φ) is a mechanism termed "supervised": input and output data is used to set, correct, and optimize the algorithm's internal criteria.

Level of ethical analysis (Φ)	Perimeter of the ethics	Gnosis (G)	Environ-ment (Φ)	Content	Shapes	Functions
Descriptive ethics (Ψ1)	Ethics of data (ED), Ethics of algorithms (EA)	Present (G1 to Gn)	Present (Φ1 to Φn)	Means, devices, ways and procedures	Practice	Application and implementa-tion
Normative ethics (Ψ2)	Ethics of algorithms (EA)	Not present	Present (Φ1 to Φn)	Norms, codes and rules	Deontology	Regulation
Reflective ethics (Ψ3)	Ethics of algorithms (EA), Ethics of practice (EP)	Present (G)	Present (Φ1 to Φn)	Principles, values and meaning	Axio-logical reflection	Legitima-tion

Table 2.2. *Model of ethical analysis (Ψ, G, Φ)*

37 We have chosen respectively the Greek letters *Alpha* (A) and *Omega* (Ω) for their symbolic value. In fact, in Christian tradition the A and the Ω symbolize Christ's eternity, the *Alpha* (1st letter of the Greek alphabet) conveys the beginning of everything (see the first chapter of the Gospel according to John) and the *Omega* (the last letter of the Greek alphabet) illustrates the end of the world (see the Apocalypse according to John). This metaphor was taken up by the Jesuit Pierre Teilhard de Chardin to represent human evolution going from A to Ω. Finally, traditional physics and chemistry uses the symbol Ω to indicate a given system's state of equilibrium [BÉR 16].

Complex thought feeds itself:

– *descriptive ethics (Ψ1)*: reflects "practice" and aims to apply rules and uses. This is based on the means, procedures, mechanisms and ways put in place to carry out the "implementation" of objectives. DE and AE are the perimeter of its ethical action. Descriptive ethics is fed by initial input knowledge (G) and environmental parameters (Φ);

– *normative ethics (Ψ2)*: can be characterized as "pragmatic". It highlights deontology, whose function is to regulate practice. AE is its field of ethical application. Normative ethics relies on and is developed from the environment (Φ);

– *reflective ethics (Ψ3)*: which aims to provide "legitimation" for any practice, any informational result (G) and any norm. This level is directed by the human values and ethical principles that serve as instances that are both normative and critical. AE and PE represent the domain of its ethical action. Reflective ethics is fed by environmental criteria (Φ).

In addition, algorithmic architectures are generally complex, formed of a large quantity of "software bricks" and should often be revised, then adjusted to improve their performance in an environment that is permanently changing. Our ethical regulation platform should develop the use of analysis algorithms that are more effective than surveillance indicators. One of these software bricks currently undergoing a meteoric growth is machine learning. Now, we can imagine the creation of an ethical machine learning to integrate ethics into processing and analysis algorithms. This learning represents part of the AI, based on a methodology of automatic education and integration of new knowledge by machines, using examples, experiments or past cases, or from the IS's own past explorations or experiences. This approach to an AI fits perfectly into a neo-Darwinian process, that is, understanding to act, learning to evolve and creating to survive in an ecosystem that is perpetually moving.

Our ethical machine learning – illustrated by this neuron network – happens through a multitude of examples of input/output, by making small, repeated adjustments at the level of the weights of individual neurons' connections. Hence, through the nature of its architecture and its performance, understanding the internal reasoning mechanism and therefore a clear explanation of the output result, will be difficult.

To do this, this platform will aim to integrate criteria and metrics that make it possible to characterize and evaluate the quality of a code (called the structural quality of the software). It is observed that the quality of a line of code can be measured automatically by static analysis tools from the source code. We have listed 27 criteria or metrics – strongly dependent on context, on the market and users of the source code. They can be listed depending on their level of benefit: 14 metrics of significant benefit, 8 metrics of moderate benefit and 5 metrics of little benefit (see Appendix A.1).

Finally, this systemic ethical learning platform (Ψ, G, Φ) must be able to take account of past experiences and integrate evolutive indicators coming from a socio-technological environment and context in perpetual motion. Our modeling is fed by data to set its operating parameters throughout the learning. This evolutive aspect is made possible by the fact that there is regular consideration of new data and, potentially, with the elimination of old data. Programmers do not have to re-add lines of code "by hand", as modifications are made automatically. Henceforth, the algorithm's criteria and the body of data form only a single whole. Such a process confirms a little more our neo-Darwinian approach, which emphasizes the fact that we make the algorithms we develop evolve and grow. This is the concept of *Ethics by Evolution*. Ultimately, the mission of this algorithmic platform is to make an algorithmic system responsible and ethical by integrating into it criteria for good practice so that it can be made to evolve and validate its own lines of code.

2.9. The systemic analysis approach centered on the individual in a digital ecosystem

Humankind's complexity comes from the fact that one of our main properties is the need for an environment (ecosystem material, individuals, situations, etc.) to be structured and to evolve. Humans are individuals through the relationships one nurtures with others. The individual has a relationship on the one hand with the world and on the other with others. They are therefore a linked, living being who is able to bring meaning to their existence through the links that unite them to other individuals. These links are rooted in the intersubjectivity and singularity of all, from which is formed the alterity of each human being to others.

Moreover, it can be observed that the digital revolution puts people at the center of society, the economy and business of our lives. The digital, by putting this power back in place, democratizes the spread of information (social networks, smartphones, WhatsApp, crowdfunding sites, etc.) and promotes freedom of expression and opinion (forums, online consultations, exchange platforms, etc.). Ethical choices are generally made unawares by individuals in their daily life. All these individual choices lead us without direction to a contemporary society that we have not explicitly chosen, and which we do not perhaps want. They can condition us, categorize us, normalize our behavior and habits, as well as shut us into ourselves, depending on the profiles that algorithms used [PIC 18].

In ethics, the word "value" is a must-have. It is a standard for measurement by which deeds can be judged. It indicates ideas to be followed. This word has a general and dynamic connotation; it first of all has a philosophical meaning before having an ethical impact. One of the foundations of ethics is this imperative to call upon actors' capacity for reasoning. This idea passes necessarily via an understanding of coordination and exchange between protagonists. Each individual contributes to seeking mutual comprehension of the situation to be analyzed. This therefore presupposes some solidarity between speakers who share the same purpose.

Any technology defines a relationship between human beings and their environment, human as well as physical. No technology can be considered purely instrumentally. This is particularly pertinent when it involves large automatic ISs, developed to contribute to the managing and integration of large organizations, such as healthcare structures. In such a context, the environment is mainly formed of human beings. By changing NICT, human factors preside simply over technical factors. Even if it is obligatory to satisfy the latter, they are never really sufficient. In any technology, the human factor and man–machine interaction are fundamental. However, in a context where there are multiple simultaneous users, man–machine interaction is the main question to be answered. The evaluation of large ISs is based on the concept of the "inter-human relationship" [FES 01] which underpins the design and the use of the system. In these conditions, NICT essentially appear as a social system, with its psychological, sociological and ethical characteristics.

Before returning directly to the heart of the subject of our systemic analysis approach to the digital, it seems vital to us to explain its final purpose, its aim and more generally the reason for its existence: that is, the individual. For Michel Ponceblanc [PON 03], all the conduct that needs to be followed to come close to an ethical ideal tends towards adequation: to act in the best interests of the individual is to find and combine the right measure and the right time. Now, company directors speak of a refocusing of their strategy onto the needs of their patients. In the medical sector, Dr. Channin even states that "the number one priority for an IS is the patient" [CHA 09]. According to François Fondard [FON 11], the technical revolution involving the information sector should be conducted in the interest of individuals and of better support. In other words, the only value to be considered, with a view to keeping it, is the individual considered, along with their dignity as a moral being. This human dignity is an absolute value that is accorded to the individual. Thus, ethical, practical, technical and ergonomic principles should be imposed so that citizens remain the main beneficiaries of this technical evolution. This is even truer, as any ethical reflection is a conflict between human values. Whatever our religious beliefs, cultures, political influences or domains of activity, it is our emotions that reveal our deeply-held values. As Pierre Le Coz [COZ 10] underlines so well in the first Cancer and fertility ethics day at the Institute Paoli-Calmettes, "if there is no emotion, there can be no formalized values and therefore no ethics". In fact, each major ethical principle that we previously described can be linked to a particular emotion. The following pairings can be made:

– *respect*: for the principle of autonomy;

– *compassion*: for the principle of benevolence;

– *fear*: for the principle of a lack of malevolence;

– *indignation*: for the principle of justice.

In addition, information expresses the act of informing. It only exists when it is transmitted and received by the individual. Its transmission can only exist in a communication that meets the criteria of truth and confidence. This essential role of confidence in communication has without doubt been needed to impose respect for fundamental ethical obligations on the entire community [CHA 98]. If we take the case of the domain of health and social care, the reception of information elicits inner reactions from the healthcare user, about a real or possible, present or future disease, and leads them to share decrypted information messages with other speakers and in other relational networks. In these conditions, individuals become the information's content, in particular vulnerable or disenfranchised individuals. From this, the consequences for NICT in healthcare seem to be the following:

– just like the entire structure, its IS should be designed and built according to the idea that "the patient and the quality of their care are at the center of concerns" [FES 01]. This involves diagnostic processes, therapy, prognosis and the monitoring of individual patients. They form the backbone of the information system. All the rest – medical research, information for management – should be drawn from it;

– the requirement for confidentiality, which is evidently very high, is only one of many ethical problems for an IS in healthcare.

The task of this chapter is to be able to reposition the individual at the center of thinking on digital challenges and risks. To do this, a model can be put in place that will have the purpose of grasping and better understanding the individual's behavior in the digital era. Thus, we were inspired in part by Aksel Tjora's [TJO 14] socio-political approach; he puts forward a typology of the emerging roles of the individual in the digital era and the era of the internet. He suggests considering a "digital patient" whose uses, behaviors and expectations are profoundly modified in often complex ways by NICT in the domain of healthcare. Our reasoning about our ethical vision is structured according to four major axes that complement each other and hinge on one another:

– the *axiological axis*: integrating human values;

– the *teleological axis*: describing the purposes of an action or deed;

– the *deontological axis*: explaining rules, norms, laws, codes, standards and limitations;

– the *axis of service and opening up to individuals*: conveying human relationships between the different actors involved.

To construct our analysis, we distinguish three categories for the effects and functions of NICT on the individual:

– *objectivation*: the mechanism by which the individual's characteristics and behaviors are transformed into digital data;

– *mobilization*: specifically involves interaction between the citizen and digital professionals and the capacity of the latter to mobilize the individual for a given project or event;

– *implication*: the steps undertaken on the individual's initiative (see Engagement).

Then we add to these three parameters with eight sociological categories:

– *consumption*: a market dynamic in which the individual can behave as a consumer;

– *communication*: the exchange of information between actors (see Exchange and sharing/concern for one's neighbors);

– *community*: actors' capacity to make their actions converge more or less strongly (see Preserving the social link);

– *increasing responsibility*: the sharing of responsibilities in building an event or action;

– *anticipation*: precaution, vigilance[38] and apprehension of all NICTs' negative repercussions, risks and consequences for the citizen;

– *social justice*: the equality and equity of a given action for the whole of society;

– *dependence*: the influence of NICT on the individual's daily life;

– *universalization*: the global, transversal and shared aspect of the nature, uses and impacts of technologies on the individual.

From this, we combine these different inputs to construct the following table, which makes it possible to highlight 24 parameters for analyzing the individual in a digitized environment (see Table 2.3).

---

38 The difficulty of apprehension and reflexivity on algorithms (especially machine learning) is part of their evolutive, unstable and shifting character. Such a characteristic reinforces the unpredictable side and the new effects of NICT. In this context, the principle of vigilance seems to be one of the collective paths for tackling the challenge of the digital world. It is a response to all the structural, technical, relational and methodological aspects and biases relating to an algorithmic device, on which our society must lean, especially to tackle the phenomenon of a lack of responsibility, resulting from AI's "black box" effect.

Functions			
Category of analysis	Objectivation	Mobilization	Implication
Consumption	Personal data such as marketing information: this data can be sold/bought	Individuals who buy business services	Individuals as informed and active consumers
Communication	Personal data as a platform support: this data can be transferred	Individuals who use information providing services	Individuals communicating
Community	Shared personal data: this data can be shared	Individuals participating in associations, forums, conferences or seminars	Individuals creating and using social media
Increasing responsibility	Traced personal data: the traceability of this data makes it possible to share or delegate all or partial responsibility	Individuals responsible (compliant) through delegation	Individuals responsible for themselves (self-management/autonomy)
Anticipation	Object personal data for precaution and vigilance: proper understanding of this data enables optimal apprehension of all the risks and consequences for the individual	Individuals who anticipate repercussions in the medium term	Individuals attentive to everything around them (environment, context, evolution)
Social justice	Personal data used fairly: this data is used in an egalitarian and equitable way	Individuals fair to society	Individuals empathetic to their neighbors
Universalization	Homogenous and universal personal data: the language and translation of this data is comprehensible to everyone	Individuals using online platforms and social networks	Individuals with the knowledge and capacity of a Community Manager

Table 2.3. *Impacts of the digital world on individuals*

This systemic approach, centered on the individual, should now be considered further by organizations and society as it has the merit of representing a tool for analysis and comprehension to grasp individuals' new behaviors, taking account of developments observed and expected from NICT.

2.10. Toward quantum ethics?

As we previously demonstrated, ethics shows us what is moral or immoral, indeed what is good or bad in a precise context. This discipline integrates a parameter of geographical but also temporal variability. Thus, an action that is beneficial at an instant will not be the next day. In other words, ethics is in perpetual motion and fluctuation, which will have the consequence of us seeing new forms of ethics appear over time. Each industrial revolution had to be accompanied by new currents of thought, then leading to new legal frameworks for societies.

Of course, there is no universal answer to these ethical questions and geographical and socio-cultural differences can cause the types of norm and behavior adopted to be modified. Ethics is therefore an empirical discipline whose postulates, based on a consensus within a dialogue, can vary over time and/or space. Our algorithmic ethics is formed from this approach, onto which is integrated an intangible and unchangeable base formed of the four ethical principles seen previously – benevolence, autonomy, lack of malevolence and justice. From these flows the significance of social and ethical questions linked to the omnipresence of algorithmic systems and digital artefacts, but also the consideration of two fundamental criteria: space and time.

Moreover, it is highly probable that the next industrial revolution is in a direct relationship with the progress and applications of quantum physics. We therefore have the right, indeed the duty, to draw up the first reflections on a quantum ethics that will accompany and frame, in as adequate and adapted a fashion as possible, the arrival of the quantum in our future daily lives. This move towards quantum mechanics and applications will follow the current digital revolution that has prepared and built the information ecosystem favorable to this revolution. From now on, quantum computing will "overwrite" time and space with its instantaneous actions and its ubiquitous spatial nature. For the first time, this quantum shift risks leading to an informational transformation of the human being, especially through the creation of a quantum avatar and quantum teleportation of individuals across space and time. Technology has become a mediation system structuring relationships between individuals who, taken in isolation, cannot claim to be masters and owners of technological wholes [POA 98]. Already, people, who were supposed to be the measure of technology, are today affected by it as well as living beings in their entirety. Anthropological and instrumental evaluation of technological innovations seems obsolete and out of date.

It is doomed to an axiological crisis and will not need the urgency and imperativity of an ethical reflection. A new approach to ethics will have to be invented to best respond to this new revolution in which – in a new spatio-temporal context governed by the laws of quantum physics – digital identities and connected relationships mingle with and confront objects and living beings. This ethics, which we will call "quantum ethics" will be able to respond to different challenges, risks, problems and repercussions especially, on the one hand, on the nature and status of people, and on the other hand, on the complexity of the duality between the real and the artificial. It is therefore important to consider, in an ethical prism, knowledge relating to the engineering of complex systems. This ethics should focus its attention on complexity[39], which will be at its peak when interweaving on the one hand, the real and the virtual on the other, time and space triggering confusion in the whole. For Blaise Pascal[40], "ethics should mobilize intelligence to brave the complexity of life, the world, and ethics itself [...] it is an ethics of understanding, which does not impose a Manichean vision of the world [...] it is an ethics that ceaselessly meets uncertainty and contradiction within itself. An ethics without any basis other than itself, but which needs support from outside itself: relying on an anthropology and on knowing the situations where it is practiced". This is why our quantum ethics turned towards complexity should link separate data, information and knowledge (of reflective, empirical or value nature) with action across space and time.

According to our systemic Neo-Platonist approach (Ψ, G, Φ), digitization – illustrated especially by the development of cognitive sciences and AI – and soon the "quantification" of our world, corroborate with the approach of

39 This term comes from the Latin word *complexus* which means "something that is woven together".

40 In his book *Pensées* (Thoughts) in 1670.

Cartesian materialism, and La Mettrie[41] according to which it is matter (and consequently information (*Gnose* (G)) that thinks.

Thought (*Psi* (Ψ)) – whose origin lies in matter – would determine the manner in which the real is built. In these conditions, the universe, environment or the ecosystem being conscious, correspond to *Phi* (Φ). At the microscopic scale of quantum mechanics, observation will break down quantum superposition, represented by *Phi* which symbolizes the wave function in Schrödinger's equation, and would thus oblige it to form reality as we know it. Ultimately, as we saw previously, everything that is matter is information (G). You just have to build a structure of ethics (Ψ) reconciling information (G) with action in a given environment (Φ).

Finally, this ethics of the future always fits the context in which it evolves. It demands an approach be carried out that re-evaluates human values and moral norms starting with changes observable in society. Ethics known as "normative" necessarily influence practices, and reciprocally, practices will enable permanent questioning of these norms. Finally, we are seeing a system of ethical reflections that are self-sustaining and fit perfectly into Leonardo da Vinci's tradition of thought.

Ultimately, quantum ethics should be directed towards the ontological problems that quantum physics will lead, to accompany current and future society [THE 90]. This quantum ethics that will serve us as a paradigm is not an "ethics in the future, or a future ethics designed today for our future descendants, but an ethics of today that is concerned with the future and expects to protect it, for our descendants, from the consequences of our present action" [JON 78].

---

41 Dr. Julien Offray de La Mettrie considers, in his books titled respectively, *L'Histoire naturelle de l'âme* (The Natural History of the Soul) (1745) and *L'Homme-Machine* (Man a Machine) (1747), that reflection has its origin in matter. He concludes that humankind is a machine and that in the whole universe there is only one substance, which is matter, variously modified and which appears in different forms.

3

The Framework for Algorithmic Processing

The emergence of new information and communications technologies (NICTs) is engendering repercussions, impacts, challenges and risks which are considerable at all levels. It is transforming the entire world by making it unstable, indeed precarious, but also transforming organizations and structures, whether public or private. It is modifying social interaction, economic behavior and even individuals. New challenges, but also new conflicts, have emerged. The use of personal digital data directly affecting the privacy of each individual means that moral dilemmas are posed about strategic choices on the subjects of algorithmic management and governance.

Moreover, because of the nature of their structure and operation, understanding the internal reasoning system of self-teaching information systems (IS) and therefore their results, seems complicated. This irremediably poses problems of algorithmic transparency, control and therefore governance which are becoming the subject of substantial attention, especially ethical attention, for the whole of society but especially for actors who design and use NICT. What society is emerging through the generalization of NICT and the big data that supply them? What form of government can be profiled though this "datafication"? Should regulation on algorithmic systems rely on greater transparency in algorithms to obtain greater loyalty? What exactly would this transparency entail for actors? And what algorithms should be transparent?

Thus, in the face of this accelerating digital shift and increasing ruptures, a framework is imposed to best accompany society's digital transition. It is essential to focus on the algorithms themselves and to establish specifications for the best practices for their construction, development, use and monitoring, while still maintaining technical progress. This new framework should be created from an ethical angle based on good, evolutive human practices via algorithmic systems and other technologies associated with digital data. This approach is based on the principles of *Ethics by Design* and *Ethics by Evolution*, that is on one hand integrating ethical demands and specifications starting with the design of NICT up to their use, and on the other hand in a more evolutive manner over time. This ethical algorithmic governance aims to integrate human principles and values from the design and implementation to the use of NICT to re-establish a relationship of confidence and reconcile and reinforce man-machine relationships with technological progress.

3.1. Characteristics of NICT essential for their use

IS should meet regulatory requirements for security and confidentiality for access to digital information, as well as for citizens' rights. NICTs aim to improve the user's transverse management by promoting information sharing between professionals, actors and networks exterior to the structure. In fact, information sharing, depending on communication and confidentiality standards, facilitates exchanges with external partners through the network. Implementing these IT applications reinforces and facilitates exchanges, coordination between services, information circulation and therefore continuity in management.

Hence, the IS tool is therefore needed to carry out the whole project. This passes as a priority through a project scheduling body and a prediction of the resources needed for implementation as well management of the target IS. We are witnessing an improvement in the quality of the structure's technico-economic direction via a good knowledge of the activity and the transmission of information within the organization put in place. NICTs thus become a support for the work process thanks to a computerized toolkit and access to references such as knowledge bases, archives, publications, and so on.

To meet all these expectations, algorithmic devices should have very precise functions and characteristics (see Box 3.1).

Produce results that are easy to access and interpret.

Be coherent, homogeneous but above all comprehensive and pertinent [TOU 04].

Reduce, indeed remove the need for re-entering information, leading to the information's greater reliability and a simplification of the tasks to be carried out.

Have the same total information, with the same degree of reliability.

Include the possibility of accessing external databases and returning information without re-entry.

Facilitate reactivity and flexibility in the organizations and actors who make up an organization.

Propose solutions in keeping with the challenges of communicating and sharing information and knowledge.

Be interoperable with other information mechanisms and mechanisms for communication internal or external to a structure (interfaces and compatibility).

Have databases that can be shared in real time between different systems and software, without having to modify them at user level.

Ensure the possibility of including different functions on single screen.

Remain simple and ergonomic to ensure good understanding by all, as well as fast reading.

Give consumers or citizens the chance to control their personal data by including rights to correct and exclude it from the databases that host it.

Possess the most automated practice possible, with a minimum of re-entry and manual formatting to be done.

Box 3.1. *An algorithmic system's functions and characteristics*

In addition, some thoughts on improving technologies are directed towards means of providing more information for users or deciders. One pertinent element is to link information to make it comprehensible and useful. This information does not have to be produced by the same sources.

Hence the need to be able to collect information from various origins, to attribute meaning to it and to understand what purpose it serves with the aim of directing it to individuals who really need it. This problem of linking information from diverse origins is thus an integration and therefore an IS problem.

Moreover, when we analyze an algorithmic system's components more deeply, we are obliged to refer to the associated applications and software. Generally, an IT code is a set of automata programmed to treat data. It is a set of data presented in two forms:

– *"binary" or "executable"*: illustrating the software so that the user's system will be able to interpret it;

– *the "source code"*: characterizing the software so that a human being can interpret it, as soon as they know the programming language in which the software is written.

The difficulty of studying software such as technical tools relates primarily to their immaterial nature. For all the material tools we use every day, a simple glance is generally enough to suggest the idea of their use to us. Even for more complex machines, their mere physical presence enables us to question them and search the mechanism, without necessarily running them: this exploration often shows us the how and the why. For software, we should on the contrary – unless one is a programmer and has the source code – expect to run them to know their usefulness.

All technical processes are hidden from us to ensure better ergonomics and a workspace clear of anything not intended to benefit the final user. Herein lies the problem of an algorithm's transparency. So we do not know very well what really "is technical" in the software, to such a point that the most esoteric will feel that everything is "magic" and the most Cartesian will see technology everywhere.

Even though it is immaterial, a piece of software is nonetheless concrete. It is not an abstract set of procedures arising out of nowhere and running everywhere. It establishes a set mode of communication between man and machine, offering the user a set number of possibilities, using a set number of functions in the system (software and hardware included) on which it is installed. What we call here the concrete character of the software is no other than this set aspect of the relationship that it makes it possible to establish between man and the machine.

In these conditions, NICT should have some major qualities for good use.

3.1.1. *Adaptability*

This may be contrary to the notion of performance. In fact, an IS built by specialists to meet professionals' demands as well as possible can prove to be very rigid and unable to absorb new IT systems to consider new needs. It may consequently perhaps be necessary to keep solutions that are less effective in absolute terms, but which are far more agile.

This brings us back to the notion of standard. One must not confuse "norm", which is defined by dominant choices on the market, and "standard" which is regulatory in character. A standard is not always a good alternative when it is confidential and shuts the user into a market that is too segmented and reduced [TOU 04]. Their adaptation to market demands is almost non-existent; they mainly meet organizational needs.

3.1.2. *Availability*

This represents the property of having information, services, resources or functions expected by users in set time conditions:

– for a function, this is the assurance of continuity of service offered respecting the expected response times;

– for information, this is the guarantee of access to data in an expected time or under timetabled conditions.

3.1.3. *Robustness*

An IS should perform without dysfunction and breakdown, especially if it disseminates personal digital data and if working methods are based on computerized transmissions or on electronic archiving. An IS's robustness is strongly linked, via its design, to its architecture, which should make it possible to change elements without bringing the entire mechanism into question. In the NICT sector, reliability is established based on the robustness and maintenance processes used by the IS. Such a process aims to reinforce the pertinence and validity of the data used. When data is entered in large numbers by users it leads to anomalies. These errors can have variable and sometimes catastrophic consequences for a patient or user.

In addition, beyond this very technical aspect on which an IS relies, the designer should still not conceal the political vision that their computing choices support and which is influential in the long term. In fact, an IS should satisfy four major concerns that are generally identified from an organizational point of view [TOU 04]. Robustness can be assimilated to a system's stability. Two types of robustness can be defined:

– a system robust in stability, if this system remains stable in the presence of uncertainties such as modeling errors, noise in measurement and external disturbances;

– a system robust in performance, if these are retained in spite of disturbances.

This latter type of robustness of course contains the former. Several types of tests can be carried out to achieve this robustness.

Beyond the heterogeneity of different types of tests mentioned above, common difficulties can be identified:

– the widening of the test's domain of entry (as much for data as for events) to consider not only the functional aspects of interactions with the environment, but even the temporal aspects of these interactions, as well as the possible occurrence of faults;

– setting pertinent trajectories in this input domain, which becomes an even more complex problem as the size of the domain has increased. The behavior to be analyzed can be linked to subtle combinations of the internal state of the system and to requirements in its environment;

– limitations relating to the commendable aspect and to the observability of the systems considered, which pose complex problems when implementing abstract test scenarios.

Thus, with evolution in the markets, just-in-time and the Internet, regulatory changes have led to adaptations in processes and imposed very high reactivity. It is the same for the evolution of user needs or the obsolescence of some technical solutions that ensure a volume of recurrent maintenance. An IS's constant evolution means implementing management of this change based on the challenges and risks linked to maintenance processes, maintenance typologies, the procedure to be followed and criteria for quality. This maintenance and evolution stage of an IS involves activities linked to an existing information system's modifications and continues until the system ceases to be used.

In IT, the notion of maintenance is not fixed and covers very varied realities. It is not reduced to purely and simply providing assistance and troubleshooting with software equipment. It can be extended to providing evolved versions of diverse software and/or software packages, indeed training services, user help and assistance depending on the evolution of user needs or technology. Indeed, maintenance professionals already speak in terms of offering "services".

Maintenance services can be carried out in different ways (by telephone, at home, etc.) and can occur on various levels (prevention, correction, evolution, etc.).

Finally, in the context of hardware maintenance and software maintenance, the activity of IT maintenance includes multiples facets. There are various levels of intervention:

– the preventive level (to avoid blockages);

– the corrective or curative level (corresponding to "repairs");

– the evolutive level (to ensure the system's sustainability).

It can be shown that this last stage relies on two essential activities:

– managing a portfolio of requests for modification;

– managing successive versions of the IT system and accompanying elements.

3.1.4. *Auditability*

Auditability (proof and accountability) ensures complete and permanent control of the mechanism and especially the ability to retrace all events over the course of a certain period. It therefore represents the ability to provide, to a competent authority, proof that the algorithm's design, performance and internal controls conform to requirements:

– for a function, it is the ability to determine the individual or automated process(es) with whom the request for processing originates and to determine the other useful circumstances associated with this demand;

– for information, it is the ability to determine the individual or automated process(es) which give access to the information and to determine other useful circumstances associated with this access.

3.1.5. *IT integration*

Integration is characterized by accepting that several different parts of a device can form part of a whole. Concretely, IT integration is based on software interfacing to guarantee dissemination of data from one to the other. The aim is to avoid re-entry and errors that arise from it and to reduce transfer delays. This integrity thus consists of determining if the data have been altered during the communication (by chance or intentionally). This requirement for interfacing leads to technical, organizational and semantic problems. It can also be noted that such an action highlights the problem of redundancy of information where the NICT designer is obliged to go and seek information to supply one or more destination software.

3.1.6. *Consolidation*

Consolidation in IT represents the coherent regrouping of data. Most often it involves data organized logically or linked to one another. This approach is essential in the context of statistics from a website, especially to measure an audience. It consists of regrouping identical data to obtain a structured relationship, which is easier to consult than raw information present on the server and means less loss of information is possible. In this example, the server's raw data detail each access to one of the files, with the name of the associated file, the date of access and the visitor's IP address. Consolidation of these types of data can occur in two ways:

– by file: there is a precise table for each file in the server and the number of times it has been accessed, over a given period of time;

– by visitor: for each IP address, the number of files accessed is obtained over a given period of time.

Thus, these two types of consolidation make it possible to retain perfectly usable audience measures by dispensing with useless data storage that consumes a great deal of disk space.

3.1.7. *Diffusion*

A major concern is that NICT may improve the transfer and dissemination of digital data. This occurs necessarily through:

– the ergonomics of consultation becoming more uniform;

– rigorous and precise confidentiality and privacy rules;

– dissemination of information to a workstation;

– IT adapted to end use;

– consideration of users' increasingly peripatetic lives;

– understanding and integration of these users' new expectations.

3.1.8. *Co-ordination*

Co-ordination is achieved in the synchronization and cooperation of actors as well as in the mutualization of resources and means of implementation. It can be noted that increasing the complexity of an organization naturally leads to it becoming disorganized. Hence this perpetual search for an equilibrium between efficiency and simplicity, which requires reflection on the mode of spreading orders and information feedback vital to managing a decision-maker.

3.1.9. *Interoperability*

The interoperability of NICT represents a fundamental challenge for policy on developing technical progress. This aims to move society into the digital era by developing communication and sharing dematerialized data between professionals, while still involving the citizen in the disposal of their personal data. As we have seen, interoperability means an IT device's capacity to function with other digital systems, existing or to come, without restricting access or implementation.

Moreover, several parameters should be considered in the subject of computer security for NICT:

– its function and purpose;

– its destination and target users;

– its mode of connection and network;

– its operating capacities;

– its possible interactions with people and/or other machines;

– the nature of possession (property, location, subscription, etc.);

– the type of data processed;

– the re-use of building blocks involved in system information, currently used or not.

Ultimately, this description of the different qualities intrinsic to NICT confirms a little more its transverse character as well as its influence and impact on the ecosystems that surround it. We can take Louis Quéré's expression "internal sociality" [QUE 89], critiquing approaches separating technology and use when analyzing a tool. Considered as a simple "black box", the very structure of a technical invention would be independent of its process of diffusion, a generalization of use that would merely be an event external to the technical object. By following the Louis Quéré's train of thought against this viewpoint, we see how software perfectly illustrates this design, as their mode of development involves users directly, and does so in multiple ways. Louis Quéré returns to the thesis, defended by Bruno Latour in his book published in 1987 and entitled *Science in Action*, for which, since a social link is in the machine, and vice versa, there is no longer space to maintain the usual distinction between the technical object and the social world. In these conditions, the innovation should be designed as technological progress endowed with a social aspect and culture. Consequently, the evaluation of algorithmic systems [GOO 16] should happen through consideration of all internal characteristics with their diverse natures, as well as the environment in which they are expressed. All risks should be studied systemically and scaled down to the technology's scale.

These risks should be considered throughout the duration of the NICT's life, depending on the evolution of the ambient threat.

3.2. Scenarios for the digital economy

The appearance of the fourth industrial revolution around the end of the 20th Century is illustrated by the fact that humanity in the western world lives in societies where the economy[1] has become an end in itself, while humanity appears to be a mere tool, still useful – but soon perhaps more indispensable with the emergence of AI – to achieve this end. This reversal of relationships between humanity and the economy necessarily creates substantial, indeed dangerous risks. Indeed, we are already right to ask if a human, previously considered as a subject, then an object, is not perceived as a product for consumption, or indeed merchandise. The economy, which has efficiency and usefulness as an engine, is at ever more risk of relying, on the one hand on data (data driven economy), and on the other hand, on "intelligent machines" evolving much more quickly than humanity, who are subject to the slow laws of biological evolution [DOS 15].

Just as the Internet has transformed in its time, the distribution, accessibility and spread of information, the blockchain should reinvent the way in which contracts, transactions and more generally confidence in autonomous and open networks, are managed. In fact, this technology in open source code, which underpins crypto-currencies (encrypted currency), compatible and interoperable with others such as Bitcoin, would form a credible alternative to the procedural, technological and organizational infrastructure essential to maintaining confidence on an institutional scale. Thus, payments – that is the transfer of financial assets (shares, obligations, debts, structured products), direct loans between individuals, or property – are immediately and instantaneously counted. This approach will reduce the cost, insecurity and complexity of transactions between different parties who do not necessarily know each other.

---

1 Etymologically, the economy is the "management of the house" (from the Greek οἶκος = house, and νόμος = law). The "house" represents a construction sheltering a person, so a means made available to them to improve their existence. Economy is therefore a science aiming to be placed at the service of a "good life". A "good life" is a life enabling humanity to develop all the faculties (physical, moral, intellectual and spiritual) forming part of their essential nature harmoniously.

Hence, it will become easier to check that a contract – which can be customized and whose parameters can be set at will – has been correctly, indeed automatically carried out, without having to divulge any confidential information about the stakeholders. This is the integration of intelligent contracts (or smart contracts).

This new disruption should impact with full force not only actors such as solicitors, insurers, banks, consumer loan organizations, stock exchanges, clearing houses, auditors and crowdlending, but also sharing economy platforms such as Airbnb or Uber. This could even have major repercussions on the entire economic system, which is based on regulators, centralization, proprietary software and states' sovereign powers.

Moreover, one can imagine a market formed of tens of billions of algorithms available through sale or on license. These algorithms – just like big data – will become an asset and an immaterial good that may even be subject to market valuation. Thus, products could be defined by the sophistication and value of their algorithms. In this context, structures would be evaluated using the big data they employ, but also the algorithms that enable data processing. Such a situation necessarily places the economy of algorithms at the center of attention, especially in machine-to-machine interaction. Since "nature always abhors a void", it inevitably runs the risk of forming markets around algorithms, generating the creation of new generations of NICT produced by large industrial groups, SMEs and start-ups. Businesses will invent new digital products and distributors will find new models for loyalty programs that will go far beyond the simple attribution of loyalty points. Supply chains will be improved for digital products and virtual currency. These new opportunities will be supported by innovative digital economic models, thus promoting connectivity and co-operation between partners. Banks and fintechs will have to offer new digital solutions to answer new customer expectations. With the emergence of connected objects and intelligent machines, businesses will have to amplify control of integration and be capable of guaranteeing a secure connection between any object and/or machine. With the constant evolution of NICT and indirectly of regulatory frameworks, organizations will be forced to accept unpredictability. Consequently, the latter will have to use integration and analytical technologies to innovate fast, but also to adapt to unforeseen situations by bringing new ideas. Many traditional sectors with a pyramidal structure such as tourism, transport, insurance, banking and the hotel industry have been the target of an "Uberization" of their activities. Other sectors are in the process of following the same trend, such as health, energy, politics[2], supply, education and training[3].

On the other hand, the generalization of architectures based on microservices will have the consequence of forcing businesses to identify new operational challenges with an approach to systemic governance. Surfing the wave of an increase in cloud services, mobile terminals and the IoT, the use and adoption of API will become obvious and automatic. Finally, this digital ecosystem will necessarily generate the expected user experience. In fact, technological progress enabling citizens to choose the closest shop or Internet site, their shopping channel, their place of delivery, and so on. Businesses should consider this new gift and be capable of providing customized and omnichannel experiences promoting the move between the real world and the virtual one.

This forces us to ask what value should be associated with algorithms and big data. What economic models, business models, and what monetization strategies should be used? Must we apply an intellectual property system in the digital economy? Can intellectual property become an instrument for protecting the service provided by digital actors?

From this observation, this period of digital transition naturally brings a host of questions and uncertainties on the future of economy 4.0 based on big data, algorithmic systems and blockchains. This exponential economy includes three major, hitherto unmentioned challenges:

– *market adjustment*: how do the markets balance out when structures are crossing over very quickly and when NICTs such as AI are never stable? Will it make prices fluctuate constantly? To differ according to their users? Can pay be stable, without leading to unemployment?

– *regulation of competition*: what are consequences and impacts for businesses whose business model is to draw income from a small number of users in an oligopolistic, indeed monopolistic, market?

---

2 Probably, policies will increasingly become open "catalysts" that will have the purpose of inciting practical action in association with citizens, rather than through restrictive laws and measures.

3 Training may begin to occur increasingly through co-education on businesses', universities' or individuals' social networks, blogs and websites, and will become more general via MOOCs (massive open online courses).

– *the geopolitical aspect*: what countries will have a monopoly on AI technologies such as deep learning? Can the regulation and global openness of these NICTs be envisaged?

To try to understand and anticipate these socio-economic changes due to the digitization of our societies, it is becoming necessary to project oneself into the short and medium term by turning to envisageable scenarios linked to the regulation it makes sense to implement. After analyzing the evolution of technological development and exchanges with the different actors involved in it, three major scenarios prevail.

3.2.1. *Scenario 1: the generalization and commercialization of algorithms combined with Platform as a Service (PaaS) tools*[4]

This trend towards the multiplication of diverse software "bricks" for a specific service raises several questions about software editors' level of engagement, the integrity of processed data, the quality of the end service, control over the use of data and about the effectiveness of algorithms. The solution that seems most suitable for this situation seems to be to develop a system for certifying software components and analysis tools. For the regulator, the difficulty of this scenario linked in the complexity of algorithmic data processing and digital services to guarantee respect for current law: responsibilities, traceability, accessibility, non-conformity, confidentiality, and so on.

3.2.2. *Scenario 2: organization into silos independent of data producers and algorithmic processing specialists*

This scenario poses questions on the ownership and portability of data as well as the conditions for access for new digital actors. This intermediate situation enables platforms (Twitter, Facebook, Apple, etc.) to deploy an independent strategy. Data silo operators will have to adopt an open innovation strategy to remain competitive, which could moderate barriers to entry for providers of new services and products. Other, smaller actors seek

4 The provision of an additional applicative platform "layer" facilitating use and running of applications.

partnerships or alliances to reach targeted, critical size. The solution would be to put in place and develop a mechanism for labeling applied directly to platforms that use digital data.

3.2.3. *Scenario 3: domination of AI leaders via proprietary algorithms with unparalleled performances*

This situation leads to problems with competition, the monopoly of certain markets and a lack of transparency towards external actors. We can take the example of the IBM platform Watson Developer Cloud, which carries 400 expert systems[5] and applications in the sectors of finance, health, distribution, sport, music, and so on. For Fleur Pellerin, the former French minister for the digital economy, "not only do we lack European champions, but we have witnessed the emergence of champions from outside Europe, such as Apple, Google, Amazon, Facebook, Alibaba, Tencent, Lenovo, Yahoo, etc."[6]. In this context, worries – about the level of competition, excessive abuse of dominant positions, or external regulation of these large businesses – are put in place.

One of the responses possible for the regulator would be to create a classification, marking or rating system with AI leaders, who would be able to bring more transparency in the actual reality of the services and products suggested.

In addition, according to work by the AXA foresight squad carried out by Cécile Wending in 2016, we see the appearance of three scenarios for AI adoption for 2030.

– *Scenario 1*: adoption limited by the monothematic criteria of AI mechanisms and by a feasible level of social acceptance (worries over jobs, fear of machines, etc.). Such a situation will not lead to massive rupture.

– *scenario 2*: a more regulated and frameworked AI, with systems that are financially more affordable. This condition advantages social acceptance and a massive use of NICT in ecosystems in direct a relationship with the customer and the individual.

---

5 We note that the expert Watson system is not a monolithic system. It contains more than 40 different algorithms each with their own method.

6 Interview in the newspaper *Le Monde* from February 11, 2014.

– *Scenario 3*: an AI strongly implanted in a country (for example China, South Korea or Japan). This situation favors trans-disciplinary development and the growing development of technical applications and competencies related to the digital.

It can be observed that these different scenarios depend in part on human factors that may or may not be able to explain setbacks in the implementation, use and therefore the adoption of a technological innovation within a business, or more generally within our society. These human parameters can come from many different sources and origins such as:

– citizens' lack of interest in NICT;

– the unsuitability of the IT device with to business's structural organization;

– poor relationships between actors;

– individuals' lack of motivation and availability;

– lack of conviction among those responsible for the structure;

– lack of training, education and sensitization among users of this technology;

– lack of recognition of the hierarchy of specialists in IS (lack of legitimacy);

– refusal to change the organization within the structure for socioprofessional or economic reasons;

– loss of confidence in the IT mechanism.

If the digital revolution disrupts and modifies our benchmarks and forces us to look afresh at our culture, our institutions and our education, ethics remain at the center of the pact of confidence. This means that a moral framework is vital to preserve society's human values. Already confronted with a new economy in the process of structuring itself, one of mobility, exchange, globalization and dematerialization, it is fundamental to better inform, sensitize, warn, train and give responsibility to all actors so they can better grasp their digital environment and master its risks and challenges.

Ultimately, whatever scenario occurs, it makes sense to instill an ethical approach in all, and this might be conveyed via three precise actions:

– establish initial relationships between humanity and the economy in which the former should again become the "end" and the second the "means";

– develop and/or systematically introduce the human sciences into primary and continued training hinging especially on NICT;

– re-introduce morals and ethics at the heart of any educative, pedagogical and professional approach.

This does not mean flying in the face of technical progress, but rather giving humanity the means to think and take its place in the digitized society now undergoing development [DOS 15]. Our ethical approach represents much more than a guardrail. The promotion of ethical rules coincides with business challenges. Big data and more especially personal data are the keystones of the digital economy. Henceforward, in a digitized universe, commercial transactions and exchanges cannot be carried out with respect for the business's image (e-reputation, trusted third party), without respect for clients (requirements and expectations) and their ethics. Consequently, the use of data-driven marketing could not be made without an ethics of digital data that is individual in character.

3.3. An algorithm's ethical rules

As we saw earlier, algorithms contain the ambivalence of being both the source of great hopes (usefulness, optimization, scientific discoveries, speed, etc.) and great concern (categorization, confidentiality and privacy, profiling, dehumanization, etc.) for society. Finally, we consider the fact that choosing the manner in which they are built and used belongs to us. This is why it seems necessary to impose ethical rules when developing, implementing and using an algorithm. Developers and editors themselves are then led to take these ethical specifications systematically into consideration. For example, it can be verified that, taking account of the geographical situation in learning an algorithm for predicting the risks of respiratory failure or myocardial infection, will remove some boundaries and places. This defect can then be compensated by initially forbidding it to process this location parameter.

Before establishing rules and an ethical framework on algorithms, it seems indispensable to provide an overview and specifications on the value of information depending on why, how and how far it is used. The algorithm is supplied by data or information that has an intrinsic base value. This value will be expressed more, and will increase and acquire its full potential when it is used in the context of an algorithmic mechanism or processing. This moves the question to an ethical terrain, which exceeds technical compartmentalization.

Hence, the "why" necessarily leads to questioning about culture. Algorithms bring classical models on making decisions and predictions into question by relying on new, inductive forms of logic. With algorithms, actors are no longer limited to data on ownership but open the field to common and open databases, notably via the Web.

As for the "how", this rather points to questions about everyday organization. Implementation is fundamental to making the use of big data possible. A business should be able to reconfigure and evolve depending on what this digital data teaches it. It is therefore led to a series of questions such as: how can my IT security system alert me quickly when an abnormal data flow forms (monitoring)? How do I follow my digital data? How to anticipate the negative repercussions, biases and risks that gravitate around my data' lifecycle?, and so on.

To finish, the subject of limits has not ceased to preoccupy society more and more. Many citizens have therefore been led to ask how far their personal data, and therefore their private life, can be exchanged for a given service or for goods.

Productive, sustainable, reliable and pertinent use of these substantial volumes of data cannot occur without a precise and coherent context for reflection on this theme. The relationship of confidence surrounding this dematerialized ecosystem comes at this price! Businesses and solution editors who work with this data on behalf of their clients will have to impose a code of good practice to reassure them. Each actor's responsibility passes necessarily through an ethics of algorithms. This is the principle of our algorithmic ethics and Responsibility (or Ethics) by Design, which we wish to foreground in this work. Our vision and ethical approach should not be summarized by confrontation between mankind and the machine but rather in the way in which it is articulated and integrated into our society. This regulation should in part be inspired by concern for transparency, often synonymous with supervision and control. Some even speak of the loyalty of algorithms, which can be expressed by institutional, indeed even citizen regulation, as is the case in the USA. The general principle of loyalty tends to force digital actors to guarantee good faith for the products and services it offers without seeking to divert them to ends contradictory to the interests of their users, whether these are professionals or private individuals.

However, application of such regulation should in our view abandon a normative and restrictive approach to tackle an ethical and flexible approach to avoid going against market dynamics. A regulation based on the message that has followed us throughout this book: "Code is Ethics and Ethics is Code".

This phrase can be considered as the contemporary version of a quotation from [HEG 21], "the real is the rational and the rational is the real". To do this, we must simply return to the postulate that we saw previously in which "code" illustrates the "real" and "nature and ethics" corresponds to the "rational". As all reality is ambivalent, like a fire that can both burn and illuminate, the same goes for IT code, which can be used both beneficially for the business and harmfully misused for the citizen.

As for ethical rules, these have the purpose of establishing order and social structure in an organization by imposing orders on individuals. They prevent anarchy[7] by refining an appropriate framework for ethical reflection. Their content is adjustable and can be revised depending on the context, the environment, space and time. Each country, via its historico-socio-cultural past, has its own ethical rules [LEC 07]. These ethical rules include an impressive structural connotation by giving ethical principles a concrete expression that makes them exist in a set situation and context. They are the adjustment variable for an ethical approach, to respond to a given problem, especially in the digital world. These rules are generally all linked to the four ethical principles seen previously. Thus, the basis for our ethical evaluation can be built from these four principles, to which 12 ethical rules are equally attached (see Table 3.1).

7 Literally "the absence of principle", *anarkhia* in Greek.

Fundamental ethical principles	Ethical rules
Autonomy	respect for the individual free will free and informed consent
Benevolence	service to the individual return usefulness and quality
Lack of malevolence	proportionality uncertainty precaution and anticipation
Justice	solidarity responsibility equity and equality

Table 3.1. *Rules that derive from basic ethical principles*

The principle of autonomy includes three main ethical rules, which are: respect for the individual by considering them as an actor in full in the decision or action, free will in particular in relation to the result of an expert self-learning system for professionals, and free and informed consent without external influence and with full knowledge. Concerning the principle of benevolence, this is linked to service to the individual, either individually and/or collectively, the return and additional profit that this should provide the individual, the usefulness and quality of the act. For the principle of lack of malevolence, ethical rules affecting proportionality (because we are always in the process of deciding between advantages and drawbacks or between costs and benefits), the uncertainty of a result or action over the medium and long term, precaution and anticipation, in particular on the repercussions or consequences of a deed over time. Finally, the principle of justice is linked to solidarity with a social approach over mutual help between individuals, the responsibility of actors, and the equity and equality of action and means of implementing it for individuals.

Moreover, this model for ethical deliberation does not aim to solve all the problems caused for society by the complexity of NICT. However, it forms an initial basis pertinent when directing thinking on the digital. These ethical rules aim to establish a rigorous schema for thought for better comprehension, grasping and guidance for the world's digital transition.

Reflecting on the nature of data that is personal in nature is, on the one hand, a cultural challenge for the individual, for whom it has become the real DNA of their digital identity, and on the other hand, a strategic advantage for businesses who integrate a culture of data science that is ever more pronounced in their economic environment. Hence, the use of data is a major pillar of value creation, as much for citizens as for businesses.

This is why it is vital to find an equilibrium between innovation and caution illustrated by these ethical rules. Couldn't one imagine a responsibility principle for digital risk on the model of environmental law [THI 04]? This approach would make it possible for digital professionals to benefit from these uses within the limit of legal data personal protection and, more generally, third party rights over data. In exchange, this would commit them to responsibility in case of major harm to others, if they have not taken the precautions needed to avoid this risk. This would lead to a win-win system based on giving actors responsibility. This responsibility principle means that the algorithm or its user considers the effects of their processes and actions.

Finally, these ethical rules on algorithmic systems include a set of involved domains, such as personal data protection and protection of privacy, legal and regulatory aspects, the opening up and sharing of data, stakeholders, data sources and analysis of the algorithm, applications, norms and protocols, technological development, man-machine interface and articulation, communication, and so on. An algorithm termed "fair" should be able to take account of its effects, as well as properly knowing the characteristics of the sectors involved.

It is noted that the notion of reliability does not belong directly to an ethical framework arising from NICTs, but illumination should be provided by three well-defined parameters:

– biases that can be generated by the data used during training, via their composition or qualification;

– the validity of the algorithms run;

– algorithms' probabilistic and therefore uncertain nature and aspect.

3.4. Ethical evaluation of algorithmic processing

In the context of ethical analysis in an algorithm's design, it is imperative to identify the latter's criteria or motives with the aim of evaluating its ethical character. Regulation work is needed for the algorithm to respect predefined values, especially for it to be non-discriminatory and non-exclusive. To do this, it is essential to fully understand the operating mode of the algorithm used. This understanding is very complicated to obtain because of algorithms' opacity level; they are considered to be a real, unfathomable "black box". This principle, of an algorithm's explicability, means that any decision taken by it must be comprehensible and accessible to individuals involved in this decision to enable them to optimally contest erroneous data or errors observed. It therefore seems very difficult to explain algorithms precisely or translate them into logical reasoning on the basis of sequencing the choices used.

Moreover, the Commission for Ethical Reflection on Research in Digital Sciences and Technology (Commission de réflexion sur l'Éthique de la Recherche en sciences et technologies du Numérique d'Allistene (CERNA)) has formulated its second report, entitled *Éthique en apprentissage machine* (Ethics in machine learning) and made public on March 15, 2017. Its recommendations on automatic learning or machine learning are formed around six main themes: learning systems' data (1–4), learning systems' autonomy (5–6), the explicability of learning methods and their evaluation (7–9), learning systems' decisions (10), consent in the digital domain (11), responsibility in man-machine relationships (12–13) and the organization of French research on digital ethics (14–17) (see Appendix A.2).

In addition, the question of ethics therefore occurs at three moments in a big data project:

– when big data are moved to a set of selected variables (see ethics of data (ED));

– when selected data are moved to results generated by an algorithm or an ethical study (see ethics of algorithms (EA));

– when these results are moved to a defined action plan (see ethics of practice (EP)).

It is therefore essential to be able to answer a number of questions such as: why select these variables and these parameters? What relationships do they have with the subject? How are data used by the analysis or processing algorithm? Does the action plan put in place respect the different ethical principles and moral rules that frame our society?

To make our remarks more concrete, we can take the example of a big data project in the domain of human resources (HR). Thus, whoever is responsible for the algorithmic system is led to ask questions at the level of each major stage listed above:

– *during the stage of selecting variables*: is it coherent and moral to select the variable "country of origin", "state of health", "gender" or "number of children" for recruitment, evaluation or promotion? However, these variables may be relevant when they are intended for an internal study on gaps in salary;

– *during an algorithm's running*: introduction of the variable "gender", after processing has ended, can lead to the reproduction of biases in the final analysis;

– *at moment of operating the action plan and practice implemented*: if an analysis of absenteeism has shown that women with young children have a higher probability of being absent than women without young children, then the business can take actions and solutions for balancing family responsibilities such as looking after sick children, setting up a crèche within the business, or providing equipment for remote working, and so on, instead of avoiding recruiting women with young children.

Finally, our ethical evaluation of algorithmic processing will be broken down into two directions, on the one hand on data and its practices, and on the other hand on the algorithm and its uses. Both these dimensions will be studied in a technical-human light (see Figure 3.1).

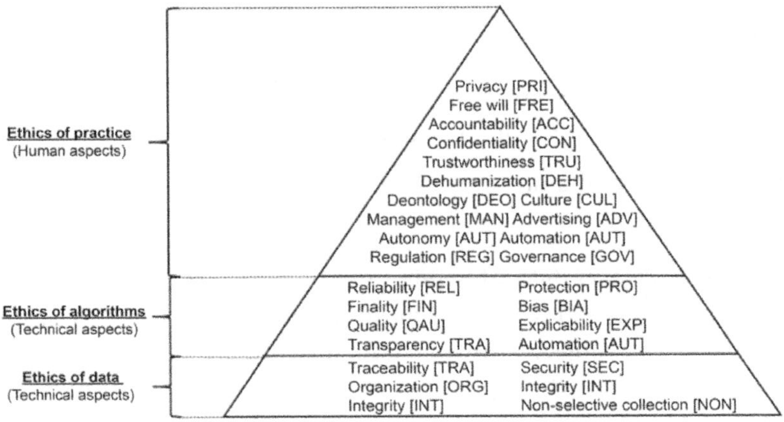

Figure 3.1. *Ethical evaluation of an algorithmic processing*

3.4.1. *Evaluation of data and practices*

This evaluation is formed, in a balanced way, of an ethics of data (ED) with six criteria that are predominantly technical, and an ethics of practice (EP) formed of six indicators with a more human aspect.

3.4.1.1. *Technical aspects (ED)*

Traceability [TRA]: the situation in which there is enough necessary and sufficient information to know (at instant or retrospectively) the nature and make-up of the data throughout its lifecycle (from its production until its destruction or recycling).

Security [SEC]: the state of situation that presents the minimum risk. It can be envisaged individually or collectively, as an objective, as a law, as a value (freedoms), as a state of what is secure and as a function or act aiming to secure the processing of digital data. Generally, security is directly linked to confidentiality, integrity, accessibility and availability surrounding the data.

Organization [ORG]: the action of structuring, delineating, matching, distributing or articulating data. This is both a social and transverse process because it requires multiple human competencies. It can be carried out according to a structural or managerial approach.

Integrity [INT]: the state of data that have all their original components without alteration in their intrinsic qualities. Above all, the data's integrity is analyzed from the point of view of its internal structure and make-up.

Accessibility [ACC]: the individual's access to data depending on some criteria and profiles. The question on accessibility is central to the risks involved in the protection, confidentiality, privacy, and security of data.

Non-selective collection [COL]: the basic concept of a big data project is to acquire a substantial volume of heterogeneous data from different sources and of different types, without prior selection, and to compare it to see if correlations emerge. More and more questions are being asked on the cleaning and hierarchical selection of data.

3.4.1.2. *Human aspects (EP)*

Dehumanization [DES]: data science can have the consequence of reducing the individual to an avatar formed of data. There is therefore a risk of depersonalizing the individual, which has a direct influence on those who handle data, who may forget that behind each digital profile there is an individual.

Culture [CUL]: the design, development and use of data is accompanied by behavior and habit in the actors responsible for activities. The culture around the management of data is built via the sensitization, training and education of the actors involved.

Confidentiality [CON]: the act of guaranteeing that data is only accessible to those authorized to access it. It is one of the keystones of data security.

Deontology [DEO]: all the ethical principles and rules (deontology code, deontology map) that manage and direct professional activity. These norms determine the minimum of duties and rights that can be demanded by professionals when carrying out their deeds and actions. This professional deontology is directly linked to the principle of individual responsibility.

Autonomy [AUT]: an individual's ability to govern themselves, according to their own rules. The individual is able to function independently, without external control. Autonomy is often linked to the individual's free and informed consent so that they can become a full actor.

Regulation [REG]: the implementation of all theoretical, material and technical means to keep each piece of data equal to a desired value, by action on a piece of regulating data, and this, despite the influence of elements disrupting the data's lifecycle. Regulation is a specific case of retroaction where the mechanism tends to decrease deviations on command.

3.4.2. *Evaluating the algorithm and its practices*

This evaluation is formed, equally, of an ethics of the algorithm, (EA) formed of eight metrics of technical origin, and an ethics of practice (EP) formed of eight parameters centered on mankind.

3.4.2.1. *Technological aspects (ED)*

Reliability [FIA]: analysis of a system's failures, in particular from a statistical point of view. An algorithm is called "reliable" when the probability of it carrying out its mission and function in given conditions over a given period corresponds to that specified in the specifications initially intended. A distinction must be made between reliability (a function of time) and quality control (static function). Reliability is established on the robustness and process of maintenance used by information systems (IS). A platform's reliability relies in part on the user's reputation, control of risk-taking and identity verification. These criteria could potentially be considered as parameters for reinforcing transparency and responsibility.

Protection [PRO]: securing an algorithm requires a study of the risks to which it is exposed, and choosing technical or organizational solutions that make it possible to guarantee its confidentiality, auditability, integrity and availability. This serves to guard against malicious actions (theft, sabotage, attacks on an algorithmic mechanism, hijackings of or deterioration of immaterial goods), accidents (partial or total destruction, or malfunctioning of the algorithmic code integrated into a platform, a connected object, an application, or an expert self-learning system), and errors (which may occur during the algorithm's operation).

Purpose [FIN]: the character of what tends towards a goal, an end in itself. One of the initial challenges of studying an algorithm is often the objective of algorithmic processing. We look at the initial objectives and results that should emanate from the use of data.

Bias [BIA]: error in the method or failure to respect the rules of protocol, which causes the algorithm to have erroneous results. The data that feed the algorithm may contain biases, notably discrimination[8], and these are consequently found in the algorithm itself. Other biases can be observed, especially linked to the fact that predictions are developed systematically from the motifs and sequences observed in a pre-existing database and therefore on data from the past. The algorithm will then tend to perpetuate the same functioning, for example by reproducing discriminatory treatment of a cohort of individuals. These biases are likely to have repercussions that may be individual or collective, intentional or unintentional. To this can be added all the biases that have, most often unconsciously, influenced developers developing their algorithms. In fact, may studies have revealed and demonstrated how online publicity could be uniquely biased by the nature and composition of names used as requests [SWE 13], and on biases on the function and behavior of algorithms, such as the newsfeed algorithm in the social network Facebook [MOR 14].

Quality [QUA]: an algorithm's internal "way of being," either good or bad. It is defined as the aptitude of a set of characteristics intrinsic to the algorithm to satisfy demands.

Explicability [EXP]: the action that implies that the algorithm's activity and operationalist are explicable. More precisely, we are capable of explaining and understanding the algorithm studied. Causal explanations that linked digital experiences to the data on which they depend can allow individuals to better grasp and understand the algorithms that surround them and influence their lives and behavior.

Transparency [TRA]: the obligation to take account of and inform the public sphere about the algorithm's content and functioning. Transparency is

8 For example, one of the sources of bias on the nature of data can be linked to an individual's age, gender and sexual preferences, which necessarily leads to a sort of exclusion by category [DIA 14].

generally based on three pillars, which are monitoring (automated or non-automated measurement), reporting (periodically considering performances), and verification. According to us, an algorithm cannot be totally transparent and at the same time in closed source (or proprietary software). Although a detailed and public documentation of the algorithm is a necessary condition for transparency, it is not sufficient. In fact, a business can write anything it wants about its algorithm in its documentation; without directly being able to analyze the source code, it seems difficult, indeed impossible, to confirm that documentation describes an algorithm correctly. The whole benefit of an audit and/or certification of algorithms is reinforced in this search for transparency. We note that the Open Data approach is often linked to transparency. This collection and processing of public data freely accessed by algorithms, inevitably gives rise to many worries and doubts on the transparency of algorithms.

Automation [AUT]: the process that enables a structure or system to have the means needed for autonomy. NICT, e.g. expert self-learning systems, AI or self-driving cars are an illustration of this automation of machines.

3.4.2.2. *Human aspects (EP)*

Automation [AUT]: the total or partial execution of a task, function, or set of technical operations by machines, acting autonomously, running without human intervention. This phenomenon has been one of the corner stones of each industrial revolution that humanity has known.

Trustworthiness [TRU]: reliability, credibility, lack of discrimination and therefore loyalty are essential components for individuals' trust in the algorithm that uses their personal data. This is achieved through a perfect knowledge and understanding of the different operations that form the processing algorithm. This notion is naturally linked to that of transparency.

Privacy [VIE]: the ability, for an individual or group of individuals, to isolate themselves to protect their interests. Privacy can sometimes be similar to forgetting, anonymity or the wish to remain removed from the public sphere. Privacy is often attached to aspects of security and to personal liberties (protection and autonomy). The degree of information privatization is influenced by the way in which the public environment might receive it, which differs according to space and time.

Accountability [ACC]: the obligation for businesses to put in place internal mechanisms and procedures making it possible to demonstrate respect for rules on data protection used by the algorithm. This is the idea of "being accountable", voluntarily or not.

Free will [LIB]: the ability an individual has to determine freely, and through themselves alone, how to act and to think. This question is asked when we study expert self-learning systems or other platforms and mechanisms for helping professionals whose job is to make decisions, to make these decisions.

Management [GES]: management of algorithmic processing makes it possible to envisage the development of architectures, practices and regulations throughout the data's lifecycle. The data are, with processing, one of the two aspects of IS identified traditionally, the two are indispensable for a coherent management of the IS. Management of algorithms is an approach to managing an algorithmic system that is structured around the nature of the algorithm and its interactions with the environment.

Governance [GOV]: the framing, direction and regulation of algorithms at a societal level. Many questions are centered on the place that algorithms take in our society and on a particular form of "algorithmic governance".

Announcement [ANN]: the divulgation of information, a result of decisions emanating from an NICT, is a decisive moment for the individual. This announcement should respect and maintain the individual's autonomy by making them share responsibility for decisions that affect them (see free and informed consent). This provision of information must be optimal, adapted to the individual, coherent in time, evolutive and shared, and above all reliable.

In conclusion, the different blocks that form this ethical evaluation provide a base on which can be structured the framework for algorithmic processing that we will describe later.

3.5. The framework surrounding algorithmic systems

In a digital context, algorithms are partially freed for mankind, but only become effective after several successive stages. Initially, their translation into computer code can be read by individuals. Then, there is a transformation of this readable code into a code that a computer or IT system can run. Then, creation of the code that can be run, resulting in an instance that acts on an infrastructure in relation to a given operational context: input, output, and interactions. Finally, a final, essential stage is carried out to avoid considerable risks. It involves maintenance of the code and infrastructure that make it possible for the algorithm to run. Thus, slow progression towards an algorithm's operational state confirms that the latter cannot be neutral and that it is inevitably impacted by mankind during its design, implementation and use. Human decisions naturally influence the technology in a masked and invisible fashion, consequently requiring regulation of their framework throughout the algorithmic stages.

In this context, governance[9] and regulation of the algorithm become a priority for attention, in particular ethical attention, for the whole of contemporary society but in particular for actors who develop and deploy NICT, that is digital researchers, designers and developers.

3.5.1. *Digital governance*

Control of ethical challenges and risks is a question of digital sovereignty and democracy. Governance of NICT can be defined as a management device, based on good practice , that enables an organization to reach its objectives of creating value, increasing the performance of IT mechanisms and customer orientation, to control financial aspects, develop solutions and competencies in IS that the organization will need in the future, and to manage risk. It can be qualified as a concept as much as a tool for policy and public actions. Governance often comes from a political judgment and sometimes becomes the victim of theories aiming to serve particular interests [RIA 09]. We are led to ask ourselves: how should fluid structures and organizations be managed optimally?

Governance should rely on an internormative approach that goes beyond the remit of merely producing laws. In fact, governance of an AI or other autonomous systems can be based on regulatory and legal models only with

9 Governance is by nature polysemic because it can be qualified as much as a concept as a public policy tool [CAP 03].

some difficulty – referring to the mechanisms managed by human operators – often offset by the latest technological innovations. A global approach to managing risks in a structure's digital strategy seems essential. It aims to identify, grasp and indeed anticipate events, actions or inactions, likely to impact implementation of the strategy on a given horizon. It should define the options for processing and ensuring that an optimal option is chosen, then implement and govern its effectiveness in meeting expectations.

In addition, it can be seen that in the majority of digital projects, the problem is not technical but very often human. Since projects are by nature transverse, it is difficult to find an overall agreement on processes of performance or control [LEB 18]. It is consequently important to accompany transverse power and manage by "catalyst".

This is why this governance relies in part on identifying a responsible team and on communicating a strong and clear "algorithmic policy" within the structures that process the big data. It is important to impose ethical rules beginning with the development and implementation of an algorithm. For example, it can be verified that, if geographical location is considered in an algorithm learning to predict defaulted payments, it will eliminate some areas. This bias can then be avoided by initially forbidding the algorithm to process location criteria.

On the other hand, the frontier between data that do not pose the problem of privacy and those that are potentially personal and/or sensitive is fairly difficult to discern. We can sense that the majority of data that form big data are, when compared and cross-checked, potentially personal. And what should be thought of data that predict behavior? These are without doubt sensitive data for which a new mode of management should be envisaged [BÉR 16].

In the light of this information, it seems vital to build regulations through real, detailed and well-founded objectives, to make good use of big data. These objectives are in part attached to a security policy on information (see Box 3.2).

Identify the main directions and priorities (proportionality).

Protect the structure's immaterial capital (security and confidentiality).

Inform and train actors at all levels.

Develop, implement and maintain a benchmark for protecting information (policy, strategy, missions and responsibilities, process, norms and codes for good practice).

Guarantee, frame and control conformity.

Respect the rights of the individuals involved: loyalty, autonomy, and transparency (right to information, free and informed consent, right to opposition, right to access, to rectification, etc.).

Define and process those weaknesses and threats given priority.

Box 3.2. *Security policy on digital data*

Beyond principles and good practice, especially on the security of NICT, vigilance on some points can avoid pitfalls and disappointments when accompanying a project depending on big data, that is:

– framing professional opportunities: identifying levers for profit from using masses of data on activities, identifying the perimeter (legal, historic, and technical) of the information available, identifying instance(s) of use;

– accompanying architecture: defining a flexible architecture adapted to instance(s) of use, validating the accessibility and usability of data sources, validating the architecture using a load test;

– testing and monitoring: regularly updating the algorithmic system used so that it remains operational in the medium term;

– considering the quality and cleaning of data as well managing the lifecycle of reference data: integrating solutions for automatic processing, qualifying and cleaning data (such as through services like Talend Data Quality).

Moreover, governance of algorithms is focused mainly on control and the role of actors in the governance. A necessary management framework of expert systems that cannot be achieved without a strong adapted governance whose aims are centered around:

– protection of data confidentiality;

– regulation of data use;

– training via massive open online courses (MOOCs) to develop a digital culture within businesses and to promote innovative systems;

– implementing the concept of data socialization[10] – very often used in the United States – of which the principle is to ensure that the right data will appear in front of the right person in the business at the right moment;

– evaluation and conformity (certification[11]/labeling, and audit[12]);

– designating a trusted third party;

– guidance on technical and legal expertise in data protection;

– regulation authority for authorization, control and sanctions linked to the use of data.

On the other hand, individual empowerment on "data capital" is becoming one of the challenges for the development of NICT. For this, it is vital that management of personal data is facilitated and free of operational, ideological or commercial bias. One response to the emergence of user empowerment may be self-data, that is the production, processing and the sharing of personal data by individuals, under their control and for their own ends. It is then a question of making ends compatible with one another, by aligning interests between the user and the business. The notion of loyalty should reconcile big data and the regulation of personal data. We can for example take the case of France and the project "MesInfos" [13] ("my data") which tests self-data that places the individual at the heart of the production and use of the data they produce.

However, the use or re-use of data via an algorithmic system stumbles too often against obstacles that prevent its optimal use: a provenance that is

10 The idea is to integrate a selective and collaborative approach to the use of digital data in business by using codes from social media platforms, based on likes and "shares". The final objective is optimizing the internal spread of good ideas on data use, whether they come from an employee or from top management. These social functions give the business a guarantee, on the one hand, on the instantaneous sharing of the latest updates, and on the other hand, on the stewardship of digital data by tagging the latter to specify who has the right to access and use them and in what way.

11 For example, this certification system will be able to analyze an algorithm depending on its trading strategy. And see if it is harmful, or indeed dangerous for the citizen and the consumer.

12 For example, algorithms should undergo a stress test to check their stability and robustness.

13 The experiment "MesInfos", Synthesis, conclusions and challenges for the future of self-data, Fondation Internet Nouvelle Génération, October 2013–June 2014.

sometimes opaque, of dubious ethics with no traceability, uncertain intellectual protection, a difficult quality to evaluate *a priori*. Hence, securing the creation of data is a factor in competitiveness, and is a duty. This does not fail to pose problems: the abundance of available information is opposed by difficulties in using it. In fact, the amount of information available is increasing considerably more quickly than mankind's ability to analyze and process it. This is the problem of the overabundance of information [OMA 02].

At the same time, society should redefine the very notion of justice and data property to guarantee mankind's freedom to act, without external influence, and with regard for responsibility. Thus, resistance to data surveillance linked to one's data does not become a phenomenon linked only to those who have something to hide: "everyone resists surveillance, as it is not a question of privacy, it is a question of control, of self-determination and autonomy" [EUB 12].

Finally, algorithmic governance can be established according to a model with four layers, like an interoperability system, to make the data's lifecycle more efficient for actors (see Box 3.3).

"Content" layer: specifications of exchanged or shared content, from a semantic, syntactical and structural point of view.

"Service" layer: specifications of usable services, their rules for use and criteria vital to corresponding transactions depending on a specific aim.

"Environment" layer: specifications for protocols for exchange and interactions in a given space.

"Relationship" layer: specifications on man-machine interfaces, human resources, organization and actors' tasks.

Box 3.3. *Model for algorithmic governance in four layers*

It is observed that consideration of security is transverse in different layers. This equally involves organization (services, processes and human resources), content (data, documents, semantics) and technology (nature and content of data, protection of IT infrastructure, etc.) Study of governance therefore extends to each aspect.

Finally, in our view, constraints and repression can only be imposed on condition that they rely on an authority coming from the code itself. It is from this perspective that we have designed our Neo-Platonist ethical systemic platform (Ψ, G, Φ) sketching the first fruits of an algorithmic governance (see section 2.8).

3.5.2. *Digital regulation*

As algorithms extend to all sectors of activity in society, the ethical challenges that result become more and more diverse. Because these algorithmic systems involve taking intrinsically subjective decisions, it appears fundamental that the underlying processes are the subject of some form of control. Regulation of algorithms is characterized by a number of problems that need to be solved. Indeed, as we explained above, algorithms are complex automated systems that have evolved beyond a response based on simplistic variables, but which on the contrary, try to respond to their ecosystem using an automatic learning mechanism or other types of complex calculation. Because of this complexity, secondary rules are sometimes introduced to modify and adjust the system's initial responses. In these conditions, several propositions are envisaged to regulate these new uses throughout the digital value chain:

– *an initial approach* would be to intervene after the event, that is by sanctioning operators in cases where there is serious harm to market equilibrium resulting from their IT power, or indeed making them responsible in case of damage resulting from use of big data and their algorithmic processing. Can regulators ask one of the digital giants such as Google or Amazon to force their algorithm to act in a certain way towards competitors? This would require regulators to have access to the algorithm, to employ people capable of understanding its properties and able to modify it effectively in the public interest. Such a regulation would also assume that it is possible to predict objectively the results of some algorithmic processes depending on different types of situation, and that evaluation resulting from this regulation is more effective that internal evaluation by those who have developed these algorithms;

– *a second approach* is directed more towards prior regulation. Many enquiries are underway on the application of some poorly adapted regulations, especially on the protection of personal data [BEN 15a]. Henceforth, other before-the-event regulation processes should be used to understand those processes that intend to impose responsibility on operators wishing to exploit big data to the maximum. In parallel, it makes sense to recognize the new obligations that are the responsibility of these operators, such as obligations for transparency and loyalty and to impose monitoring on the use of algorithms, for example through a third-party certifier, an "algorithm specialist", on the model of auditors [ZOL 15].

On the other hand, the real power to take decisions is in the hands of those who control the processing algorithm. Finally, the opening up and accessibility of data for all only plays a secondary role, real dominance lies in controlling the processing algorithms that use this data. In these conditions, it seems vital to access the source code to control decision-making, especially for a public actor. The citizen should be able to understand how such a massive processing algorithm functions when it has repercussions for privacy. In fact, misunderstanding of the way in which a public action is taken will inevitably contribute to doubt that it really seeks a general objective benefit for society. Transparency is therefore a gauge for levels of respect for the general interest. Indeed, a source code for massive operating algorithms is rarely put online in open source by businesses for intellectual property reasons. Thus, it is very unusual to be able to know precisely the rules that formalize the transformation of input data into output data. Such rules are often the choices of software protected by the designer. For example, the Predpol solution, which relies on a closed algorithm, uses only data on location and criminality and not social and economic data. Since this methodological and strategic choice is crucial, it is worth knowing and discussing.

In addition, another solution that could enable individuals to better control their personal data in terms of accessibility and purpose, could consist of using data storage spaces or sorts of "safe" for digital data. This method would integrate security processes making it possible to guarantee that only bodies to which the individual concerned has given permission can have access to data, and that these bodies can only access data for which they have been given clearance. These data storage spaces would have great benefit in the case of current, and constantly updated information such as geospatial and health data. Besides providing technological guarantees, data users would be obliged to respect rules linked to the sharing and use of data. Finally, recent developments in AI and neuron networks are leading, through their capacity for self-learning, to questions on our ability to control their functioning and so are giving our debate a new dimension.

On the other hand, the proper use of NICT is the businesses of all living forces in our society, because:

– ethical choices about the digital world are omnipresent and often arise from small decisions in individuals' daily lives;

– the digital makes it possible less to dissociate ethical decisions and action, highlighting the algorithm coder's role of as actor–decider (see "Code is Ethics");

– the relative autonomy of self-learning systems, and often their opacity, requires ethical choices to be made at the level of their technical design (see "Ethics by Design", in, for example, section 2.6) and for technological advances to be made in the subject of the fundamental science of mathematical logic [PIC 18].

Thus, regulation should become one of the keys for successful adoption of NICTs. Systems need to be framed to be accepted to be able to be developed. This regulation on algorithmic processing involves a multitude of challenges (see Box 3.4).

An algorithmic system's pertinence and coherence.

Support and purpose of collecting and exploring data.

Management and traceability of an analytical tool's lifecycle.

Understanding and adaptation of advanced analytic environments.

Conservation and recycling of digital data.

Responsibility of actors involved directly or indirectly in NICT.

Organization and roles clearly defined on the subject of data management.

(Prospective) management of required competencies on data is in place.

Rules on personal data protection and security that are considered from design (see Privacy by Design, section 2.6).

Free and informed consent for the individual concerned, regarding their personal data.

Management of accessibility of data.

Structuring of merged data coming from distinct sources destined for more exhaustive analysis.

Integration of ethics throughout the digital data development chain, of the practices carried out.

Assurance that forms of human and contradictory deliberation surround and accompany the use of algorithms, via supervision and auditing of parameters but also of all the latter's effects – both direct and indirect.

Establishing transparency and readability via better explicability and intelligibility of rules and hypotheses that underpin functions of the data going in and out, and the objectives of algorithmic processing. This operational rationale should be declared verbally or in writing – and not in the form of lines of code – to be understood by all citizens.

Considering the design of algorithmic systems, in other words, the man–machine interface, to counter-balance the "black box" effect and the informational asymmetry of algorithms, by reinforcing individuals' autonomy and reflectiveness (see data visualization).

Making data anonymous from the source code.

Ethical rules on the use and exploitation of data which are defined, applied and shared internally, and communicated to the individuals involved (final customers and/or partners).

Guarantee of the reliability and quality of data (see "data repository") approaches.

Cultural and socio-professional diversification through the involvement of individuals in developing algorithmic systems to avoid a form of ethnocentrism.

Reduction in categorization and discrimination in society.

Monitoring interconnections and interactions between different processing systems.

Strategy and policies to value data.

Compliance with mechanisms involved.

Open data policy that is implemented both internally and externally (open data/publication of data and/or algorithms).

Guaranteeing reciprocity in the sharing and accessibility of data for citizens to reduce societal inequalities (see social justice).

Continuous improvement, which is applied to the quality of data.

Development of reliable results that properly convey reality at instant and for a given situation.

Respect for citizens' expectations and requirements of digital professionals.

Box 3.4. *Challenges for the regulation of algorithmic systems*

As for the study of regulation on algorithms, it can be observed that dispositions and actions vary from one country to another and from one actor to another. When the General European Data Protection Regulation (GDPR) came into force on May 25, 2018, France was positioned in a European regulation framework. We note that France had already pioneered and been at the forefront of this subject with the application of its Digital Republic law which already emphasized the nature of platforms, the obligation for algorithms to be transparent and public, experimentation on platforms and collaborative space and public debates on the ethics of algorithms run by CNIL.

In parallel with this, we can cite two foreign initiatives that have been carried out. First, in Germany (in the *Länder*), with the financing by the ministry of Justice of two platform networks – the "market watchers" (*Marktwächter*) – which rely on consumer associations, respectively for financial services, and for the digital economy. Secondly, in the United States, with the creation of an Office of Technology Research and Investigation (OTRI) within the Federal Trade Commission (FTC) for the development of research on algorithm tests.

To this must be added the actions of digital actors such as the collective Partnership on AI which is formed of Facebook, Apple, Google, Microsoft, IBM, and Amazon, as well as six NGO representatives or universities (OpenAI, University of California Berkeley, Peterson Institute of International Economics, Advancement of Artificial Intelligence and ASU, ACLU, and the MacArthur foundation). This collective aims to develop the ethics of AI to solve major problems with purposes, transparency, security, confidentiality, equity and influence engendered by NICTs to come.

Finally, each large digital business has its own mechanisms for internal control, but good professional practices are rare and recent (e.g. the code for voluntary engagement in advertising – Digital Advertising Alliance (DAA) from 2015).

3.5.3. *Digital confidence*

Codes for rules on internal good practice in businesses, certification and labeling – more or less restrictive and above all with respect for the individual – can contribute to building solid confidence in the digital ecosystem (see Table 3.2).

Demand	Supply	Law	Finance	Organizations	Ethics
Requesting an ethical charter on algorithmic data processings for businesses, establishments or structures	Explaining what will be evaluated in ethical labeling	Sanctioning poorly developed algorithmic processing	Integrating ethical aspects in annual reports	Adopting a language and models for shared risks	Drawing out a common standard for question-naires and rating systems
Requiring proof that an independent external analysis on the ethical approach used in the processing and manipulation of personal digital data has been carried out by the business, establishment or structure	Providing a guide for good practice and specifications on data. Promoting and certifying independent bodies or independent private societies empowered to perform these independent analyses	Making recourse to independent external analyses obligatory via subscrip-tion to an ethical label or certification for processing personal digital data	Predicting a financial initiative for carrying out these studies via tax credit of the innovation tax credit kind	Placing ethics at the center of business governance, establishments, or structures	Having a trusted third party to evaluate the level of businesses' ethics

Requiring transparency on processing algorithms from businesses, establishments or structures	Sensitizing, educating, training and accompanying businesses and citizens in an ethical approach to their digital activity	Establishing a more flexible and evolutive legal framework suitable for techno-logical innovations	Creating a specific budget to anticipate digital changes in the market	Creating the post of director of digital ethics (DDE) in charge of ensuring ethics in the business', establishment's or structure's digital activities	Making processing algorithms loyal and trans-parent, with attention on respect for and the well-being of the individual

Table 3.2. *Market regulation on digital confidence*

As for demand, the citizen has the right to ask businesses to describe, transparently, the processing of their digital data. They could request for there to be an ethical charter and declaration of subscription to an ethical label within the business.

On the side of supply, it can be imaged that this should be covered and analyzed by an ethical label, especially transverse aspects on the use of digital data. This supply should develop a good recommendations guide for data with concern for culture and ethical accompaniment of the digital business. It must tend towards an Ethics by Design, starting with the design of algorithmic systems. In parallel with this, it is important to educate, inform, accompany and train businesses and citizens in an ethical culture on their digital activity. This should result in the development of initial and/or continuous training (universities and higher education establishments) on an ethical digital culture for actors and future actors in the digital world.

In terms of law, it seems fundamental to be able to sanction businesses who integrate malicious algorithms to control systemic risks affecting data. To do this, it is necessary to make subscription to an ethical label on data processing obligatory to permit a more flexible and evolutive legal framework, dependent on technical progress.

Concerning finance, all French annual reports already have several pages on an organization's social and environmental responsibility (SER). Ethical criteria should be added to this to reinforce the business's level of confidence and sustainability. In parallel to this, we urge the installation of a specific fund for technological damage to cover part, or indeed all, these systemic risks linked to NICTs within an organization. This fund could be created from a tax on liability contracts and/or on digital products and services. Finally, one could envisage freeing up specific capital to better understand and follow technical evolutions in the market.

On the subject of organizations, big data projects are by nature transverse. It would make sense to adopt a shared language between different actors in the data's lifecycle and to place ethics at the heart of the business' governance. For an approach to data valuation to be implemented and for "data culture" to be spread within the structure, it would be necessary to promote a post for a director of digital ethics (DDE) within the management committee, to:

– orchestrate an ethical approach at all levels of the business;

– to bear responsibility for the entire governance and strategy for algorithmic processing.

In addition, the ethical approach is fundamental to drawing out a shared standard to facilitate dialogue between different digital protagonists. This occurs via pluridisciplinary analysis questionnaires and the development of adapted rating scoring systems. In parallel, even though standard ratings agencies – such as Standard and Poor's, Moody's and Fitch – are beginning to consider digital risk evaluation, there is no structure specifically designed for an ethical evaluation of digital data. Hence, the need to have an independent, trusted third party for ratings to make algorithms more loyal, considerate and transparent with respect for and in the interests of the individual. In this context, we recommend the creation of a ratings agency for algorithmic ethics at a European or indeed global level, which would have a positive effect on the digital economy by giving it more meaning, loyalty to and confidence for and from citizens. This agency could rely especially on reputation as a lever for action via loyal algorithm labels, platforms, IS, or connected objects, considered by private and public investors. Such a labeling mechanism would as a consequence "on the one hand guarantee non-discrimination and loyalty in algorithms; on the other hand, also provide visibility for efforts in view of implementing a design, as well as in view of putting in place proactive and adapted information, thus in conformity with previous recommendations, and even beyond strictly legal obligations"[14].

We note that practices for third-party testing or certifying of algorithms are still embryonic [PAV 16]. We can cite a French initiative with the launch of ADEL[15] (Algorithm Data Ethics Label) which is the first ethical label with a global mission on digital data and processing algorithms. This label aims to provide a context for ethical reflection and good practice on the development, implementation and use of algorithmic systems and big data projects to better manage, control and follow them within businesses. The aim is to give the actors involved with these "megadata" the first key to understanding which would enable businesses to acquire an ethical approach to NICT, to define a moral and human framework that working in the public interest and individuals' rights to personal data on health, and to draw up a new space for the confidentiality of our data by focusing more on taking responsibility in the use of data than on individual consent when collecting it. ADEL includes a committee of multidisciplinary, independent experts formed of twenty members, such as data scientists, big data security professionals, members of institutions, mathematicians, healthcare professionals, legal experts, philosophers, sociologists, entrepreneurs and networks of e-patients and e-doctors. This committee of experts has two honorary presidents who uphold this ethical approach: Cédric Villani (Fields Medal 2010 and French representative), and Gilles Babinet (Digital Champion for France in the European Commission).

By highlighting a background based on new ethico-technical reflection, the ADEL label is providing the first elements plan for evolution contributing to substantial changes in mindsets and in working practices to result in NICT that is loyal to the "human face" as well as better use of big data and the algorithms that use it in our society. The aim is to find some coherence and meaning in a landscape in constant technological evolution to provide the best support possible for citizens. This ethical certification applied to processing algorithms and big data is the basis for a new approach, which respects all actors, and is directed towards human responsibility (see Appendix A.3).

---

14 Comment permettre à l'Homme de garder la main ? Rapport sur les enjeux éthiques des algorithmes et de l'intelligence artificielle, CNIL report, December 2017.

15 Available at: www.adel-label.com.

Finally, for some years we have seen the appearance of classification, ranking and rating systems in all sectors of activity in society. We can take the example of the University of Shanghai, which publishes an annual classification of higher education establishments and which exercises a form of control over the data published by them. The same goes for various classifications established with hospitals by the press in the medical sector. These classification mechanisms lie outside the remits of labeling or certification, and lack a contractual basis.

This approach to evaluation is instantly grasped by some businesses or administrations as they were not initially intended or prepared for it. Data previously considered as being of little importance can appear non-negligible, indeed fundamental, after being benchmarked. Thus, rating systems can be considered as the revealers of reality and enable organizations to evolve to remain in tune with their environment and their time. From this observation, a regulation can be imagined enforcing an algorithm's loyalty, or even the implementation of mechanisms making it possible to verify its operationalist and functioning, such as a ratings agency or a committee of experts on algorithms ("algorithmists") available on the request of a digital environment regulation agency.

3.5.4. *Algorithmic responsibility*

Philosophical reflections on responsibility are traditionally directed towards the human components of moral action. Generally, when it comes to designating moral responsibility, we presuppose human actors who carry out actions with immediate and well-defined consequences. Indeed, in a society that is becoming ever more digitized and in which technology is assuming a pre-eminent place, human activity cannot be understood properly without referring to technical artefacts, which has the consequence of complicating the assignment of moral responsibility [NOO 14]. Thus, the emergence of AI, of machines and robotics as new agents inevitably upsets the attribution of individual or even collective responsibility. Where the machine's results are studied by a competent person – for example, a medical diagnosis generated by Watson and supervised by a doctor – can this person be required to not follow the expert system's recommendations? This question about the attribution of responsibility is crucial. In fact, a democratic society only progresses by calling further on ethics and on the responsibility of its fellow citizens. Thus, the way in which a person reflects on existence, on the meaning of things, returning to a contingency will contribute to returning it to a reflective ethics based on values and ends. Welcoming the presence of and having openness to the interhuman or man–machine relationship makes it possible to be aware of the value of the things that surround us and opens up responsibility and interdependency.

In the context of technology, ethics deals with actions, actions that have an incomparable causal affect governing the future and which are accompanied by a provisional knowledge that, no matter its incomplete nature, also spills over onto everything that was known before. To this must be added the order of size of long-term actions and also, very often, their irreversibility. All this places responsibility at the center of ethics, including the horizons of space and time, which correspond to those of the four ethical principles seen previously. Awareness of our past actions is effectively a message to us of responsibility and hope, which prompts us to make more effort for our future.

For the philosopher Emmanuel Levinas, responsibility is the fundamental structure of subjectivity, which means that mankind is a subject. Here too, responsibility is not reciprocal: one is responsible for others, for things that are not our doing. With the arrival of autonomous machines, the boundary between objectivity and subjectivity is more and more ambiguous. This brings the initial benchmarks into question, where robots are already becoming subjects and agents in full. In fact, because robots are replacing some professions, we are right to ask ourselves if a movement from a responsibility for the machine's actions to a responsibility "of" the machine itself is necessary, which would mean ceding a value traditionally associated with mankind to robots. Some have even suggested creating a specific legal status for NICTs. One is the lawyer Alain Bensoussan [BEN 16] who is advocating and fighting to endow robots with rights and responsibilities. In these conditions, the law could extend the category of "legal identity" so as to include non-human actors such as businesses (called "moral beings"). This information makes it possible to reflect on the question of algorithmic responsibility [DEW 26] and to apply the principle of Ethics by Design within structures and organizations.

The idea may at first sight seem utterly abusive, provocative and indeed disturbing. Is this the first stage before saying that machines are equal to mankind, before they surpass mankind? In our opinion, the problem should not be approached from this angle but rather we should say that the attribution of an established legal status for autonomous devices will make it possible to provide clarification on the perimeter of each protagonist's responsibilities. The designation of a legal profile makes it possible to clarify the status of the agent or/and artificial agent and to accord them rights but also duties. Given that algorithmic responsibility is revealed in an actor's digital duties, this designation appears decisive when considering tomorrow's world! This approach would have the advantage of being able to propose a plausible alternative to another idea according to which, behind each machine, is hidden a human being, otherwise a single "legal identity" cannot be envisaged. In fact, this vision ignores the fact that complex devices are mainly the product of a multitude of authors, and that human beings and machines do not operate in separate environments. Exchanges, mediation and man–machine interfaces are so intimately linked that the very notion of a "sovereign human agent" appears utterly improbable [GER 14].

Hence, such a reflection leads us to ask about the importance for the citizen of being, from a legal point of view, the real owner of their personal data. In fact, it may be thought that such a status could lead the individual to pay more attention to the importance of the digital, because they may already consider it to be an immaterial good with a precise value. In this context, the individual becomes more of an actor and more autonomous (see empowerment) in the digital economy, and consequently more responsible in the decisions they make about their personal data.

We note that at present, from a legal point of view, European nationals are not owners of their data. Since digital data is not considered to be an immaterial good, but rather as an extension of the individual, the individual has only a subjective right[16] or a right of use. It is safe to bet that this legal situation will have to evolve in the coming years to be consistent with the digital reality of the market.

Moreover, the notion of precaution[17] is mentioned increasingly often in political and legal decisions where risk has to be evaluated in the medium

---

16 Subjective right is a legal prerogative attributed to an individual by the right to govern their relationships in society, from which they can draw advantage in their own interest. This right may differ in nature: the right to freedom of expression, rights to debts (positive rights), right to property, and so on.

17 From a literal point of view, precaution comes from the Latin word *praecavere* ("take care") which implies a danger that has just appeared. In English, this word has two major

and long term for the whole of society, in a context fraught with uncertainties. It therefore engages also with real philosophical problems, of an epistemological but also an ethical kind. Elevated to the status of "rule", precaution takes a greater dimension here. It is therefore a question of making it a general theoretical rule that guides conduct. This brief definition contains all the ingredients of the problem, such as risk, the uncertainty of knowledge, legitimacy and therefore responsibility.

Thus, precaution is an act of prudence enacted in a specific case. This means that, for antiquity, prudence was a general virtue of which precaution was effectively the consequence. Thus, prudence is the calculating and predicting part of moral virtue and therefore of wisdom. We note that Cicero's *prudentia* is the direct heritage of Aristotle's *phronesis* in his *Nicomachean Ethics*. Faced with serious and irreversible but potential risks, the absence of scientific certainty should not delay the adoption of measures that have been judged legitimate if such certainties had been acquired.

In addition, most authors place the notion of precaution in direct descent from ethical reflection, opened by the German philosopher Hans Jonas, the founder of the concept of responsibility and who inquired about the evolution of our modes of action within a technical civilization. Hans Jonas's heuristics of fear is therefore the origin of a possible awareness of the long-term effects of our present technical and scientific innovations. The author advocates for an "ethical oversight" that should accompany "technical oversight": the combination of the two creating a real "legal and jurisprudential oversight". According to him, one must "surround oneself with precautions" in the face of future risks, then insist on the need to mobilize reason and willpower so as not to slide into a sterile state of fear [JON 98]. The ethics of the future is renewed with Cicero's *prudentia* and Aristotle's *phronesis*: the long-term is the basis for the shorter-term and the common interest carries the individual benefit. It is therefore a question of combining precaution and prudence. Its general acceptance indicates a social behavior confronted with the uncertain nature of scientific and technical evolution [VAN 04].

Already, the ethics of benevolence, foresight and prevention are succeeding the ethics of precaution – and therefore of responsibility – which is

meanings which echo the Latin meaning: a person who takes precautions senses danger but also knows how to predict it.

introducing this obligation inherent for digital professionals to predict inherent risk by considering all foreseeable consequences. This leads to an obvious statement of an ethics of the future, believing that what is possible is not inherently "ethically acceptable or without risk" and the principle of evaluating our responsible acts in the long term; hence it is not only a problem for the medical profession, it is a problem for the collective as a whole to consider the nature of the responsibilities that can be attributed to actors in the digital world.

It is really from this point of view that we must consider the importance of the principle of precaution from the design of NICTs, which would eventually have fewer unduly rigid and fixed legal implications than a flexible and evolutive ethical framework. In fact, faced with rapid technological developments, we can legitimately be worried about the level of reactivity or indeed inertia in legal rules in terms of their ability to adapt quickly and to make algorithmic processing subject to regulation and governance mechanisms in force. This is why we suggest an approach centered on an evolutive digital ethics, that is Ethics by Design or Responsibility by Design.

More significantly still in terms of legal responsibility, a system's completely automated decision-making process also depends on the device's ability to educate itself: that is the possibility for the algorithms to learn and to adjust the sequences they code, independently of any human control [GER 14]. It is in these conditions that our systemic ethical learning platform (Ψ, G, Φ) takes it full meaning to make the autonomous machines that will constantly inject new information into its operating process more ethical and so more responsible. This ethically acceptable decision-making necessarily occurs through feedback loops directly linked to our AI (Ψ, G, Φ).

Finally, the answers to questions arising from the digital do not rely only on the adoption of restrictive legal frameworks. It would therefore be essential to integrate an instrument, on the declaratory mode including all ethical–legal aspects, to anticipate the challenges to come surrounding NICT. In this governance to be built, the place of public and private institutions – as trusted third parties – will have to be classified.

Ultimately, the digital revolution imposes a framework via ethical and moral rules that are clear and coherent in relation to all the common legal rules with which they interact, to give confidence and meaning that citizens expect of these NICTs. These ethical specifications cannot be applied without an individual given specific responsibility for this. It is therefore the role of the Chief of Digital Ethics (CDE) – to watch over the ethical impacts of algorithms, that we will describe in the following chapter.

3.6. Ethical management and direction framing algorithmic systems

One of the possible paths to avoid the risk of dehumanizing the digitized society would be to review the notion of an "individual" by emphasizing its relational aspect and ability to bring meaning to our existence. Such an approach could lead, within managerial practices, to a renewal of the uses and means according to which human relationships are formed in the area of work. This method would make it possible to experiment with or structure, not an ethics of management, but ethical management, that is a way of working and of managing individuals both with respect for their individuality and with consideration for their shortcomings.

Already, businesses are increasingly interested in the ethical problems and dilemmas that management involves. They formulate constraints that emanate from society as well as autonomous commitments that they impose daily. Reflections on the ethics of management and direction have developed considerably during the last ten years. As we mentioned previously, an organization's ethics covers a set of principles, associated values and visions that govern the line of directing individuals. Research on identity is the very motor and essence of an adapted management aiming to bring importance to individuals with the goal of getting them to work together. The aim is therefore to give some identity to the business in terms of social and moral values. To do this, it is vital to instill an internal digital culture that is structured via the organization's continuous learning mechanism and which forms in line with its reactions, faced with new situations.

A business' digital culture can be described according to seven dimensions[18] that aid the structure to be more effective in a digital ecosystem, that is:

---

18 These seven dimensions are inspired by the document published by CIGREF which is titled "Cadre de référence CIGREF sur la culture numérique" (The CIGREF reference framework on digital culture), 2014.

– *reliability*: makes it possible to guarantee continuity of activities and the confidence of customers, collaborators and other stakeholders;

– *openness*: makes it necessary to manage and value different types of information available both inside and outside the business;

– *knowledge*: requires the ability to produce value by using available information;

– *agility*: requires the ability to transform, permanently, and to experiment, which involves taking the initiative and accepting the right to make mistakes;

– *confidence*: makes it necessary to meet commitments, based on authenticity and exemplary performance inside and outside the structure;

– *interdependence*: involves a more transverse and co-operative internal functioning;

– *responsibility*: requires risks and challenges relating to the digital to be considered and understood within the business.

Hence, we can develop each of these dimensions via three cultural practices and characteristics. Thus, each dimension is revealed within the reality of an organization via associated values, challenges and risks, behaviors, practices, and needs (see Table 3.3).

Dimensions	Cultural practices and characteristics
Reliability	Security/protection Continuity/monitoring Risk management
Openness	Connectivity/networks Fluidity Accessibility of data
Knowledge	Sharing/exchange Transversality Value creation
Agility	Innovation Flexibility Anticipation

Confidence	Coherence/meaning Ethics Cohesion of common human values
Interdependence	Cooperation Partnership Alliance
Responsibility	Collective and societal responsibility Solidarity Well-foundedness

Table 3.3. *Dimensions forming a digital culture in a business*

Hence, culture represents the structure's mode of operating, it is part of tradition and is the way in which things are achieved. IT does not make it possible to explain why only an ethical approach to the subject makes it possible to respond to this concern. By nature, a business' ethical identity only has meaning through the human values, norms and culture it delivers. Ethics is perceived as an engine for quality: only structures and organizations that have been able to identify then clarify their morals can respond to environmental requirements.

Already, an ethical approach has become a new dimension for business policies, complementing strategy. It creates a common language, culture, and set of values to develop membership of the establishment. Ethical reflection is therefore a federative discourse that incites each actor to direct and adapt their professional behavior. It makes it possible to respond to its environment's different protagonists who run the risk of calling the structure's very identity into question. It is also an element of stability aiming to meet the perpetual and constant changes affect the life of organizations. The aim is to make behavior predictable within the organization.

To do this, it seems essential to revisit the notion of the "individual" to bring meaning to work and to turn managers into people who create meaning, rather than the wielders of power who give more thought to economic efficiency than to respect for the individual. It is in these conditions that questions on the nature of management can be supplied. Should this meaning be imposed at the risk of turning the individual into an instrument? Should it be co-constructed and shared between the manager and the employee? Indeed, if we make the hypothesis that efficiency at work tends to increase when personnel are motivated, in this case, it is difficult to say that this could come from an external injunction that would escape whoever carried it out. Thus, ethical management inevitably happens via listening and teaching to give meaning to actions to be taken.

In addition, internal communication makes it possible to accompany this management. In fact, the overlap between communication and management results from the daily enactment of relationships organized at different hierarchical levels between different teams at work. The role of management is to reach an equilibrium between all the different groups of individuals who play a part in the business, to retain their participation. Relationships should be managed while respecting the other party and by seeking the collective well-being of all the parties concerned. Recourse to ethics therefore becomes a challenge for survival. In this context, ethical formalization indicates the way in which stakeholders' rights are respected.

In these conditions, the success of change happens through the involvement of the same people who must carry it out: the involvement of management can only result in their association with "managerial transformation" directly linked to the emergence of NICT. For this, the notions of meaning, rules stakes, anticipation, engagement and responsibility must be considered from a more global view of ethics. In an institution whose purpose is to listen to others, "to take care", to pay attention to management, this means fully building its future. In this context, the manager is placed at the heart of a system of perpetual interaction. They participate fully in building a coherent system of exchanges. Their communication actions both start communication with others and are induced to start by them. The articulation of information and knowledge is a strategic end for managers. Thus, these characteristics have an impact on organizations' structures.

In addition, management of digital processes is an essential challenge for the business' actors. The aims are multiple and can tackle:

– the productivity of internal performance;

– the efficiency and quality of digital tools such as expert systems for aiding medical decisions with an effective interpretation of tests, a systematized use of earlier tests and a reduction in time taken for tests and reports;

– faster management and accessibility of big data;

– co-operative work reinforced between actors, which facilitates organization within the structure.

To effectively reach these objectives, a real reconfiguration must be made of processes linked to the digital in the organization and direction of "professional" actions. The real object of direction is to reach the performance objectives that the structure has fixed from the strategy in place. This management makes it possible to plan, enact and follow these achievements. It can be variable, though it nevertheless meets three ends:

– ensuring the quality of the business' services;

– meetings the structure's needs and conforming to regulatory requirements;

– optimizing its organizational and economic effectiveness.

These three aims are multidisciplinary and transverse. They involve administration, the operational and "professional" team and IT services. It is therefore vital to identify and instill IS tools for direction and management to enable protagonists at each level of decision-making to obtain complete, reliable and easily accessible data. The aim is to have a transverse and interoperable IS to be able analyze existing deviations from initial objectives. This differential is measured especially with the aid of performance indicators. This search for "efficiency" makes it possible appreciate, afterwards, the effects of the strategy in place. This cannot be achieved without an innovative approach in managerial terms with the aim of acquiring a change in management, motivating action, and linked to the IS. It may be noted that the materialization and evolution of methods and means of management are more often linked to strategic, management or organizational changes rather than to technology and computerization. Such management is essential to lead to better management of digital data. This direction of data makes it possible to explain it better (use, discovery of causes and effects, targeted exploration, visualization and reporting), monitor it better (profiling, calculating quality dimensions, detecting anomalies, definition of key performance indicators (KPI), monitor of deviations), improve it (enrichment, consolidation, use of sources and external databases), and to clean it (unification, formatting, standardization, duplication, statistical corrections, repair) [BOU 17].

This is why businesses or administrations need to define well-identified and pre-established objectives and strategies to break them down to all levels in their organization. We will speak here of the notion of "pertinence" to convey the fact that these criteria should be adapted to the nature of the problem. In this context, the IS becomes the "conductor" and the preferred tool for this management policy. Such a mechanism cannot be achieved without solid resources in terms of processes, materials or competencies.

Moreover, the commissioning of management accompanying NICTs means acting on four precise and complementary domains:

– the evolution of the management type by instilling an approach to change with the aim of mastering all mechanisms;

– the improvement and/or development of the methodology according to different levels of management and use of the IS for strategy, operations or performance;

– the evolution of computer methods with the reliability, robustness and completeness of information. On the other hand, the adjustment of the IS to enable the development of business intelligence, completing the development of production intelligence;

– changes in the organization by providing greater transversality and mastering the human resources used by adjusting competencies and the organigram.

Such an approach to the direction of technological innovations can only materialize with rigorous project management in which these four domains of action should be carried out jointly and simultaneously. Already, businesses should be developing and structuring a real management strategy. It is becoming necessary for them to be able to explain their priorities and thus precisely identify the actions that must be developed, produced or reduced or indeed removed. Management is only the support for turning the strategy into action.

In fact, management of a project should involve a shared and federative dynamic, a real multidisciplinary exchange. In this context of direction, digital mechanisms are the vector by which information circulates and is spread at all levels of the organization. Generally, it can be observed that interconnections between different sectors of activity are often victim to many dysfunctions. Reducing their number generally leads to an improvement in the fluidity of working mechanisms, transmission, access to information and the consumption of resources, while still respecting social and moral obligations such as confidentiality or autonomy. Thus, the IS should also be studied in the context of each structure that has its own history, its own strategy, its own axes of progress. The aim is to be able to monitor the management and objectives that the structure has defined. The entire benefit of ethical management lies in the fact that it brings meaning and purpose to the organization implemented (see Table 3.4).

Types of measures	Questions
Vision	What does the organization wish to become?
Mission	What is the reason for the structure's existence?
Values	What are the principles for conduct and for decisions in the business?
Medium-term strategic axes	What are the medium-term strategic axes and their coherence?
Dominant annual strategies	What are the strategic priorities that should be present in everyone's minds
Overall objectives	Do the business' aims fit the digital environment and the market?
Objectives by process	What are the annual performance and digital process progress objectives?
Objectives by team	What are the shared objectives and targets piloted at the first leadership level?
Individual objectives	What are the individual objectives or contribution of each person to their team's objectives

Table 3.4. *Strategic deployment of the digital*

Finally, the digital framework is by nature polymorphous, heterogeneous and multidisciplinary. Consequently, those responsible for digital governance within a structure should have these characteristics. This is a necessity if we wish to create a form of management with transverse range on the principles and norms that control the use of the digital. Refocusing on the ethics of NICT has the virtue of saving them from themselves and their offshoots to lead to transparency, confidence, sincerity and acceptability.

To do this, businesses are led to create and integrate a new function within their organigram, the Chief Digital Ethics (CDE). Their role is multifaceted is (see Box 3.5).

Be a guarantor for the purpose and well-foundedness of their business' digital mechanisms.

Guarantee the sincerity of digital mechanisms integrated into the establishment.

Identify and understand the ethical challenges and risks inherent in their structure's digitization.

Guarantee the protection of their establishment against inappropriate use of the digital applications and supports it is likely to provide.

List and understand optional norms and their rules on posting to which the business may be exposed and which are not judged to be a priority, indeed which are sometimes neglected by technical services.

Ensure that data, particularly quantitative data, affecting their business or administration are justified with regard, on the one hand, to the norms that govern their production, and on the other hand, the rules that govern their diffusion [ADA 17].

Have a precise understanding of the digital data development via an inventory of digital circuits (quality, documentation and use) by relying on the competencies of the professional teams around them.

Manage conditions for the communication and diffusion of digital usages and defend the associated information that is transmitted publically.

Structure and frame the strategy and policy for digital innovation within the business.

Verify and justify the integrity of the processes and elements that form NICT conform to protocols defined outside its structure and which are imposed on it.

Respect standards for conformity, regulatory, methodological and deontological requirements fixed by public and or professional powers.

Plan and direct data circuits and flows impacting the organization's reputation and image in an operational way.

Monitor, identify and correct points of dysfunction and deviations from the norms in force and professional diligence (from the "professional" and communication angle).

Take care that the use of NICTs always fits with the opinions of society at that time (see space–time parameters).

Forestall the risks of theft, misuse and appropriation of digital data by the wrong stakeholders.

Anticipate and prepare the evolution, internally, of regulation, law and of legal uses in the digital domain.

Acquire and understand the different operational roles that form their business' digital processes to properly identify the mechanisms, good practices, behavioral trends and distinctions between different actors.

Evaluate the repercussions, consequences and risks of administrative, judicial and extrajudicial sanctions.

Co-ordinate the increasing autonomy of the daily organization of work with the progressive unification of data management.

Box 3.5. *Missions for the Chief of Digital Ethics (CDE)*

The DDE's transverse functions reflect the complexity and variability of the digital environment in which the business is situated. This function is still emerging and will have to develop very quickly. For a long time, large structures and administrations have integrated ethical or deontological references into their organization but their perimeter for intervention was quite limited for the digital, due to the presence of a management for information systems. Sometimes indeed, since there is no ethicist or deontologist, this mission is carried out by individuals in charge of other, related actions.

Moreover, although their field of action is very different, the CDE's mission, especially in the internal surveillance of production and the transmission of digital data, is similar in shape to that of an IT and freedoms advisor (CIL). However, unlike a CIL, it seems hard to envisage that the CDE is a moral being or an actor external to the structure. In fact, their functions require a profound and precise knowledge of the organization and processes and a personal authority that only a permanent presence can guarantee. It is preferable for the CDE to be linked to the business' general management to accompany, develop and manage the strategy and policy for digitizing the structure. Because of their transverse functions, they should not intervene hierarchically in digital processes.

Finally, this function should not be reduced to a simple coordination of operational services involved in the organization's digital circuit. Its added value would be reduced by this and its presence would become unstable, fluctuating with trends in the business' governance and managerial policy. This leads us to ask about the positioning of this role, especially within the business' social and ethical responsibility (SER). What are the good practices to be carried out? What are the skills, experience, and training that a CDE should have?

Conclusion

Technical progress has been the driver of multiple changes in the ways we interact, acquire knowledge, work and design the world. By opening the way for new possibilities, technical innovations are structuring the evolution of our behavior, while generating new mores, habits, usages and dependencies. The digital revolution that the society is undergoing therefore supposes the acquisition of new competencies. Technological advances and digital data processing are a real asset but also present ethical risks. One of the challenges in improving an algorithm lies in machine learning technologies that enable the machine to learn from its errors. It is vital for algorithm designers to be aware of the value judgements that impact their design. The way in which the algorithm is formed is underpinned by values and imagined by people. For this, it is essential to list the different families of algorithms according to their purpose, to better understand them, challenge them and adjust them to improve them. In fact, big data run the risk of accentuating discrimination and the categorization and individualization of society. In the medium term, they could endanger one of the pillars of human dignity, in this case its responsibility and free will.

Data will be linked to us more and more, as a second skin, to better classify and discriminate between us with the abuses associated with this. This is why we must not underestimate the risk of a “digital fracture” illustrated by several lines of separation (social, industrial, economic, indeed spatio-temporal) and covering multiple realities.

In this light, it makes sense to rethink our way of tackling digital life and the uses of our NICT. Protecting privacy means that users of the tools of this digital revolution become more responsible for their acts and deeds. The individual should be able to understand their digital environment to master its applications. If a detailed ethical framework is not put in place, then the ethical glass ceiling will be broken and we will not be able to change anything. The survival of the human race – as we now know it – will be guided only by the rationalization of intelligent autonomous systems that are part of our environment.

In these conditions, it is necessary to provide a framework and an ethical accompaniment that articulate human processes and technologies. Our digital ethics is therefore an adequate mode of regulation for man-machine behaviors based on respect for moral values that are judged indispensable. Ethical thought is about decisive societal choices that affect all citizens. It cannot be structured independently of consideration of a collective, transverse and pluralist dimension. It should not be considered as a constraint on the digital economy but rather as a source of opportunities and expansion. Algorithms should be ethical from their development to their use, because responsibility belongs both to designers and owners. This acquisition of responsibility also occurs via quite particular attention on the design of the algorithmic mechanism playing a central role in the man-machine interface. Thus, it is vital to give a moral personality to these NICT by means of an algorithmic ethical conscience. In our opinion, this notion of responsibility is the cornerstone of the framework around algorithms: it is Responsibility by Design or Ethics by Design!

The majority of digital choices in daily life are generated at the level of the individual, the level where the ethics of the digital belong. This is why education on this new digital responsibility is needed. For this, the requirement for responsibility must be imposed socially on citizens by abandoning too normative an approach for a more ethical one. Consequently, campaigns for sensitization and education will have to change to ensure education and training for new generations to understand these new technological innovations and the challenges of the types of decision associated, but also the use and securing of their personal data. Digital lessons will identify the strengths and weaknesses of each student and will discern their preferences to move towards better training and an adapted and better targeted orientation. Hence, our educational system should as such make the transmission of expertise and knowledge its priority which will enable each individual to find their place in society, as much as a future worker as an active citizen.

Used ethically, NICT could mark important, indeed primordial progress for humanity. For this, the audit of algorithmic processing via instances of labeling, certification and regulation seem indispensable.

Today, we are observing a tissue of complex interactions between people and their environments at all levels. We run the risk of descending into the oversimplification and false ease of an obsolete Lamarckism, so present in our culture. Our "digital evolutionist" makes it possible to better understand digital innovations, their origins and their histories in different parts of the world but it also makes it possible to suggest new understandings of the relationships between mankind and its technical progress, since science is advancing, creating new paradigms, making already-known facts more heuristic and above all, suggesting new paths for research for digital innovation. Antoine de Saint-Exupéry [DES 39] stated that "man's most beautiful possession is the job of uniting men". From this observation, the digital must be considered as a fantastic opportunity for humanity to create a greater global link between us.

Trouble, indeed fear, might arise from the prospect of an AI that might have its own projects developing new algorithms without human intervention by 2030–2040[1]. According to Google's directors, from the 2030s, the problem of algorithms may move into our brains, due to future intracerebral implants and nano-implants that will be directly connected to it. Our brain will probably be more intelligent with better access to knowledge, but will it still be governed by our free will? Such a situation reinforces a little more the idea of the loyalty of algorithms and the repercussions their popularization may have. In these conditions, it is essential to properly understand the entirety of algorithmic processing (formed of a triptych: data, algorithm and practices), and guarantee that it will also be as transparent as possible and to understand what it is capable of doing and not doing, with respect for the individual and the individual's dignity. Hence, collaborative and transverse work should be started between the world of scientific research, business, government institutions, education and the whole of civil society to ensure that digital giants do not become the sole guarantors of ethical rules that will affect tomorrow's world: "Code is Ethics"!

---

1 According to the celebrated physicist, Stephen Hawking and the principal founder of Microsoft, Bill Gates.

As code is a source of value for businesses and institutions, this value should be preserved by putting in place practices for developing quality. To improve the code's quality, it is necessary to observe and intervene in the system in its entirety, especially by integrating ethical rules (via our systemic platform for ethical learning (Ψ, G, Φ)) into it and creating a context that promotes the improvement of practices by giving them back their meaning and a well-founded: "Ethics is Code"! In fact, in our view, the future of humanity really lies in its capacity to retain on the one hand, a human thinking and conscience, and on the other hand, interhuman communication [COL 16]. This will probably happen via a progressive digitization of all information and reflection indeed in the medium term, of the human conscience.

On the other hand, governance of digital data belongs to a governance for a near future that urges the redefinition of today's ethical dimensions and aspects. Thus, it is therefore the whole of our society that should define an ethics of the digital centered on Responsibility by Design. To do this, scientific institutions and experts should define and apply shared moral values, citizens should be aware of new digital challenges, digital professionals should be directed in their work closer to action and researchers in logical science (fundamental mathematics and theoretical computing) should carry out this coding of the hierarchical complexity of ethical principles and human values from a neuron-network type system with a dynamic logic, in other words, an AI with an ethical purpose. This should lead to the design of a universal AI that would audit and would make all IT programs follow predefined ethical rules written in their source code. It can be imagined that this global AI could be managed and directed by an institution such as the UN.

As François Rabelais – the French Renaissance Humanist writer – said so well "algorithms without conscience are merely the foreshadowed ruin of our society". This is why ethics applied to NICT fully concern mankind's future, our freedom of determination, judgment and free will, as much individual as collective.

Finally, humanity has always been subject to industrial revolutions that have socio-cultural and economic repercussions and consequences on the global population. These cyclical ruptures are part of an uneducable global Darwinian evolution. Concerns in the immediate future may focus on discoveries in quantum physics. To understand, prepare for and accompany them as well as possible, our society will have to develop an adapted human and moral framework by creating a new schema of thought, reflection, responsibility and a new way of designing value and work. Hence new meaning must be brought to data, algorithms and their use, to create a real value added for the NICT that is invading our society. This necessarily happens through the planning, construction and development of a quantum ethics that we will describe in more detail in a further book on the subject. Since, in our view, writing and thinking about the future of an algorithmic, then a quantum ethics, is to make it possible!

Appendix

A.1. Criteria for evaluating the quality of a source code

Evaluation	Definition	Interest
Cyclomatic complexity	Measure of the number of possible linear paths in a function	Substantial
Code coverage	Proportion of the source code that is covered by tests (unitary, functional, and validation tests), that are generally automated	Substantial
Afferent coupling	Number of references to the class measured	Substantial
Efferent coupling	Measure of the number of types that the class "knows"	Substantial
Instability	Level of resistance to change	Substantial
Abstraction	Level of abstraction in relation to other classes present in the code	Substantial
Distance from the main sequence	The module's balance between abstraction and instability	Substantial
Lack of cohesion of methods (LCOM)	A class's level of cohesion	Substantial
Relational cohesion	Average number of internal relationships in a module	Substantial
Specialization index	A class's degree specialization	Substantial
Number of rules on violating the coding	Alerts on violations affecting the code	Substantial
Maintainability	Capacity for components or applications to be maintained, coherently and at least cost, in operating condition	Substantial

Scalability	The code or software's potential to change code	Substantial
Reliability	Number of failures encountered in a given time span	Substantial
Density of commentary	Ratio between the number of lines of code (SLOC) and the number of commentaries (CLOC)	Average
Performance	Capacity to create a result, an achievement and a finalization of the code or software	Average
Pertinence	A code or software's logic, appropriate aspect and accuracy	Average
Style and readability	Structuring the text component of lines of code: each paragraph is physically distinct and punctuation correctly used	Average
Technical documentation	Documents that should enable the developer to configure their working environment to be able to begin work on the code	Average
Portability	Capacity of a software to run on different systems	Average
Security	State where dangers and conditions that can trigger physical or material damage are controlled so as to preserve the code or software	Average
Number of bugs	Number of problems disrupting normal use of the software	Average
Source lines of code (SLOC)	Measure of the size of part or whole of a software based on the number of lines of code	Weak
Size of the instance	Number of bytes of memory used by an instantiated object	Weak
Number of variables	Number of variables declared in the body of a method	Weak
Number of parameters	Number of parameters in a method	Weak
Number of overloads	Number of methods with the same name	Weak

Table A.1. *Evaluation metrics on the quality of a source code*

A.2. CERNA's recommendations on machine learning

1) Designers and teachers of learning systems take care of the quality of learning data and of the conditions it is collected in.

2) Teachers should guarantee that the data represent a mirror of cultural diversity.

3) Teachers should take care that the variables by which the data are regulated are not discriminatory (age, sex, race, etc.) while still respecting the principle of data confidentiality.

4) The designer of an automatic learning system should provide mechanisms for system traceability.

5) The machine should not introduce characterization bias and mislead the user on the state of the system.

6) The designer should maintain a level of vigilance in communication on a learning system's capabilities so as not to leave any room for misinterpretation, "specters" or irrational fears.

7) The designer should consider the explicability and transparency of their learning system's actions, while still maintaining a sufficient level of performance.

8) While still guaranteeing better explicability of the system, the designer should describe the limitations of the system's explanation heuristics, especially while avoiding the creation of bias.

9) A learning system's designer brings their own contribution to the development of norms and protocols for evaluating the learning machine.

10) The designer should guarantee the place of humanity in decisions assisted by learning machines, in particular to avoid the creation of bias or the establishment of humanity's dependency on machines' decisions.

11) Memorization of traces of personal data used in the learning process will occur by obtaining the consent of the user and in agreement with current legislation on the protection of personal data.

12) The system's designer should include mechanisms for automatic or supervised control.

13) The designer should provide a declaration of intentions for using an IT system "sincerely, loyally and completely" over the course of its learning.

14) The creation of a national research network called "Federal Initiative for Digital Research, Ethics and Society" would make it possible to draw out a French (or other nations) position on questions on the societal and ethical impact of digital sciences and technologies.

15) The creation of operational ethics committees for establishments in digital science and technology is advised.

16) Establishments are also encouraged to launch initiatives on legal aspects of the uses of digital innovations, through working groups and research projects with any other involved actors.

17) Awareness-raising actions and researcher support from establishments should be put in place.

A.3. The ADEL's objectives and contributions

A.3.1. *Providing an ethical framework for automated information systems (IS) to guarantee meaning, confidence and security for society*

The ADEL (Algorithm Data Ethics Label) label leads businesses that process digital data to ask themselves questions about human values and ethical principles involved in the design and use of automated information systems. One of the major questions is knowing how technical modernization of the use of digitized information and big data can be accompanied by ethical awareness for drawing an IS with a "human face". What are the repercussions for an IS on actors' mentalities and social values, from a structural, technological, strategic, methodological, organizational, relational and cultural point of view?

A.3.2. *Accompanying the evolution of IS and associated processing on an ethical level*

We could then replace this ethical reflection from the perspective of an evolution in IS, since currently both recent technological developments and new medical communication tools are linked to big data, as well as new organizations that are being put in place. It is questions on this subject that we are relying on to develop an intellectual approach to questioning, turned towards an ethics of algorithmic treatment of big data. The aim of this tool is to provide not only the appearance of phenomena but to go beyond this to perceive their real meaning.

A.3.3. *Provide ethical evaluation tools (ratings) to serve businesses*

Hence, ADEL's tool makes it possible to provide an ethical reflection and evaluation of an IS, processing algorithms and big data existing within a structure so as to obtain a cartography and a guide to good practice on the situation of the latter. This evaluative approach is illustrated by a system of scoring and ratings for different domains involved throughout the digital data's lifecycle. This is one of the main challenges of such an approach.

A.3.4. *Evolving a universal ethical requirement into a practical and concrete ethics*

Thus, in the domain of health, we will cover, from an ethical angle in particular, the acquisition, sharing, transmission, storage, and processing of medical big data for managing patient support and diagnosis. One of the major challenges is to establish a framework for analysis starting from a universal, abstract and rational ethical requirement to lead to a practical and concrete ethics hinging on the labelled business' daily life on the ground to guarantee its customers total confidence in how their personal data is processed.

A.3.5. *Providing ethical recommendations and specifications*

The objective is not to publish directives on the achievement, implementation and use of big data via NICT but to draw out their challenges and provide recommendations and a roadmap for ethical principles. This enhancement of an IS's ethical dimension thus forces us to work on two levels simultaneously, that of the individual, and of the system itself, with the aim of ensuring the minimum coherence required. This is why transforming an IS into an ethical system will depend on the nature of the ethical norms that surround that "system". This ethical framework will help you to detect directions dictated by short-term pragmatism, by power-seeking, by solely economic benefits, and so on. The objective is to know whether the objectives and means used meet the same ethical requirements on the subject? What methods for spreading big data are favored? Does the regulation of digital healthcare data necessarily happen with ethical concerns in mind?

A.3.6. *Towards an algorithmic ethics*

This ADEL labeling enters into an approach that is disruptive to auditing, and which aims to evolve in accordance with constant technological advances. This leads to the development of recommendations for achievement, use, methodology and means to be implemented to ensure the efficient running of your automated information system.

The ADEL objective is therefore to give actors affected by the use of big data the first keys to understanding, which will enable readers to acquire an ethical approach to NICT, to define a moral and human framework that manages the general interest and individual rights to health data of a personal nature, and to draw up a new space for confidence and for the confidentiality of our data, by focusing more on responsibility in the use of data than on individual consent, that is only read and given at the point of collecting this data.

List of Abbreviations

A

A to B: Administration to Business

ACLU: American Civil Liberties Union

ADEL: Algorithm Data Ethics Label

AI: Artificial Intelligence

ARPANET: Advanced Research Projects Agency Network

ASU: Arizona State University

B

B to B: Business to Business

BATX: Baidu, Alibaba, Tencent, Xiaomi

C

CB: Citizen-Band

CDE: Chief of Digital Ethics

CEEEN: *Confiance et évaluation éthique de l'économie numérique* (Ethical confidence and evaluation in the digital economy)

CERNA: Commission for reflection on the ethics of research in digital sciences and technologies at Allistene

CIGREF: *Club informatique des grandes entreprises françaises* (IT club for large French businesses)

CIL/IFC: *Conseiller informatique et libertés* (IT and freedoms correspondent)

CLOC: Count Lines of Code

CNIL: *Commission nationale de l'informatique et des libertés* (French National Commission for IT and Freedoms)

COMEX: Executive committee

CRM: Customer Relationship Management

CSA: *Conseil supérieur de l'audiovisuel* (French Higher Audiovisual Council)

D

DAA: Digital Advertising Alliance

DAO: Decentralized Autonomous Organizations

DCO: Decentralized Collaborative Organizations

DDE: Director of Digital Ethics

DI: Digital Infosphere

DNA: Deoxyribonucleic Acid

DVD: Digital Versatile Disc

E

EA: Ethics of Algorithms

ED: Ethics of Data

EP: Ethics of Practices

ERP: Enterprise Resource Planning

G

GAFA: Google, Apple, Facebook, Amazon

GAFAM: Google, Apple, Facebook, Amazon, Microsoft

GAFAMITIS: Google, Apple, Facebook, Amazon, Microsoft, IBM, Twitter, Intel, Salesforce

GDP: Gross Domestic Product

GDPR: General Data Protection Regulation

GPS: Global Positioning System

H

HR: Human Resources

HSS: Human and Social Sciences

HTML: HyperText Markup Language

HTTP: HyperText Transfer Protocol

I

IAEA: International Atomic Energy Agency

ICT: Information and Communication Technology

IIoT: Industrial Internet of Things

IMEI: International Mobile Equipment Identity

IoT: Internet of Things

IS: Information System

ISO: International Organization for Standardization

K

KPI: Key Performance Indicator

L

LCOM: Lack of Cohesion of Methods

M

MIT: Massachusetts Institute of Technology

MOOC: Massive Open Online Course

N

NATU: Netflix, Airbnb, Tesla, Uber

NBIC: Nanotechnologies, biotechnologies, IT and cognitive sciences

NEAC: National Ethics Advisory Committee

NGO: Non-government organization

NPT: Treaty on the non-proliferation of nuclear weapons

NICT: New Information and Communications Technology

O

OTRI: Office of Technology Research and Investigation

P

PAAS: Platform as a Service

PLC: Programmable logic controller

R

R&D: Research and development

RFID: Radio Frequency Identification

RSA: Rivest, Shamir, Adleman

S

SCM: Supply Chain Management

SIM: Subscriber Identity Module

SLOC: Source Lines of Code

T

TCP/IP: Transmission Control Protocol/Internet Protocol

U

UID: Unique Identifier

UN: United Nations

URL: Uniform Resource Locator

UV: Ultraviolet

W

WWW: World Wide Web

References

[ADA 17] ADARY A., *Big ou Bug Data? Manuel à l'usage des datadéontologues*, Éditions du Palio, Paris, 2017.

[ALE 16] ALEXANDRE L., La santé face au tsunami NBIC et aux plateformistes, Study report, Digital New Deal Foundation, 2016.

[ALE 17] ALEXANDRE L., *La guerre des intelligences*, Éditions JC Lattès, Paris, 2017.

[ALI 17] ALIZART M., *Informatique céleste*, PUF, Paris, 2017.

[ATO 06] ATOUI H., "Conception de systèmes intelligents pour la télémédecine citoyenne", *The Informatique INSA,* Lyon, 2006.

[AZI 42] AZIMOV I., "Runaround", *Astounding Science-Fiction*, vol. 29, no. 1, p. 94, 1942.

[AZI 50] AZIMOV I., *I, Robot*, Gnome Press, New York, 1950.

[AZI 85] AZIMOV I., *Robots and Empire*, Doubleday, New York, 1985.

[BAD 15] BADILLO P.-Y., PÉLISSIER N., "Usages et usagers de l'information numérique", *Revue française des sciences de l'information et de la communication*, no. 6, p. 4, 2015.

[BAL 18] BALAGUE C., De l'éthique des algorithmes et de l'intelligence artificielle, vade-mecum sur la gouvernance des traitements de données numériques, White paper, ADEL, 2018.

[BAR 15] BARD A., SÖDERQVIST J., *Les Netocrates II*, Éditions Léo Scheer, Paris, 2015.

[BEA 01] BEAUCHAMP T.L., CHILDRESS J., *Principles of Biomedical Ethics*, Oxford University Press, Oxford, 2001.

[BEN 14] BENSABAT P., GAULTIER D., HOARAU M. *et al.*, Du Big Data au Big Business. Livre 1 : Phénomène de mode ou facteur de performance ?, White paper, Business & Décision, 2014.

[BEN 15a] BENSAMOUN A., ZOLYNSKI C., "Cloud Computing et Big Data : quel encadrement pour ces nouveaux usages ?", *Revue Réseaux*, vol. 1, no. 189, 2015.

[BEN 15b] BENSOUSSAN A., "Droit des robots : science-fiction ou anticipation?", *Recueil Dalloz*, no. 28, July 2015.

[BEN 16] BENSOUSSAN A., "Pour une éthique des algorithmes et des robots", *DSIH*, no. 19, p. 22, 2016.

[BÉR 14] BÉRANGER J., "Big Data et données personnelles : vers une gouvernance éthique des algorithmes", *ParisTech Review*, available at: www.paristechreview.com/2014/12/22/big-data-ethique, 2014.

[BÉR 15] BÉRANGER J., *Medical Information Systems Ethics*, ISTE Ltd, London and John Wiley & Sons, New York, 2015.

[BÉR 16] BÉRANGER J., *Big Data and Ethics*, ISTE Press, London and Elsevier, Oxford, 2016.

[BLO 13] BLONDEL V., "Big Data : traitement massif des données, que peut-on en attendre ? Faut-il le redouter ?", *La Recherche*, no. 482, pp. 26–32, 2013.

[BOI 03] BOISVERT Y., JUTRAS M., LEGAULT G.A. *et al.*, Raisonnement éthique dans un contexte de marge de manœuvre accrue : clarification conceptuelle et aide à la décision, Research report, Centre d'expertise en gestion des ressources humaines, Quebec, 2003.

[BOL 10] BOLLIER D., *The Promise and Peril of Big Data*, The Aspen Institute, Washington, D.C., 2010.

[BOU 17] BOUZEGHOUB M., MOSSERI R., *Les Big Data à découvert*, CNRS Éditions, Saint-Étienne, 2017.

[BOY 12] BOYD D., CRAWFORD K., "Critical Questions for Big Data: Provocations for a cultural, technological, and scholarly phenomenon", *Information Communication & Society*, vol. 15, no. 5, pp. 662–679, 2012.

[BRO 13] BROWN I., MARSDEN C., *Regulating Code: Good Governance and Better Regulation in The Information Age*, MIT Press, Cambridge, 2013.

[BUT 15] BUTTARELLI G., Vers une nouvelle éthique numérique : Données, dignité et technologie, no. 4/2015, EDPS, Brussels, 2015.

[CAL 12] CALLEBAUT W., "Scientific perspectivism: A philosopher of science's response to the challenge of Big Data biology", *Studies in History and Philosophy of Science Part C: Studies in History and Philosophy of Biological and Biomedical Sciences*, vol. 43, no. 1, pp. 69–80, 2012.

[CAM 04] CAMBON-THOMSEN A., "Médecine de prévision, génétique et santé publique", *Observatoire de la génétique*, no. 19, 2004.

[CAP 03] CAPELLER W., SIMOULIN V., "La gouvernance : du programme de recherche à la transdisciplinarité", *Droit et société*, vol. 2, no. 54, pp. 301–305, 2003.

[CAR 13] CARDON D., "Dans l'esprit du PageRank", *Réseaux*, vol. 177, no. 1, pp. 63–33, 2013.

[CAR 15] CARDON D., *À quoi rêvent les algorithmes*, Le Seuil, Paris, 2015.

[CHA 13] CHAZELLE B., *L'Algorithmique et les sciences*, Éditions Fayard, Paris, 2013.

[COL 08] COLLOC J., LÉRY L., "Un métamodèle d'aide à la décision en éthique médicale SDM", *Médicament, éthique et PED*, vol. 11, nos 1–2, pp. 255–274, 2008.

[COL 14] COLL S., "Power, knowledge, and the subjects of privacy: Understanding privacy as the ally of surveillance", *Information Communication & Society*, vol. 17, no. 10, pp. 1250–1263, 2014.

[COL 16] COLLOC J., "L'éthique des systèmes d'information autonomes vers une pensée artificielle", *Les Cahiers du Numérique*, vol. 12, nos 1–2, pp. 187–211, 2016.

[COL 18] COLLOC J., De l'Intelligence Artificielle mimétique aux systèmes autonomes : Quels objectifs ? Quels enjeux éthiques ?, vade-mecum sur la gouvernance des traitements de données numériques, White paper, ADEL, 2018.

[COU 07] COUDERC B., PREVEL L., "La maîtrise du cycle de vie du document numérique", *Aproged*, vol. 1, pp. 1–4, 2007.

[CIG 14] CIGREF, Éthique et Numérique : Enjeux et recommandations à l'intention des entreprises, Report, 2014.

[CIG 16] CIGREF, Gouvernance de l'intelligence artificielle dans les grandes entreprises : Enjeux managériaux, juridiques et éthiques, Report, 2016.

[DAV 12] DAVIS K., PATTERSON D., *Ethics of Big Data: Balancing Risk and Innovation*, O'Reilly Media, Sebastopol, 2012.

[DEF 16] DE FILIPPI P., HASSAN S., "Blockchain technology as a regulatory technology: From code is law to law is code", *First Monday*, vol. 21, no. 12, 2016.

[DEG 17] DE GANAY C., GILLOT D., Pour une intelligence artificielle maîtrisée, utile et démystifiée, Report, L'office parlementaire d'évaluation des choix scientifiques et technologiques, 2017.

[DEM 17] DEMOULE J.-P., "La révolution néolithique n'a pas de comparaison dans l'histoire", *Le Monde Science et Techno,* no. 22644, October 2017.

[DEN 15] DENG B., "Machine ethics: The robot's dilemma", available at: https://www.nature.com/news/machine-ethics-the-robot-s-dilemma-1.17881, 2015.

[DER 17] DE ROSNAY J., "Ce sera quoi un territoire positif en 2517 ? Comment y vivra-t-on ?", *Positive Economy Forum*, Le Havre, France, October 2017.

[DES 39] DE SAINT-EXUPERY A., *Terre des hommes*, Gallimard, Paris, 1939.

[DEV 15] DE VAUPLANE P.-A., BERNARD J.-B., ROBLOT E., Fintech 2020 : reprendre l'initiative, Comment la technologie Blockchain peut permettre à la France et à l'Europe de prendre l'avantage en matière de banque et de finance ?, Report, 2015.

[DEW 26] DEWEY J., "The Historic Background of Corporate Legal Personality", *Yale Law Journal*, vol. 35, no. 6, pp. 656–669, 1926.

[DHE 07] DHERSE J.-L., MINGUET D., *L'éthique ou le chaos ?*, Presses de la Renaissance, Paris, 2007.

[DIA 15] DIAKOPOULOS N., "Algorithmic Accountability: Journalistic investigation of computational power structures", *Digital Journalism,* vol. 3, no. 3, pp. 398–415, 2015.

[DOD 05] DODGE M., KITCHIN R., "Code and the Transduction of Space", *Annals of the Association of American Geographers*, vol. 95, no. 1, pp. 162–180, 2005.

[DOS 15] DOS B., "Quel modèle d'enseignement au XXIe siècle en Occident pour un développement harmonieux de l'Homme, de la société et de l'économie ?", *13th International Conference, Lifelong Learning : Continuous education for sustainable development*, Saint-Petersburg, pp. 1–8, May 2015.

[DOS 18] DOS B., Vers une voie européenne de la révolution numérique ?, vade-mecum sur la gouvernance des traitements de données numériques, White paper, ADEL, 2018.

[DOU 11] DOUEIHI M., *Qu'est-ce que le numérique ?*, PUF, Paris, 2011.

[EAG 06] EAGLE N., PENTLAND A., "Reality mining: sensing complex social systems", *Journal Personal and Ubiquitous Computing*, vol. 10, no. 4, pp. 255–268, 2006.

[EIS 91] EISENSTEIN E., *La révolution de l'imprimé, dans l'Europe des premiers temps modernes*, La Découverte, Paris, 1991.

[EUB 12] EUBANKS V., *Digital Dead End: Fighting for Social Justice in the Information Age*, MIT Press, Cambridge, 2012.

[FER 15] FERRY L., L'humain dans le numérique… et le Big Data, White paper, EPA, Paris, 2015.

[FLO 98] FLORIDI L., "L'éthique télématique", *L'Agora*, vol. 5, no. 4, pp. 19–20, 1998.

[FLO 02] FLORIDI L., "Éthique dans l'infosphère", *Blesok*, no. 24, 2002.

[FLO 07] FLORIDI L., "A look into the future impact of ICT on our lives", *The Information Society*, vol. 23, no. 1, pp. 59–64, 2007.

[FLO 14] FLORIDI L., *The Fourth Revolution*, Oxford University Press, Oxford, 2014.

[FLO 18] FLOREONI S., L'Humain au cœur du digital, vade-mecum sur la gouvernance des traitements de données numériques, White paper, ADEL, 2018.

[GAD 76] GADAMER H.G., *The Historicity of Understanding*, Penguin, London, 1976.

[GER 14] GERBER L., "Mortels algorithmes : du code pénal au code létal", *Radical Philosophy*, no. 187, pp. 1–7, 2014.

[GHE 18] GHERNAOUTI S., Homo Numéricus et hyperconnectivité, résister à la colonisation numérique, produire du bien commun, vade-mecum sur la gouvernance des traitements de données numériques, White paper, ADEL, 2018.

[GOO 16] GOODMAN B., FLAXMAN S., "European Union regulations on algorithmic decision-making and a 'right to explanation'", *AI Magazine*, vol. 38, no. 3, pp. 50–57, 2016.

[GRI 16] GRINBAUM A., "Gouverner le code qui nous gouverne", *Congrès scientifique, Gouvernance des algorithmes*, Institut Mines-Télécom, Paris, February 2016.

[HAB 84] HABERMAS J., *The Theory of Communicative Action: Reason and the Rationalization of Society*, vol. 1, Beacon Press, Boston, 1984.

[HAL 12] HALEVI G., MOED H., "The evolution of Big Data as a research and scientific topic: overview of the literature", *Research Trends Issue*, vol. 30, no. 1, pp. 3–6, 2012.

[HAM 07] HAMID N., *Information Security and Computer Ethics, Tools, Theories and Modeling*, IGI Global, Hershey, 2007.

[HAR 17] HARARI Y.N., *Homo Deus : une brève histoire de l'avenir*, Albin Michel, Paris, 2017.

[HEG 99] HEGEL G.W.F., *Principes de la philosophie du droit*, Flammarion, Paris, 1999.

[HER 97] HERVÉ C., *Éthique médicale ou bioéthique ? L'éthique en mouvement*, L'Harmattan, Paris, 1997.

[HER 17] HERVÉ C., "L'impératif éthique pour la médecine de demain, à l'aune de nos grands anciens", *Bulletin de l'Académie nationale de médecine*, vol. 201, nos 4–5, pp. 1–8, 2017.

[JON 78] JONAS H., *Pour une éthique du futur*, Éditions Rivages, Paris, 1978.

[JON 98] JONAS H., *L'éthique du futur*, Éditions Rivages, Paris, 1998.

[KHA 15] KHARE R., GOOD B.M., LEAMAN R. *et al.*, "Crowdsourcing in biomedicine: challenges and opportunities", *Briefings in Bioinformatics*, vol. 17, no. 1, pp. 23–32, 2015.

[KIT 11] KITCHIN R., DODGE M., *Code/Space: Software and Everyday Life*, MIT Press, Cambridge, 2011.

[KIT 14] KITCHIN R., "Big Data, new epistemologies and paradigm shifts", *Big Data & Society*, pp. 1–12, 2014.

[LAC 06] LACHIEZE-REY M., *L'espace physique entre mathématiques et philosophie*, EDP Sciences, Les Ulis, 2006.

[LAZ 98] LAZARE M., "Les tâches d'une philosophie pratique à l'âge des technosciences", *Philosophie*, vol. 21, p. 101, 1998.

[LEB 18] LE BARS H., Gouvernance des données, RGPD et éthique pour le futur, vade-mecum sur la gouvernance des traitements de données numériques, White paper, ADEL, 2018.

[LEC 07] LE COZ P., *Petit traité de la décision médicale*, Le Seuil, Paris, 2007.

[LEC 09] LE COZ P., "Place de la réflexion philosophique dans la décision médicale", *Bulletin de l'Académie nationale de médecine*, vol. 193, no. 2, pp. 499–510, Paris, 2009.

[LES 99] LESSIG L., *Code and Other Laws of Cyberspace*, Basic Books, New York, 1999.

[LÉV 54] LÉVI-STRAUSS C., "Les mathématiques de l'homme", *Bulletin international des sciences sociales*, vol. 6, no. 4, p. 644, 1954.

[LOI 15] LOISEAU G., *Des robots et des hommes*, Dalloz, Paris, 2015.

[LUS 03] LUSSAULT M., "Spatialité", in LUSSAULT M., LÉVY J. (eds), *Dictionnaire de la géographie et de l'espace des sociétés*, Belin, Paris, 2003.

[LUS 10] LUSSAULT M., STOCK M., "Doing with space: towards a pragmatics of space", *Social Geography*, vol. 5, no. 1, pp. 11–19, 2010.

[LYO 03] LYON D., *Surveillance as social sorting: Privacy, risk, and digital discrimination*, Routledge, London, 2003.

[MAC 13] MACCORMICK J., *Nine Algorithms that Changed the Future*, Princeton University Press, Princeton, 2013.

[MAR 04] MARCINKOWSKI A., WILGAUX J., "Automates et créatures artificielles d'Héphaïstos : entre science et fiction", *Techniques et Culture*, no. 2, pp. 43–44, 2004.

[MAR 14] MARKOWETZ A., BŁASZKIEWICZ K., MONTAG C. *et al.*, "Psycho-informatics: Big Data shaping modern psychometrics", *Medical Hypotheses*, vol. 82, no. 4, p. 308, 2014.

[MCL 77] MCLUHAN M., *La galaxie Gutenberg : la genèse de l'homme typographique*, Gallimard, Paris, 1977.

[MÉN 15] MÉNARD B., *L'entreprise numérique : quelles stratégies pour 2015 ?*, CIGREF, Paris, 2015.

[MEN 16] MENDOZA-CAMINADE A., *Le droit confronté à l'intelligence artificielle des robots : vers l'émergence de nouveaux concepts juridiques ?*, Dalloz, Paris, 2016.

[MOR 05] MORIN E., "Complexité restreinte, complexité générale", *Colloque Intelligence de la complexité : épistémologie et pragmatique*, Cerisy-La-Salle, June 2005.

[MOR 14] MORGAN E., "I Quit Liking Things on Facebook for Two Weeks, Here's How It Changed My View of Humanity", *Medium*, 2014.

[MOW 76] MOWSHOWITZ A., *The Conquest of Will: Information Processing in Human Affairs*, Addison-Wesley, Boston, 1976.

[NAG 12] NAGEL T., *Mind and Cosmos; Why the Materialist Neo-Darwinian Conception of Nature is Almost Certainly False*, Oxford University Press, Oxford, 2012.

[NOO 14] NOORMAN M., ZALTA E.N., "Computing and Moral Responsibility", *The Stanford Encyclopedia of Philosophy*, 2014.

[NOU 02] NOUVEL P., *Enquête sur le concept de Modèle*, PUF, Paris, 2002.

[OGI 07] OGIEN R., *L'éthique aujourd'hui : Maximalistes et minimalistes*, Gallimard, Paris, 2007.

[OMA 02] OMARJEE S., *Le Data Mining : aspects juridiques de l'intelligence artificielle au regard de la protection des données personnelles*, ERCIM, Biot, 2002.

[PAR 11] PARISER E., *The Filter Bubble: What the Internet is Hiding from You*, Penguin, New York, 2011.

[PAV 16] PAVEL I., SERRIS J., Modalités de régulation des algorithmes de traitement des contenus, Report, French Ministry of Industrial and Digital Economy, 2016.

[PIC 18] PICARD F., Une éthique du numérique centrée sur les citoyens et orientée vers des solutions techniques, vade-mecum sur la gouvernance des traitements de données numériques, White paper, ADEL, 2018.

[PON 09] PONÇON G., "Système d'information : vers une éthique de l'usage ?", *Revue hospitalière de France*, vol. 531, p. 74, 2009.

[PRE 16] PREDON, Approches contemporaines en hébergement et gestion de données, White paper, 2016.

[REY 12] REYNAUDI M., SAUNERON S., Médecine prédictive : les balbutiements d'un concept aux enjeux considérables, note d'analyse, centre d'analyse stratégique, 2012.

[ROS 14] ROSKI J., BO-LINN G.W., ANDREWS T.A., "Creating Value In Health Care Through Big Data: Opportunities and Policy Implications", *Health Affairs*, vol. 33, no. 7, pp. 1115–1122, 2014.

[ROU 14] ROUVROY A., "Des données sans personne : le fétichisme de la donnée à caractère personnel à l'épreuve de l'idéologie des Big Data", *Étude annuelle du Conseil d'État: le numérique et les droits fondamentaux*, pp. 407–422, La Documentation française, Paris, 2014.

[RIA 09] RIAL-SEBBAG E., Implications juridiques des nouvelles formes de gouvernance en bio-technologie : l'exemple des biobanques utilisées en recherche, Thesis, Paul Sabatier Toulouse-3 University, 2009.

[RIA 17] RIAL-SEBBAG E., "La gouvernance des Big Data utilisées en santé, un enjeu national et international", *Journal international de bioéthique et d'éthique des sciences*, vol. 28, no. 3, p. 46, 2017.

[RIF 11] RIFKIN J., *The Third Industrial Revolution*, Palgrave MacMillan, 2011.

[SAL 15] SALLES M., *Decision-making and the Information System*, ISTE Ltd, London and John Wiley & Sons, New York, 2015.

[SCH 00] SCHWANDT T.A., "Three epistemological stances for qualitative inquiry: Interpretivism, hermeneutics, and social constructionism", in DENZIN N.K., LINCOLN Y.S. (eds), *Handbook of Qualitative Research*, SAGE, Thousand Oaks, 2000.

[SCH 13] SCHULER M., ZNATY B., "La propriété intellectuelle et la transformation numérique de l'économie, quelle protection juridique pour l'algorithme ?", *INPI*, Paris, 2013.

[SER 16] SERVY H., "Big Data : jouer au jeu de go pourrait-il donner du temps au médecin ?", *La Lettre du Rhumatologue*, no. 424, pp. 20–26, 2016.

[SHA 48] SHANNON C.E., "A Mathematical Theory of Communication", *Bell System Technical Journal*, vol. 27, 1948.

[SPR 13] SPRANZI M., "Clinical ethics and values: how do norms evolve from practice?", *Medicine, Health Care and Philosophy*, vol. 16, pp. 93–103, 2013.

[STI 15] STIEGLER B., *Dans la disruption. Comment ne pas devenir fou ?*, Les liens qui libèrent, Paris, 2015.

[SWE 13] SWEENEY L., "Discrimination in Online Ad Delivery", *Communications of the ACM*, vol. 56, no. 5, pp. 44–54, 2013.

[TEN 13] TENE O., POLONETSKY J., "Big Data for all: Privacy and user control in the age of analytics", *Northwestern Journal of Technology and Intellectual Property*, vol. 11, no. 5, pp. 239–272, available at: http://scholarlycommons.law.northwestern.edu/njtip/vol11/iss5/1, 2013.

[TER 14] TERRY N., "Health privacy is difficult but not impossible in a post-HIPAA data-driven world", *Chest*, vol. 146, no. 3, pp. 835–840, 2014.

[THE 90] THEVOZ J.-M., *Entre nos mains l'embryon : recherche bioéthique*, Labor et Fides, Geneva, 1990.

[THI 04] THIBIERG C., *Avenir de la responsabilité, responsabilité de l'avenir*, Dalloz, Paris, 2004.

[THO 84] THOM R., *Stabilité structurelle et morphogenèse*, Dunod, Paris, 1984.

[TOU 04] TOURREILLES J.-M., *SIH : 1, 2, 3 ... partez !*, Éditions ENSP, Rennes, 2004.

[VAL 41] VALÉRY P., *Les carnets de Léonard de Vinci*, Gallimard, Paris, 1941.

[VAL 48] VALÉRY P., *Vues*, La Table Ronde, Paris, 1948.

[VAN 04] VAN GRIETHUYSEN P., "Le principe de précaution : quelques éléments de base", *Les cahiers du RIBios (Réseau interdisciplinaire biosécurité)*, no. 4, 2004.

[VAY 18] VAYRE J.-S., Élément de réflexion éthique sur la socialisation algorithmique, vade-mecum sur la gouvernance des traitements de données numériques, White paper, ADEL, 2018.

[VOD 10] VODOZ L., "Fracture numérique, fracture sociale : aux frontières de l'intégration et de l'exclusion", *SociologieS*, 2010.

[WEI 76] WEIZENBAUM J., *Computer Power and Human Reason: From Judgment to Calculation*, W.H. Freeman & Co Ltd, San Francisco, 1976.

[WIE 50] WIENER N., *The Human Use of Human Beings: Cybernetics and Society*, Houghton Mifflin, Boston, 1950.

[WIL 18] WILLIATTE L., Le cadre légal et réglementaire : les exigences du Règlement européen du 27 avril 2016 et la loi française pour une République numérique du 7 octobre 2016, vade-mecum sur la gouvernance des traitements de données numériques, White paper, ADEL, 2018.

[ZOL 15] ZOLYNSKI C., "Big Data : pour une éthique des données", *I2D – Information, données et documents*, no. 2, pp. 25–26, 2015.

[ZOU 18] ZOUARHI S., Éthique et TIC, la Blockchain comme outil de Gouvernance des Données, vade-mecum sur la gouvernance des traitements de données numériques, White paper, ADEL, 2018.

[ZUB 15] ZUBOFF S., "Big Other: surveillance capitalism and the prospects of an information civilization", *Journal of Information Technology*, vol. 30, pp. 75–89, 2015.

Index

I, J, L

M, N

P

Q, R

S, T

Other titles from

iSTE

in

Science, Society and New Technologies

2018

BARTHES Angela, CHAMPOLLION Pierre, ALPE Yves
Evolutions of the Complex Relationship Between Education and Territories
(Education Set - Volume 1)

DUGUÉ Bernard
Time, Emergences and Communications
(Engineering, Energy and Architecture Set – Volume 4)

GEORGANTOPOULOU Christina G., GEORGANTOPOULOS George A.
Fluid Mechanics in Channel, Pipe and Aerodynamic Design Geometries 1
(Engineering, Energy and Architecture Set – Volume 2)

GEORGANTOPOULOU Christina G., GEORGANTOPOULOS George A.
Fluid Mechanics in Channel, Pipe and Aerodynamic Design Geometries 2
(Engineering, Energy and Architecture Set – Volume 3)

LELEU-MERVIEL Sylvie
Informational Tracking
(Traces Set – Volume 1)

SALGUES Bruno
Society 5.0: Industry of the Future, Technologies, Methods and Tools (Technological Prospects and Social Applications Set – Volume 1)

2017

ANICHINI Giulia, CARRARO Flavia, GESLIN Philippe, GUILLE-ESCURET Georges
Technicity vs Scientificity – Complementarities and Rivalries (Social Interdisciplinarity Set – Volume 2)

DUGUÉ Bernard
Information and the World Stage – From Philosophy to Science, the World of Forms and Communications (Engineering, Energy and Architecture Set – Volume 1)

GESLIN Philippe
Inside Anthropotechnology – User and Culture Centered Experience (Social Interdisciplinarity Set – Volume 1)

GORIA Stéphane
Methods and Tools for Creative Competitive Intelligence

KEMBELLEC Gérald, BROUDOUS EVELYNE
Reading and Writing Knowledge in Scientific Communities– Digital Humanities and Knowledge Construction

MAESSCHALCK Marc
Reflexive Governance for Research and Innovative Knowledge (Responsible Research and Innovation Set - Volume 6)

PARK Sejin, GUILLE-ESCURET Georges
Sociobiology vs Socioecology – Consequences of an Unraveling Debate (Interdisciplinarity between Biological Sciences and Social Sciences Set - Volume 1)

PELLÉ Sophie
Business, Innovation and Responsibility (Responsible Research and Innovation Set - Volume 7)

2016

BRONNER Gérald
Belief and Misbelief Asymmetry on the Internet

EL FALLAH SEGHROUCHNI Amal, ISHIKAWA Fuyuki, HÉRAULT Laurent, TOKUDA Hideyuki
Enablers for Smart Cities

GIANNI Robert
Responsibility and Freedom
(Responsible Research and Innovation Set - Volume 2)

GRUNWALD Armin
The Hermeneutic Side of Responsible Research and Innovation
(Responsible Research and Innovation Set - Volume 5)

LAGRANA Fernando
E-mail and Behavioral Changes – Uses and Misuses of Electronic Communications

LENOIR Virgil Cristian
Ethical Efficiency – Responsibility and Contingency
(Responsible Research and Innovation Set - Volume 1)

MAESSCHALCK Marc
Reflexive Governance for Research and Innovative Knowledge
(Responsible Research and Innovation Set - Volume 6)

PELLÉ Sophie, REBER Bernard
From Ethical Review to Responsible Research and Innovation
(Responsible Research and Innovation Set - Volume 3)

REBER Bernard
Precautionary Principle, Pluralism and Deliberation – Sciences and Ethics
(Responsible Research and Innovation Set - Volume 4)

VENTRE Daniel
Information Warfare – 2nd edition

Printed and bound by CPI Group (UK) Ltd, Croydon, CR0 4YY